Robert Herrick

Revised Edition

Twayne's English Authors Series

Arthur F. Kinney, Editor

University of Massachusetts, Amherst

TEAS 34

Engraved frontispiece from *Hesperides; or, The Works Both Humane and Divine of Robert Herrick, Esq.* London, 1648.

Robert Herrick

Revised Edition

Roger B. Rollin

Clemson University

Twayne Publishers • New York
Maxwell Macmillan Canada • Toronto
Maxwell Macmillan International • New York Oxford Singapore Sydney

Robert Herrick: Revised Edition
Roger B. Rollin

Twayne Publishers   Maxwell Macmillan Canada, Inc.
Macmillan Publishing Company   1200 Eglinton Avenue East
866 Third Avenue   Suite 200
New York, New York 10022   Don Mills, Ontario M3C 3N1

Macmillan Publishing Company is part of the Maxwell Communication Group
of Companies.

Library of Congress Cataloging-in-Publication Data

Rollin, Roger B.
    Robert Herrick / Roger B. Rollin. — Rev. ed.
        p.   cm. — (Twayne's English authors series ; TEAS 34)
    Includes bibliographical references (p.   ) and index.
    ISBN 0-8057-7012-7
    1. Herrick, Robert, 1591-1674—Criticism and interpretation.
I. Title. II. Series.
PR3514.R64   1992
821′.4—dc20   91-33734
                                               CIP

10 9 8 7 6 5 4 3 2 1

Printed in the United States of America

L.E.R.

Bid me to live, and I will live,
Thy Protestant to be:
Or bid me love, and I will give
A loving heart to thee.

Contents

Editor's Note

The astonishing and strikingly undeserved fate of *Hesperides,* Robert Herrick's lifelong miscellany of poetry, according to Roger B. Rollin, has been to be "damned with the faint praise of the fastidious, distorted by enthusiasts, or bowdlerized by the censorious." That is no longer true. What in 1966 was a mere scattering of publications on the poet has taken a quantum leap. Rollin's careful reassessments of Herrick's secular and sacred works and of the scholarship and criticism that have emerged in the last quarter century reveal an extraordinary poet whose talents were applied to one of the widest ranges of English lyric poetry in the entire seventeenth century. From his close exegesis of *"The Hock-cart"* to his serial examination of the various genres of Herrick's writing—country life poems, epigrams, love poems, fairy poems, and songs—with their recurring themes of love, faith, art, and the good life, Rollin describes a major artist whose self-reflexivity, whose guidance from his model Ben Jonson, and whose repeated concern with the act of mediation in his writing all help make this self-conscious poet one of the finest of his age. His genres and themes, Rollin argues, do not so much order and regulate *Hesperides* and *His Noble Numbers* as they orchestrate a grander body of work that moves from the secular to the sacred in ways at once moving and memorable. Rollin's fully revised study of Herrick for this series promises to be as useful and as influential as his original ground-breaking book on the poet.

Arthur F. Kinney

Preface

The Church of St. George the Martyr, whose vicar Robert Herrick was for 31 years, still stands in a green Devonshire valley near the village of Dean Prior. Inside, just beyond the church door, the visitor will find a glass-front bookcase. It contains copies of a few modern editions of Herrick's poems and a collection of critical works about the poet, including the first edition of this book. Installed in the late 1960s, this cabinet is now too small to hold all the books, scholarly articles, master's theses, and doctoral dissertations on the poet that have appeared since the publication of the 1966 edition of *Robert Herrick*. Indeed, Herrick has likely been more widely read and more closely studied in the period since 1966 than in all the rest of the nearly 350 years since the publication of his collected poems, *Hesperides*. Space does not permit taking this wealth of new scholarship and criticism fully into account here; nevertheless, this revised edition of *Robert Herrick* has benefitted more from that valuable body of work than its bibliographical apparatus can adequately indicate.

The reader who compares this book with the original edition will find that, although the latter's organization by chapters and within chapters remains pretty much intact, the text itself has been almost completely rewritten. The 1966 edition still serves reasonably well as a critical introduction to Herrick for the general reader, students, and the occasional teacher; however, times have changed, and so have I. While I still stand behind most of what I wrote 25 years ago, my sense of Herrick and his poetry has, I trust, been broadened and deepened by a quarter century of teaching and writing about seventeenth-century British literature. His *Hesperides* has not changed, of course, but a Herrick for our time would seem to call for a substantively revised study.

Nevertheless, the methodology of this new book remains in most respects that of the 1966 study. The quantum leap taken by literary and critical theory during the last two decades has created numerous new possibilities for approaching even a traditional poet like Robert Herrick. Some of these possibilities are explored in the pages that follow. I believe, however, that the first edition's approach, combining traditional historicism—attempting to place Herrick as man and poet in the context of his time—with the then still fairly new New Criticism (featuring the "close reading" of selected poems) remains an effective way of helping readers relatively unfamiliar with Herrick to understand and appreciate his art and to put it in cultural perspective. Although this is, then, in many ways a new book, its predecessor continues to shape its design and inform its approach.

A specific aspect of that critical approach, derived from genre studies, also reappears here—the idea of pastoral. Viewing Herrick's collection of 1,402 poems in the light of the bucolic tradition still seems to me to be a useful way of achieving a perspective on this elusive poet. Moreover, Herrick invites us to do so himself: as I show in chapter 1, he presents himself as something of a pastoral poet at the very start of his collection and reinforces that impression throughout both his secular and his sacred verse. Similarly, he shows a decided tendency to think of his book as representing a kind of pastoral world (in his phrase, a "*Sacred Grove*") that both encompasses and transcends the seventeenth-century world of material reality. Reading *Hesperides* in the light of the pastoral tradition, originally a suggestion of my early mentor, Louis Martz, has not been greeted with universal approval since the publication of the 1966 edition, as subsequent discussions reveal. Yet this approach has been neither disproved nor ignored; indeed, the idea of pastoral figures importantly in the most recent major study of the poet to appear, Anne Baynes Coiro's *Robert Herrick's "Hesperides" and the Epigram Book Tradition*. As its title suggests, however, Coiro's estimable work emphasizes *Hesperides'* link to another literary mode and tradition, that of the short, pithy poem. Two earlier full-length studies, by A. Leigh DeNeef and by Robert Deming, presented Herrick as a "ceremonial" poet, yet to varying degrees both also acknowledged his pastoralism. As the chapters that follow make clear, each of these ways of reading *Hesperides* has considerable merit.

Another aspect of the first edition's critical approach, one drawn from intellectual history, has also been retained here—the hypothesis that Herrick's poetry presents a relatively consistent vision of life, a unique synthesis of classical Stoicism, serious Epicureanism, and flexible Anglican Protestantism. This proposition and its corollary—that from this vision Herrick's vast and diverse collection of poems gains unity and coherence—have provoked fewer exceptions than the 1966 volume's hypothesis about the pastoral. More important, demonstrating how these classical and Christian attitudes, beliefs, and values shape poem after poem helps make Herrick more accessible to modern readers, for the poet's doctrine of moderation and tolerance may still have much to recommend it.

Pastoral and philosophical themes combine to frame and structure the discussion that follows. In chapter 1, I outline the critical controversies that have swirled about Herrick and the critical consensus that is finally beginning to emerge; then I set forth the argument and methodology of this book. Subsequent chapters are arranged thematically. For example, in chapter 2 I treat poems dealing with transiency and death—two facts of existence to which Herrick directly or indirectly responds in his poems of "the good life" (discussed in chapter 3), in his love poems (chapter 4), in his devotional poems (chapter 5), and in those poems that affirm the power of poetry (chapter 6). By way of conclusion, in chapter 7 I attempt to put the preceding discussion in perspective and to situate Herrick in the general context of seventeenth-century English poetry.

The first edition of this book used as its source L. C. Martin's Oxford University Press edition of Herrick's poetry. For this edition I have chosen J. Max Patrick's more accessible edition, *The Complete Poems of Robert Herrick,* which conveniently assigns an *H*-number to poems in *Hesperides* and an *N*-number to those in *Noble Numbers.* (It is a scandal of scholarly publishing that both of these works—the only definitive modern editions of Herrick—are at this writing out of print. The majority of academic libraries, however, will have a copy of Patrick's edition, which most Herrick scholars now use because of its superior notes and format.)

A change in terminology from the first edition should be noted here. In 1966 I used the term *neoclassical* to describe poets like Herrick and his mentor, Ben Jonson, those "new classicists" of later English Renaissance poetry whose primary models were the poets of ancient Greece and Rome. I did so even though I recognized that confusion might arise because the term *neoclassical* is commonly used to designate such Restoration and eighteenth-century poets as Dryden and Pope. Having belatedly come to recognize the folly of doing battle with usage, in this edition I simply label earlier seventeenth-century poets like Jonson and Herrick *classicists.*

My original preface concluded with an expression of gratitude to Louis Martz, who first led me to the "fresh woods and pastures new" of *Hesperides;* for me he remains the model of the meticulous scholar, elegant critic, and patient, humane, and knowledgeable teacher. Now, however, I also owe a debt of gratitude to my other mentor in Herrick, J. Max Patrick, whose mighty erudition and intellectual rigor have contributed so much to my continuing education, even as his wit, his friendship, and his indomitable spirit have been my delight and my inspiration. Since the 1960s I have also been fortunate to gain the friendship of a host of scholars who have been unfailingly generous in sharing with me their knowledge and insights about seventeenth-century literature generally and about Herrick in particular. I honor and appreciate them all, though I can name only a few: the late

Shonosuke Ishii, Leigh DeNeef, Robert Deming, Jay Gertzman, and Ann Coiro—all of whom have given so much of themselves to Herrick scholarship; Ted-Larry Pebworth and Claude Summers, who graciously hosted the 1974 Herrick Tercentenary Conference at the University of Michigan–Dearborn and have energized seventeenth-century scholarship with their biennial meetings ever since; outstanding "occasional Herrickeans" like John Shawcross, Bob Hinman, Helen Roper, Gordon Braden, Achsah Guibbory, Leah Marcus, and Norman Farmer; a legion of admirers of Herrick, like John Idol, Tom Hester, Arlene Stiebel, Jim Simmonds, Gale Carrithers, Wally Kerrigan, and Peter Rudnytsky; and last, but never least, Bob Fallon, whose persistent failure to accept my pronouncements on literature and life has kept our friendship lively and kept me honest. To paraphrase Frost, "Good scholars make good friends."

Chronology

1591   Robert Herrick, seventh child of Nicholas Herrick, a goldsmith and banker, and Julian Stone Herrick, baptized in London on 24 August.

1592   "Sick in body," Nicholas Herrick makes out his will on 7 November; two days later he dies in a "fall" from an upper window of his house.

1607   After a period of schooling Robert apprenticed to an uncle, Sir William Herrick, a successful London goldsmith.

1613   Matriculates at St. John's College, Cambridge. Later transfers to Trinity Hall.

1617   Admitted to the degree of Bachelor of Arts at Cambridge.

1620   Receives the degree of master of arts.

1623   Ordained a deacon and a priest of the Church of England.

1625   Praised in print (*The Muses Dirge*) by Richard James by being compared to Michael Drayton and Ben Jonson. By this time probably admitted to "the tribe of Ben," the young poets and wits whom Jonson called his "sons."

1627   Serves as a chaplain to the Duke of Buckingham, leader of an ill-fated expedition to the French Isle of Rhé.

1628   Buckingham assassinated. Julian Herrick dies. Herrick nominated to the vicarage of Dean Prior, an obscure parish in rural Devonshire, between Exeter and Plymouth.

1630   Installed as the vicar of the Church of St. George the Martyr.

1640   Probably visits London to arrange for publication of *The severall Poems,* apparently an early, never-issued version of *Hesperides.*

1647   Expelled from his vicarage for his Royalist sympathies and refusal to submit to ecclesiastical authority. Probably returns to London as a private citizen.

1648   *Hesperides* published as the Civil War winds down.

1649   Charles I, celebrated by Herrick in several poems, is executed.

1655   "Young Heric" (now 64) said "to entertaine / The Muses in a sprightly vein" in an anonymous poem in *Musarum Delicae: or, The Muses Recreation.*

1658   In a left-handed compliment, described as the English Horace in an anonymous poem in *Naps upon Parnassus.*

1660   English monarchy restored with the return from France of Charles II, to whom (as Prince of Wales) *Hesperides* had been dedicated. Herrick petitions successfully to have the vicarage of Dean Prior restored to him and returns to "dull Devonshire."

1674   Buried in the churchyard of the parish church of St. George the Martyr on 15 October. Where his "bones [have] . . . their rest" is unknown, but a commemorative tablet has recently been installed at the base of the church tower. Now in private hands, his parsonage, enlarged and remodeled over the centuries, still stands across from the church. (A four-lane motorway now rushes Plymouth–Exeter traffic directly past the front gate of the church.) The poet is commemorated in a series of small stained-glass windows (installed after World War I) behind the altar.

Chapter One

"This Sacred Grove": The Problem of Herrick's *Hesperides*

In a letter that had the ulterior motive of asking his uncle (yet again) for money, young Robert Herrick, then a Cambridge University undergraduate, wrote, "Are the minds of men immutable? and will they rest in only one opinion without the least perspicuous shewe of chaing? O no they cannot, for . . . it is an old but yet yoong saying in our age: as times chaing so mens minds are altered."[1] Although such self-conscious rhetoric served mainly to lead up to a painful financial request, it contains an accurate if unintentional prophecy about the rhetorician. For when it comes to literary history, at least, "the minds of men" have indeed changed with the times, and Robert Herrick's reputation as a poet has ultimately been a beneficiary of those changes.

Today Herrick's poems are more widely and more appreciatively read than they were in his own lifetime. No anthology of English verse would be complete without at least several of them, and occasionally Herrick is accorded more space than poets with loftier reputations. In addition to diverse selected editions, the latter half of this century has produced two superb scholarly editions of his collected works, *Hesperides*.[2] A recent full-scale bibliography bears witness to the outpouring of scholarly publications about Herrick, the master's theses and doctoral dissertations, and the numerous references to his poetry that have appeared, particularly in the last quarter century.[3] In 1974 the tercentenary of his death was marked by a conference that brought together Herrick scholars from all over the world, and papers from that conference were collected and published.[4] In addition, a society honoring the poet and his family has been formed in England, and at this writing the dean of Westminster Abbey has been petitioned concerning the placing of a memorial to Herrick in the "Poet's Corner."[5]

All this activity surely would have pleased Robert Herrick—gentleman, scholar, priest, and would-be immortal poet. The literary fame he so much desired and that was denied him while he lived is now assuredly his. Even the following epigrammatic prophecy has been completely fulfilled, for not only does Herrick's love poetry continue to find appreciative readers but his

1

lyrics continue to be set to the music of his day (and our own) and recorded:[6]

> THou shalt not All die; for while Love's fire shines
> Upon his Altar, men shall read thy lines;
> And learn'd Musicians shall to honor *Herricks*
> Fame, and his Name, both set and sing his Lyricks.
> (*"Upon himself,"* H-366)

The Critical Controversy

Although Herrick's fame and reputation may now be at their height, that height has not been easily or quickly gained. One American scholar, invited to appear at the 1974 Herrick Memorial Conference, replied that Herrick was not worthy of a conference. Attendance at that meeting and the growth of interest in Herrick that followed it has proved that scholar wrong; but his view—that Herrick, however pleasing some of his verses may be, is in the end a poet of little consequence—can be traced back to a strain of nineteenth- and earlier twentieth-century criticism. For example, the prominent critic of the 1930s and 1940s, F. R. Leavis, while acknowledging the "charm" of Herrick's poetry, judged his talent to be at best trivial.[7] Likewise, T. S. Eliot, while acknowledging that Herrick's poems are well crafted, charged that *Hesperides* is lacking not only in high seriousness but also in the "continuous conscious *purpose*" and "unity of underlying pattern" that should characterize the collection of a major poet.[8]

In the second half of the twentieth century, both of these influential pronouncements have undergone reconsideration and, as a consequence, a critical consensus that takes a different view from them has emerged. This consensus holds that, in a golden age of important poets, Herrick is a more significant poet than has previously been recognized; that his poetry merits reading for its "instruction" as well as its "delight" and merits reading in the order that *Hesperides* sets forth rather than in selections; and that his artistic achievement, being not yet fully understood or appreciated in its depth, breadth, and structure, requires further scholarly and critical study.

Such a view might well have surprised Herrick himself, but it is certain that it would also have gratified him, for over the centuries literary history and criticism have been less than evenhanded with him. J. Max Patrick, who has carefully investigated the evolution of the poet's reputation, concludes that Herrick's rise to "the fame that he now enjoys" was "slow." Patrick demonstrates that although Herrick's individual poems were relatively popular in the seventeenth century, published in such collections as *Witts Recreations* and copied down in various manuscript collections, the poet himself seems not to have been very well known. Also, his *Hesperides* appears to have sold comparatively well in the quarter century after its publication, but "its greatness was inadequately recognized while [Herrick] lived and for more than two hundred years after his death."[9]

There are several reasons for this failure of perception. Although Herrick seems to have written some well-received poems as early as the 1620s, he published none of them before he left the center of England's literary cosmos, London, in 1630 to take up residence in culturally remote south Devonshire. Moreover, when he finally did publish his collected works, his timing could scarcely have been worse, for his likely audience, cultured gentlemen and ladies, must have been much preoccupied with the wrack and ruin of the Civil War and its aftermath. The execution of Charles I in 1649 could also have made it a risky proposition to sell—or buy—a book in which the Stuarts were so fulsomely celebrated. Of course, none of this would have come as much of a surprise to a poet who could pen an epigram like "*Posting to Printing*" (*H*-1022): "LEt others to the Printing Presse run fast, / Since after death comes glory, *Ile not haste.*"

Literary glory for Herrick, however, would be more than two centuries in coming. The poet's death in 1674 attracted little attention, and in time even the location of his grave was lost. Interest in Herrick, almost totally dormant during the eighteenth century, began to awaken in the nineteenth. But that sometimes constrained era was often inclined, after proclaiming the "beauties" of some of Herrick's lyrics, to parade its rectitude by roundly condemning his more naturalistic epigrams and more explicitly erotic love poems. Still, one eminent Victorian, Swinburne, gave Herrick his loftiest tribute, calling him "the greatest songwriter—as surely as Shakespeare is the greatest dramatist—ever born of English race."[10] Other literati of the nineteenth and early twentieth centuries, however, criticized Herrick for what they regarded as a lack of originality, emotional and intellectual shallowness, and obscenity. Nevertheless, Herrick was also celebrated for his poetic craftsmanship and lyricism, was favorably compared to Burns and Shelley (Hageman, xvi), and was admired for his command of the classics and his absorption of their spirit.

Recent Herrick criticism, recognizing the subjectivity and relativity of literary taste, puts less emphasis on evaluating the poet's achievement and more on understanding and interpreting it, enabling a more balanced perception of his place in English literary history to emerge. Moreover, the surprisingly complex nature of his talent and of his collection has been clarified by scholarship and criticism produced in the 1970s and 1980s. Thus, the readings that this book offers are to be regarded, not as definitive, but as approaches to a body of poems that readers ultimately can experience and appreciate only for themselves. Those in search of biographical studies or analyses of sources and influences can find such studies in this volume's selected bibliography. In this book my focus is upon the poems themselves, their relationships with other seventeenth-century verse, and on their places within the general context of *Hesperides* itself. Since there are more than 1,400 of them, attention can be paid only to representative works, some of them familiar anthology favorites, others known mainly to scholars, as well as a number of poems that for one reason or another are of special interest.

Herrick His Own Critic

Readers new to *Hesperides* will find Herrick himself quick to assist them in developing an approach to his verses. No other seventeenth-century poet, possibly no other poet writing in English, exhibits more awareness of his readers or makes more of an effort to have them respond "appropriately" to his poetry than does Herrick. In over a dozen poems he addresses the reader directly. Sometimes he provides footnotes or marginalia, and he arranges poems in certain configurations in an effort to guide the reader's responses. A good example is the famous poem that serves as the introduction to *Hesperides*.

"*The Argument of his Book*" (*H*-1) is not, as its title might suggest, a poetic thesis statement nor a disputation but rather a versified catalog of what purports to be the main subjects treated in *Hesperides*. (I say "purports to be" because as a catalog it is by no means comprehensive; for example, most of the subjects dealt with in Herrick's hundreds of epigrams are not covered in his listing.) "*The Argument*" also hints at the general areas of the human condition on which the poet will focus. For example, the opening couplet emphasizes the fact that the natural world is to figure importantly in this collection: "I Sing of *Brooks,* of *Blossomes, Birds,* and *Bowers:* / Of *April, May,* of *June,* and July-*Flowers*" (ll. 1–2). The alliteration of the first line contributes to the effect of a formal catalog, in which items are systematically ordered. Catalogs, however, normally make for dull reading; this one does not because the items it lists are not ones we would normally inventory. Together they represent the milder seasons, spring and early summer, when brooks race, blossoms emerge, birds (like the poet himself) "sing," and bowers beckon with their cool shade. Thus, the poem's initial line prepares the reader for the second, which suggests that the poems of *Hesperides* are typically set in that idyllic time of year, the seasons of rebirth and new growth.

This couplet also introduces Herrick's idealized self-image: he is a "singer," a lyric poet (no hint of Herrick the epigrammatist here) who celebrates nature in its most benign aspects. That clue helps place Herrick in the long line of "pastoral" or "bucolic" poets. Pastoral poetry is based on an opposition between the rural and the urban—between the vision of a simple, quiet, and virtuous life lived close to nature and the notion of a complex, hectic, and morally imperiled existence in the city. Perceiving Herrick's unique relationship to this ancient literary tradition is, as this book will try to show, important to understanding and appreciating his poetry.

The second couplet of *"The Argument,"* with its repetition of the word *"May,"* effects a transition between the natural and human realms: "I sing of *May-poles, Hock-carts, Wassails, Wakes,* / Of *Bride-grooms, Brides,* and of their *Bridall-cakes"* (ll. 3–4). Both maypoles and hock carts (used for bringing in the harvest) are intimately associated with natural events—the renewal of the earth's fertility in the spring and the fulfillment of that renewal in the fall. The antique rituals in which the maypole and the hock cart figure combine pagan and Christian elements to celebrate a fundamental connection between humans and nature, an association that the pastoral tradition poetically affirms.

With wassails (drinking rituals) and wakes (local festivals), Herrick shifts his focus from nature to humanity (although he will soon shift it back to nature). Weddings are sanctified human rituals and, like May Day, they are celebrations of renewal and fertility. These ceremonies and others, as A. Leigh DeNeef and Robert Deming have shown, are frequent subjects or structural devices of Herrick's, sometimes to the extent that a poem itself becomes a kind of ceremony.[11] DeNeef goes so far as to suggest that Herrick's characteristic mode of expression—his way of interpreting, ordering, and poeticizing experience—is, in fact, "ceremonial" (4). According to Deming, "Ceremony is Herrick's usual mediating device between classical and Christian, between play and seriousness, between Nature and Art" (81–82). It is clear that social and religious ceremonies and rituals from the amatory to funerary to the cultural are important to Herrick's poetry. There is even a sense in which the formal relationship between poet and reader makes a ritual of *any* poem. But the latter view becomes a kind of reductio ad absurdum: the act of reading rather than the poem itself constitutes the ritual. Accordingly, subsequent discussions regarding Herrick and the ceremonial, although indebted to DeNeef and Deming, will take a less complicated view than theirs, emphasizing a poem's ritual character chiefly when a ritual figures importantly and explicitly in the text.

To return to "*The Argument*," despite Herrick's reputation as a love poet, even a risqué poet, in this introductory poem he refers to marriage (line 4) *before* he refers to love and sensuality: "I write of *Youth, of Love,* and have Accesse / By these, to sing of cleanly-*Wantonnesse*" (ll. 5–6). "Cleanly-*Wantonnesse*" is a phrase coined by Herrick to announce that his amatory verse will be love poetry with a difference. Denotatively, the phrase seems oxymoronic—as in "chaste lasciviousness" or "innocent unchastity"; but connotatively, it implies sinless sexuality, a radical idea for Herrick's time. His phrase then constitutes a bold challenge to prevailing morality, for every permutation of "wanton" in the seventeenth century is pejorative, expressing the age's ambivalence toward human sensuality. As chapter 4 suggests, however, "cleanly-*Wantonnesse*" implies an attitude that derives from Herrick's liberated view of human nature and from his aesthetic sense of life. The phrase implies the possibility of a valorized sensuality, even of sex without guilt. In a single couplet, then, Herrick prepares his reader to expect not only love poetry but love poetry informed by a distinctive ethical theory of love.

The next couplet shifts the focus to the sensuous in nature: "I sing of *Dewes, of Raines,* and piece by piece / Of *Balme, of Oyle, of Spice,* and *Amber-Greece*" (ll. 7–8). For an Englishman to celebrate rain may seem incongruous, but preceded as it is in Herrick's catalog by dew, rain becomes one of nature's gifts and life's pleasures. The more exotic items listed in the next line are also natural things, but they have been refined by humans for sensual pleasure or for ceremonial purposes. In another of the poet's memorable phrases, found in the next couplet, the reader may be reminded that, like dew and even rain, these exotica are highly transitory: "I sing of *Times trans-shifting;* and I write / How *Roses* first came *Red,* and *Lillies White*" (ll. 9–10). Again, Herrick surprises: to celebrate the cause of so much late-Renaissance melancholy, the transiency of existence, might seem radical or even perverse. However, Herrick cushions the shock of his statement somewhat by following it with examples of benign, even beautiful, change, alluding to folklore and legends about how flowers received their distinctive hues. Worth noting at this point is how large the theme of the transiency of existence, and particularly of human life, looms in *Hesperides.* This theme is expressed in poem after poem dealing with cycles in nature and in the human world, and it becomes a fact of life that links the two. Nevertheless, change is also paradoxical: although it is both familiar and natural, it is also mysterious, since neither its origins nor its ends can be known. For human beings, moreover, change all too soon comes to mean atrophy or decay and, ultimately, death. Nature may well "die" during the winter, but spring and rebirth are never far behind, whereas men and women can never be certain about resurrection. This problem, with all of its attendant ironies, is repeatedly raised in Herrick's secular verse. To resolve it humans have turned to myth, religion, and philosophy, and Herrick is no exception. However, while he is able to find answers to such fanciful questions as how flowers received their hues, the more pointed question of mankind's fate is, in *Hesperides,* less readily resolved.

Beyond the effects of *"Times trans-shifting"* is the realm of the supernatural, the next item in Herrick's index of poetic subjects: "I write of groves, of *Twilights,* and I sing / The court of *Mab,* and of the *Fairie-King"* (ll. 11–12). In our own age we are accustomed to relegating the "little people," who come out of the woods at sunset, to the custody of imaginative children and quaint Irish folk, but in Herrick's time fairies were more consequential. Occupying a place between the human and the divine worlds, the realm of faerie could become a convenient myth through which poets like Spenser and Herrick were able to comment on their own world. In addition, it offered a challenge to these poets' imaginations and to their technical virtuosity. Although Herrick published only a few fairy poems, they are quite ambitious ones. The fact that he devotes a couplet in his introductory poem to this popular form of folklore indicates his participation in what Robert Deming has called the "folk mind" (81) or that, at the very least, he shares a special artistic interest with other seventeenth-century authors, Michael Drayton and William Shakespeare among them.

Although *His Noble Numbers,* the part of *Hesperides* devoted to his Christian verse, numerically constitutes about 20 percent of Herrick's collected works, only the final couplet of *"The Argument"* alludes to it: "I write of *Hell;* I sing (and ever shall) / Of *Heaven,* and hope to have it after all" (ll. 13–14). Herrick's sacred poetry has not been as highly esteemed as his "profane" verse (not altogether justifiably, as chapter 5 proposes), and there have been speculations that the poet himself may have devalued them; hence, the relegation of these poems to a separate section at the end of his book and the brevity of his allusion to them in *"The Argument."* On the other hand, it could be maintained that Herrick actually enhances the value of *His Noble Numbers* by alluding to it in the climactic couplet of his introduction and that he is simply being accurate about where his Christian poems are to be found in his volume. In any case, these lines are of greater interest than simply being a declaration that Herrick is a religious as well as a secular poet; after all, so were most of his fellow poets in the earlier seventeenth century. More important, it is here, for the first time in the poem, that a distinctively personal note is sounded: the couplet hints at the preoccupation with death, which is central to Herrick's consciousness. Moreover, these lines evoke the seemingly simple Christian faith held by the man behind the sophisticated poet "*The Argument*" has presented to us—a poet equally adept at pastoral, social, ceremonial, amatory, philosophical, folk, and devotional poetry, among other kinds.

Not only does "*The Argument of his Book*," with its careful structure, precise diction, and sophisticated adaptation of the catalog convention, provide an example of Herrick's unique craft and art, it also serves as a guide to a collection that is both sizeable and, in its considerable variety, complex. Moreover, the poem suggests that, as one scholar has put it, Herrick treats "nothing less than the whole universe; his theme is, in a sense, no narrower in range than that of *Paradise Lost*."[12] Furthermore, "*The Argument*" tells readers that they will find the poet playing many roles in this collection, although how many and how often as himself, how often as some sort of persona, the poem barely hints at. Herrick has presented himself as a poet who takes the whole "Great Chain of Being" (which links the natural, human, and supernatural realms) as his province; whose moods can range from the grave to the frivolous; and whose personality encompasses both the spiritual and the sensuous, the philosophical and the practical. What Herrick does *not* indicate at the outset is that he is also a student and admirer of the classics, an amateur but keen psychologist, an incisive social critic, a shrewd political analyst, a perceptive aesthetician, and a loyal citizen, family member, and friend—all of which indicates that Herrick is something more than the merely charming "Cavalier Poet" he is sometimes accused of being.

That accusation, however, may not seem entirely inappropriate after a casual reading of the seven poems that follow "*The Argument*." All of these are self-reflexive works, addresses to the poet's muse, his book, and his audience. But despite their apparent slightness, they are, in fact, designed to put readers on the defensive and thus, presumably, to render them more open to Herrick's art. The best known of these is the last of the series, the ebullient "*When he would have his verses read*" (H-8). Unlike the "*The Argument of his Book*," whose mode is descriptive, this poem is prescriptive, aggressively stipulating the time, place, and mood most conducive to appreciating Herrick's poetry:

> IN sober mornings, doe not thou reherse
> The holy incantation of a verse;
> But when that men have both well drunke, and fed,

Let my Enchantments then be sung, or read.
When Laurell spirts 'th fire, and when the Hearth
Smiles to it selfe, and guilds the roofe with mirth;
When up the *Thyrse is rais'd, and when the sound
Of sacred *Orgies flyes, A round, A round.
When the Rose raignes, and locks with ointments shine,
Let rigid Cato read these Lines of mine.

*A *Javelin* twisted with *Ivy* [Herrick's note]
*Songs to *Bacchus* [Herrick's note]

It might be inferred that Herrick is deliberately trivializing his poetry here, that he regards it as merely diversionary, an added attraction at parties. Well-schooled seventeenth-century readers, however, would recognize that Herrick is actually imitating the Roman poet Martial (*PW,* 499) and the Greek poet Anacreon, legendary lyrist of wine, women, and song. Thus, his poem aligns itself with an ancient tradition that celebrates poetry as not only one of life's pleasures but also a kind of secular religion. In this religion the recitation of poetry becomes a "holy incantation" that "enchants" listeners, transforming them into a temporarily altered state. Herrick's scholarly footnotes explicitly remind readers of the poem's antique—and, thus, eminently respectable—roots, as well as making sure that a bawdy interpretation is less readily imposed upon it. Nonetheless, the spirit of the poem is decidedly comic: read this book, Herrick urges, after a good meal, in a cozy room, at a gathering of convivial spirits as ready for a lyric as for a jest or a toast. Then, when the party mood (symbolized by the rose and the pomaded coiffures of the guests) is in full swing, even puritanical types can appreciate *Hesperides.*

Many of the poems in Herrick's collection—some of his love lyrics, his celebrations of the good life, and some of his comic-satiric epigrams—are in fact well suited to the mood of a carouse, and, taken together, such poems contribute to a light and spirited vein that is particularly noticeable in the earlier part of *Hesperides.* However, the atmosphere and mood recommended by "*When he would have his verses read*" would be inappropriate for reading the 20 percent of Herrick's poems that are *His Noble Numbers*—not to mention many pieces, some of them his most admired, in his secular collection as well. Indeed, the two poems that immediately follow "*When he would have his verses read*"—"*Upon* Julia's *Recovery*" (*H*-9) and "*To* Silvia *to wed*" (*H*-10)—which are relatively serious pieces, undercut and problematize the seemingly straightforward message of their predecessor. The reader,

then, is warned that Herrick cannot always be trusted—that, like all crea-
tors of fictional worlds, he transcends contradiction, giving and taking away,
disposing as he chooses. *Hesperides,* then, resists reduction and easy catego-
rization: no one critical approach to that world of poetry can accommodate
and account for it in its entirety.

A Critical Approach to *Hesperides*

It could be argued that, in some ways, it is more difficult to confront
Robert Herrick's collected poems than John Milton's. The order in which
Milton wrote his poems, for example, has been fairly well established, and
to read them chronologically is to experience the evolution of a genius. But
how to deal with a poet who writes many short poems in a variety of genres
and who seems to arrange them, not in chronological order, but in an order
whose principle—or, more likely, principles—is unclear? One suggestion
comes from T. S. Eliot, who proposes that:

> a work which consists of a number of short poems, even of poems which, taken in-
> dividually, may appear rather slight, may, if it has a unity of underlying pattern, be
> the equivalent of a first-rate longer poem in establishing an author's claim to be a
> "major" poet. That claim may, of course, be established by *one* long poem, and
> when that poem is good enough, when it has within itself the proper unity and vari-
> ety, we do not need to know, or if we know, we do not need to value highly, the po-
> et's other works. (44)

More than 30 years after Eliot wrote these words, they lack the ringing authority they once had. Contemporary literary criticism has properly given
the coup de grace to aesthetic evaluation, except as a phenomenon of cultural history. Thus, words like "slight," "first-rate," and "good" mean little
today, except as expressions of the personal taste of one critic at one point in
time. Even Eliot's need to classify poets, like baseball players, into major
and minor leaguers now seems misplaced, the compulsion of the quintessential elitist. Nonetheless, pared down to its essentials, Eliot's notion can
offer a key to the problem of comprehending the bulk and multiplicity of
Hesperides. Herrick's collection does consist of "a number of short poems,"
and, since they are the work of one mind, it is reasonable to expect that they
may exhibit "a unity of underlying pattern." The discovery of such a unity,
however, will not make a poet "better" or "major," nor will it necessarily
make a body of poems more gratifying to the reader. Nevertheless, an
awareness of such a unity may foster a reader's perception of a poet's

achievement and may encourage its fuller examination. For Eliot goes on to claim that if a collection of poems exhibits such "unity in variety," it follows that readers should read "a great deal [of it, if] not always the whole" in order to be able to put the poet in proper perspective. Since Herrick is a poet who deliberately arranges the poems in his collection and since today he is a poet read mainly in selections in anthologies, Eliot's point about the need for comprehensive reading is well taken.

Accordingly, this study tries to determine what kinds of subjects, themes, moods, and modes *Hesperides* exhibits and to discover aspects of its unity and coherence—as well as elements that work against such unity and coherence. An approach of this kind must take into account both the uniqueness of any individual poem and its relationship to the poet's other poems (and to similar poems by other poets). Since Herrick is, more than most poets, explicitly identified as a speaker or character in a surprising number of his verses and yet is, as artist, more than their sum total, this dual approach has much to recommend it.

Additional justification for this approach is provided by no less an authority than Herrick himself. His address *"To the generous Reader"* (*H-95*), despite its ingratiating title, is comically peremptory in its issuance of instructions:

> SEe, and not see; and if thou chance t'espie
> Some aberrations in my Poetry;
> Wink at small faults, the greater, ne'rtheless
> Hide, and with them, their Father's nakedness.
> Let's doe our best, our Watch and Ward to keep:
> *Homer* himself, in a long work, may sleep.

Noteworthy for its illustration of Herrick's special awareness of his readers and their critical tendencies, for its demonstration of the poet's objectivity about his art, and for its good humor (he sees himself "exposed" by poems the reader perceives as failures), this apostrophe is of special relevance to the discussion of an approach to *Hesperides,* for its final couplet suggests something about Herrick's conception of the scope and character of his book. Since he obviously cannot be associating himself with Homer as one epic poet to another, the basis of the association must be that each of them has written "a long work." The very phrase "a long work" implies something more than a mere gathering of short poems: it suggests a literary whole that the poet sees as "epic," even though it is not *an* epic or, as Eliot says, a whole that "is more than the sum of its [poetic] parts" (44). That such is indeed

Herrick's settled view of his *Hesperides* can be inferred not only from *"To his generous Reader"* but also from certain other poems in which he characterizes the "world" of his collected works.

The Pastoral Criticism of Life

It is ironic that, although T. S. Eliot's theory about unity in variety in collections of short poems serves as the foundation for this study, his application of his theory to Herrick is wrong—not because Eliot insists that Herrick is a "minor poet" (for whatever that classification may be worth) but because, as most critics now agree, he fails to see that *Hesperides* does exhibit a "unity of underlying pattern" and a "continuous conscious purpose." He is wrong, moreover, because he fails to see that Herrick's "personality," the sum of his personae, is well defined enough to lend ample coherence to his collection. The rest of this study constitutes in part the proof of these arguments and a refutation of Eliot. To do both seemed, in the first edition of this book, a pressing need; today that is no longer the case, for Herrick has outlasted both his detractors and his defenders.

Earlier in this chapter it was noted that in *"The Argument of his Book"* Herrick presents himself as something of a pastoral poet. That self-presentation largely sets him apart from the other prominent poets of the seventeenth century. Some of them, like Donne, attempt the pastoral mode hardly at all; others, like Jonson, do so only on occasion. In the Renaissance hierarchy of poetic modes, pastoral ranked low in terms of difficulty, seriousness, and style. However, a few poets, such as Milton and Marvell, have, like Herrick, a longer view of pastoral's potential. If this were not the case, it would have been simply foolish or whimsical of Herrick to have introduced his magnum opus with not one but two poems that associate him with pastoral. But whereas *"The Argument"* emphasizes pastoral subjects, *"To his Muse"* (*H*-2) personifies Herrick's poetic imagination as a bucolic deity. The poet urges her to "stay at home" with common rustic folk who appreciate her *"Eclogues"* (pastoral dialogues). Acknowledging that pastoral is a "meaner Minstralsie" (l. 6)—poetry with fewer pretensions than the epic, for example—he claims it is a happier and more innocent kind of poetry, "smooth, and harmlesse" (l. 10). While "such Lines as These" (l. 15) are bound to appeal to country people, endeavoring to write poetry to please the urban and the urbane—his witty epigrams, perhaps, or his encomia in praise of worthy persons—is to invite rejection: "Contempts in Courts and Cities dwell" (l. 21).

To some extent such admonitions are ironic, for as Thomas R. Whitaker observes, "Herrick's world is decidedly complex and courtly."[13] Ann Baynes Coiro also stresses the poem's wit and humor, even seeing it in part as a "tongue-in-cheek mockery of the poet's preference for a pastoral stance."[14] On the other hand, poetic closure can go a long way toward fixing a work's tone, and in the last five lines of *"To his Muse"* a certain anxiety about the reception of his book appears to surface—and not without reason; after all, Herrick had to have been aware that even his eminent literary "father," Ben Jonson, had not been immune to vicious attacks:

> No *Critick* haunts the Poore mans Cell:
> Where thou mayst hear thine owne Lines read
> By no one's tongue, there, censured.
> That man's unwise will search for Ill,
> And may prevent it, sitting still.
>
> (ll. 22–26)

"To his Muse" no more proclaims that Herrick sees himself *solely* as a pastoral poet than *"The Argument of his Book"* lists all the subjects and themes his poetry will treat. But just as Herrick in *"The Argument"* gives his readers a reasonable indication of what *Hesperides* will be like, *"To his Muse"* is by no means a misleading characterization of the poetic imagination whose nature is explored in this study.

Succeeding sections demonstrate that the pastoral tradition, whose potential Herrick explores and exploits, is a very rich one, with roots in the Bible, in ancient Greek and Roman poetry, and in native British folk culture. Herrick, like Milton, his contemporary, continues a trend begun by Sidney and Spenser and carried on by Shakespeare and Jonson—the "domestication" of the pastoral tradition, transforming the latter's idealized rural vision by blending into it the real sights and sounds of the English countryside. In such poetry and drama the classical nymphs and swains of Arcadia take their place beside, or sometimes become, Devonshire dairy maids and Kentish field hands.

If the two poems that Herrick places first and second in his collection clearly participate in the pastoral tradition, the next five introductory pieces just as clearly do not: four are terse epigrams to his book—one of them amusing (*H*-4), one scatalogical (*H*-5)—and another is an acerbic address *"To the soure Reader"* (*H*-6). None of them is as close to the spirit of traditional pastoral as the exuberant *"When he would have his verses read."* Such is the pattern of *Hesperides:* it occasionally features poems in the bucolic mode—some in the Old Style (the classical tradition), some in the New Style (the more modern, "synthesized" mode); there are poems that are not distinctively pastoral (love lyrics, for example, or encomia) but that can be and have been "pastoralized"; finally, there are other works, like many of Herrick's epigrams, that are not usually associated with the pastoral tradition at all. Indeed, a few of his poems, pieces celebrating London or denouncing Devonshire, are actually "antipastorals." Nevertheless, approaching the fictional world of Herrick's poetry in general as a pastoral world remains justifiable for two reasons: (1) in its long history, pastoral has accommodated a wide range of poetic modes, from love lyrics to satire, from elegies to encomia, from epitaphs to epigrams, from devotional verse to bawdry, from dialogues, debates, and descriptions to ceremonies and narratives; (2) as noted earlier, Herrick himself conceives of his Hesperidean world in terms of what he has called "pleasing Pastorall" (*H*-955.6).

A case in point is an important cluster of three commendations to the royal family. These three epigrams, observes Coiro, are "marked typographically and thematically as central to *Hesperides*" (1988, 189). The first of them, "TO THE KING" (*H*-264), is a conventional verse-compliment in which Herrick submits his "Lyricks" to Charles I in the hope that at least one will find royal favor. A poem so honored, the poet proclaims, will become "The Heire to This *great realm of Poetry*" (l. 6). The italicized phrase is significant because it makes explicit what has been implicit in *Hesperides* from the start—that Herrick thinks of his collection, not as a mere miscellany, but as an organic whole, a total achievement of which he can be proud. He is, after all, this little world's creator, and like the Creator he can decree who shall rule over it and who shall succeed to its "throne." It is Herrick's unifying personality that imposes order on this imaginary realm and promulgates its "laws" and that lends it a distinctive character and ambience. Herrick's metaphor, then, like the title of his book, yields a crucial insight into what he thinks art, or at least his art, ultimately represents. This insight is reinforced in the poem that follows, a verse compliment addressed to Henrietta Maria.

The political overtones of the image of the Hesperidean "realm" are transformed into more pastoral ones in the central image of "TO THE QUEENE" (*H*-265):

> GOddesse of Youth, and Lady of the Spring,
> (Most fit to be the Consort to a King)

> Be pleas'd to rest you in *This Sacred Grove,*
> Beset with *Mirtles;* whose each leafe drops Love.
>
> (ll. 1–4)

Whereas "TO THE KING" is a straightforward apostrophe that presents and celebrates Charles I as a poetry reader, "TO THE QUEENE" is a miniature masque: Herrick welcomes Henrietta Maria as if she were making a progress through his "*great realm of poetry,*" presenting her as a mythological figure associated with youth, love, and springtime—all conventional elements of pastoral. She is attended by such standard pastoral figures as "*sweet-fac't Wood-Nymph*[s]" and, in the tradition of masques and entertainments, becomes their queen (ll. 5–6). The poem concludes with a series of masquelike movements, with the nymphs strewing their new ruler's path with flowers and, after she has ascended her "Leavie-Throne (with *Lilly-*work)," presenting her with their own crowns of flowers (ll. 6–9). The effects of Herrick's 10-line ritual are quite similar to those Milton attains (in many more lines) in his pastoral entertainment *Arcades.*

The controlling image of "TO THE QUEENE," "*This Sacred Grove,*" is an allusion to the mythical garden of the Hesperides, with its fabled grove of golden apples planted by the queen-goddess Juno (*PW,* 522; *CP,* 148). Like Herrick's title for his book, this pastoral image suggests that Herrick's "poems are golden apples, fruits, at least in part, of Devonshire; collectively they constitute a garden of poetry" (*CP,* 5). A new Eve (Hesperides is also associated with the Garden of Eden),[15] Henrietta Maria now adds to her royal titles two others: Herrick invites her to "be both *Princesse* here, and *Poetresse*" (l. 10). These roles, it could be inferred, are viewed by the poet as being of about equal importance. As in "TO THE KING," Herrick decrees who will symbolically hold sway over this pastoral realm of *Hesperides,* and in the final poem of the triad he will determine its line of succession.

Patrick's speculation that "*The Poets good wishes for the most hopefull and handsome Prince, the Duke of York*" (H-266) was written to celebrate the birth (in 1633) of the future James II or an early birthday of his is apt (*CP,* 149): this poem, unlike those to the prince's mother and father, is not addressed to the personage named in its title, presumably because he would be too young to read it. The bucolic rhetoric, however, continues: Herrick's wishes allude to flowers; to those fixtures of classical pastoral landscape, "the Graces, and the Howers"; to the nine muses and the springs sacred to them; and to gardens and meadows (many of which are represented in the frontispiece to *Hesperides*). Among his other wishes the poet hopes that the young duke may grow up to become the Prince of the Muses, the master of arts and letters, perhaps even a poet like Robert Herrick, who can magically create a "*Sacred Grove*" whose fruits and flowers are poems:

> May his soft foot, where it treads,
> Gardens thence produce and Meads:
> And those Meddowes full be set
> With the Rose and Violet.
>
> (ll. 13–16)

Implicit here may also be the hope that James will be a good prince to the green and pleasant land that is England and that he will, like the heedful husbandman, ensure that his realm remains fertile and productive. As Claude J. Summers implies, like its companion pieces, "*The Poets good wishes*" helps establish the centrality of "the poetic ideal of pastoral" in *Hesperides*.[16]

The vision of "This *great Realme of Poetry*" (*Hesperides* as a world of art), "*This Sacred Grove*" (*Hesperides* as a bucolic realm sanctified by the "religion of poetry"), and "my rich Plantation" (*H-392*) may be represented iconographically in the frontispiece to Herrick's book (and to this one). It is reasonable to assume that, as the poet supervised the printing of his volume, its frontispiece also was his conception. The background of the engraving is a rural scene, to the left and center of which are a grove, hills, meadows, a large tree, and shrubs; the landscape to the right contains traditional images such as Mt. Parnassus and the Spring of Helicon (both sacred to the Muses) and Pegasus, the symbol of poetic inspiration. Nine winged figures—the Muses, suggests Patrick (*CP*, 7)—complete the picture: five dance in a circle beneath the large tree in the left midground and two, bearing wreaths of flowers, wing their way toward what is undoubtedly a bust, possibly somewhat "Latinized" (note the toga) of Herrick himself.[17] This bust—representing a massive man with a "Roman" nose, a moustache, and a mane of curly hair—dominates the pastoral landscape in the background. He is clearly the *genius loci* of "*This Sacred Grove*," as a poet second only to Phoebus Apollo, the god of poetry himself (at least according to the neo-Latin poem inscribed on the tomblike structure on which the bust sits).[18] The opening lines of this poem conflate the trees, which in the engraving partly frame Herrick's bust, and the wreath, which traditionally crowns the head of the true poet:

"A denser shade of leaves thy brows should bind; / A laurel grove is due to such a mind."[19]

That mind is the mind of a poet, yet it has something of the philosopher's self-consciousness and power of conceptualization. If *The Temple,* George Herbert's carefully structured collection of short devotional poems, expresses a mind that has been called "architectonic," *Hesperides,* that carefully designed collection of short secular and devotional poems, may be said to express a mind that is "creational," in the sense of being able to conceptualize a world and through art bring that world into existence.

Chapter Two

"Putrefaction" and *"This Sacred Grove"*: Themes of Transiency

One of the best-known of all seventeenth-century English poems is the Holy Sonnet of Herrick's older contemporary, John Donne, that begins: "Death, be not proud, though some have called thee / Mighty and dreadful." Death figures prominently in Donne's secular as well as his devotional poetry, and his prose is dominated, in the words of Frank Kermode, by "terrible sermons on death, full of the poetry of charnel house and worm," leading Kermode to conclude, "There is truth in the oft-repeated charge that Donne was preoccupied with sin and death; he confesses his melancholy temperament (calling it 'a disease of the times')."[1]

Authors in other ages have been preoccupied by death, but such a preoccupation is characteristic of English writers of the seventeenth century. From the soliloquies of Shakespeare's Hamlet to the meditations of Sir Thomas Browne to the cry of Andrew Marvell's persona to his coy mistress, "But at my back I alwaies hear / Times winged Charriot hurrying near," the literature of the period is pervaded by death's dark presence. Whether or not this preoccupation was, as Donne claimed, "a disease of the times," seventeenth-century Englishmen were predisposed by their religion, their education, and the vicissitudes of their existence to contemplate death seriously and often. Medicine of the time was primitive, and the average lifespan was, by modern standards, exceedingly short. Life's precariousness and brevity were further underscored by a Christianity whose prevailing themes were that earthly existence was primarily a preparation for death; that holy living was a prerequisite for holy dying; and that since the only true life lay beyond the grave, one's inevitable end was something to be continually confronted. Whatever the extent of their faith, citizens of seventeenth-century England could no more avoid contemplating the grave than citizens of the late twentieth century can avoid contemplating nuclear holocaust. Death, paradoxically, was central to the seventeenth-century way of life: "TIme is the Bound of things, where e're we go, / *Fate gives a meeting. Death's the end of woe*" (*"Death ends all woe,"* H-766).

The Occasion of Death

Herrick has been popularly associated with the poetry of life, love, joy, and beauty. That popular image is fundamental to the character of his poetry, but there is also another Herrick. As Allen H. Gilbert once pointed out: "Herrick is hardly to be appreciated unless he is seen to be aided by two muses, one jocund, the other diviner, inspiring him to sing of 'death accursed,' and of the victory over death."[2] This rectification of Herrick's popular image, although much needed, had the disadvantage of reinforcing a simplistic portrayal of the poet as a dual figure, half "pagan," half Christian. Gilbert's characterization, moreover, implies an attitude of despair about death that is not in fact characteristic of Herrick's secular collection, as this chapter will show.

Of the first 50 poems that follow Herrick's eight introductory pieces, more than a quarter treat the inevitability of change and death. That the poet himself is aware of his preoccupation with death is indicated in an epigram that serves as a kind of negative *"Argument of his Book."* Situated at approximately the half-way point in *Hesperides,* *"On himselfe"* (H-658) itemizes some of the volume's chief subjects, subjects about which Herrick, in a melancholy mood, vows he will no longer write or sing; there will be no more encomia or commendatory poems to "that sweet Lady, or that gallant Knight" (l. 2), no more pastorals of "Frosts" and "Flowers" (ll. 3–4), no more love poems, and in the climactic couplet, no more poems about death: "Ile sing no more of death, or shall the grave / No more my Dirges, and my Trentalls have" (ll. 7–8). He fails to keep his vow, of course, but his own words amply demonstrate how misleading was the widely held notion that "Herrick is all delicacy and delight."[3]

Some of the poems in *Hesperides* that deal with death are "occasional" in nature; that is, they are ceremonial pieces written not so much about the idea of death as about a particular death, real or imagined. To Herrick such an occasion sometimes calls for an epitaph, as in *"Upon a child"* (H-180), a poem reminiscent of Jonson's touching commemorations of his son and daughter. The first two couplets in Herrick's poem suggest a corollary of the concept of *"Times trans-shifting"*—the theme of the brevity of human existence:

> BUt borne, and like a short Delight,
> I glided by my Parents sight.

> That done, the harder Fates deny'd
> My longer stay, and so I dy'd.
>
> (ll. 1–4)

In the abrupt, clipped alliteration of "But borne," Herrick conveys the sense that something has been cut short, ended almost before it has begun. This feeling is reinforced by the six simple words that make up the characteristically Herrickean iambic tetrameter line and by its terse simile. Yet Herrick's verb, "glided," connotes a natural, easy motion: this child was like a bird in flight, seen for a moment, then gone, but all the more valued because its appearance was so brief. It is only human to want such precious moments to last, and so the mysterious, irrevocable cosmic plan, symbolized by the Fates, seems "hard." These lines do not imply that the speaker, the child himself, is railing against his fate; the tone is rather one of calm acceptance of what is natural and inevitable: "and so I dy'd."

In keeping with one of the conventions of the epitaph genre, the poem's last four lines are addressed to readers as if they were passersby who have stopped to peruse the tombstone on which the words of the poem have been engraved. These strangers are invited to involve themselves in this untimely death by empathizing with the bereaved parents, an empathy symbolized by performing certain traditional funerary rituals:

> If pittying my sad Parents Teares,
> You'l spil a tear, or two with theirs:
> And with some flowrs my grave bestrew,
> Love and they'l thank you for't. Adieu.
>
> (ll. 5–8)

Such a direct appeal to the reader suggests that this poem is something more than a simple epitaph for an anonymous, possibly imaginary, child: it becomes an implicit reminder that, in Donne's words, we all are "involved in mankind."[4] The death of a child not only deprives the parents of something precious; it diminishes everyone. Such an event poignantly reawakens our awareness of the brevity of human life. (That note is most memorably sounded by Herrick in the poem "Corinna's *going a Maying*," which precedes this epitaph by only two places in *Hesperides;* the lines of the love poem, "Our life is short; and our dayes run / As fast away as do's the Sunne," echo in the commemoration of the child's untimely death.)

Like the epitaph, an elegy is a poem of mourning; but whereas an epitaph is conventionally a brief poem appropriate for being inscribed on a tombstone, an elegy is by convention a ritual utterance recited over a grave. *"To the reverend shade of his religious Father"* (*H*-82) is an elegy in which Herrick brings his creative imagination and his concern for ceremony to bear on a personal situation, translating that situation into a moving literary experience. Herrick's use of the word *shade* (a spirit dwelling in the underworld) in his title foreshadows the poem's classicizing tendency, in which Christian elements are, as J. Max Patrick says, translated into their "Graeco-Roman equivalents." At the same time, as Patrick also suggests, the title's emphasis on Nicholas Herrick's piety may indicate that Herrick wanted to believe that his father's mysterious death (when the poet was an infant) was due to an accident and not to the sin (in the Christian view) of suicide (*CP*, 40–41). That the poem opens with an apology lends credence to such a view:

> THat for seven *Lusters* I did never come
> To doe the *Rites* to thy Religious Tombe:
> That neither haire was cut, or true teares shed
> By me, o'r thee (*as justments to the dead*)
> Forgive, forgive me; since I did not know
> Whether thy bones had here their Rest, or no.
>
> (ll. 1–6)

If we assume that Herrick is being historically accurate, the elegy was written about 1626, when he was 35. (*Lustre* is a Roman term for a five-year period.) Because of the suspicious circumstances of his father's death, which might have required that the location of the grave be concealed, it is quite possible that Herrick could have remained long in doubt about where Nicholas Herrick's remains "had their Rest." Such biographical details, however, are in the end irrelevant to a first reading of the poem, for the poet would not expect—doubtless would not want—most readers to know about the tragedy that had struck the Herrick family in 1592. The more general thrust of the elegy is clear enough from its opening lines: the poet seeks forgiveness because he has inadvertently failed to do a son's duty to his father—ensuring that the proper funeral rites have been performed. That these are represented as "pagan" rituals (cutting one's hair to commemorate the death of a loved one was an ancient Greek custom) may be of less significance than the fact that Herrick feels so very strongly— "Forgive, forgive"—that these rites are something owed to the dead by the living (*justments* means "due ceremonies").

As noted in chapter 1, the poet's almost anthropological fascination with ceremony has been the focus of a good deal of recent criticism. Today it is possible to take pride in doing things "without ceremony," but Herrick and his age believed that the observance of countless ceremonies, large and small, is essential to the conduct of civilized life. Rituals can formalize and sanctify profound feelings and thoughts associated with events such as bereavement. This is why Herrick invests so much emotion (conveyed by the repetition of "Behold; behold") in the laying of plants symbolic of death on his father's tomb: "I bring . . . Smallage, Night-shade, Cypresse, Yew" (ll. 5–9). Since this grieving son is also a poet, he can perform an additional ritual:

> I come to pay a Debt of Birth I owe.
> Thou gav'st me life (but Mortall;) For that one
> Favour, Ile make full satisfaction;
> For my life mortall, Rise from out thy Herse,
> And take a life immortal from my Verse.
>
> (ll. 12–16)

At this point the apologetic and regretful tone of the elegy changes to one of relief, even of exhilaration: under normal circumstances children cannot pay their parents back for the gift of mortal life, but a poet can give the gift of eternal life. Immortalized in this poem, his father will "live" as long as Robert Herrick's verses are read—which will be, he boldly claims, forever. Nicholas Herrick, then, in a sense will have two monuments—a physical one that "*Times trans-shifting*" must eventually overthrow and obliterate and a poetic one that, transcending earthly flux, will perpetuate his memory. This almost religious faith in the immortalizing power of poetry, which turns the tragedy of this poem into triumph, is (as I show in chapter 6) one of the major themes of *Hesperides*. That it may also be true can be inferred from this very discussion: were it not for the fact that his second son turned out to be a poet, after four hundred years who would remember the London goldsmith, Nicholas Herrick?

The Fact of Death

The death of a child, a parent, or other personally significant individual can prompt even the least reflective of mortals to contemplate their own mortality. Poets, of course, by their very nature are inclined to engage in such contemplations. What sets Herrick apart from many poets is the frequency and intensity with which he expresses the irony that death is ever imminent in life—that the bloom all too quickly leaves the rose, that just beneath the creamy cheek lies the whitened skull. This irony is compounded in his secular poems about natural phenomena by an acute awareness that the world of brooks and blossoms is cyclical, with death invariably succeeded by rebirth, whereas in the human realm regeneration is by no means foreordained.

Such ironies disqualify Herrick from being labeled (as he sometimes is) a "nature poet"; for if by that term is meant one whose favored subjects are natural phenomena, who describes them accurately, and who celebrates their qualities, Herrick does not fit the category, in spite of what may be inferred from the bucolics of *"The Argument of his Book."* Although the natural realm is the setting for many of his poems, few of them focus on that realm to the exclusion of the human dimension. In addition, while Herrick can take flowers or birds, for example, as his subjects, his images of them are never presented with a naturalist's loving precision—he is not a poet to number the stripes of the tulip. Finally, while a reading of his *Hesperides* can give the impression that Herrick the man found pleasure in nature, generally speaking Herrick the poet has less concern for the intrinsic qualities of natural objects than for their usefulness as metaphors for the human condition. For him, the important point is not that "a rose is a rose is a rose" but that a rose is, like a child or a lovely woman, a thing of beauty and a joy—not forever, but for all too brief a span.

Like Sir Thomas Browne, Milton, and most other learned and devout men of his day, Herrick could view nature, with its infinite variety but apparent order and purpose, as God's other book, the "Book of the Creatures," from which the divine plan could be read. Since humans, being part of the Great Chain of Being that links earth and heaven, were part of nature, their destiny figured in that plan. It is for this reason—and because natural objects are grist for his poetic mill, and because nature, as heightened by the pastoral tradition into *"This Sacred Grove,"* provides a mythic framework for his book—that the world of brooks, blossoms, birds, and bowers is important to Herrick.

Although traditional pastoral, except in its elegaic mode, tends to gloss over the fact of death, in the more realistic pastoral world of *Hesperides* death is omnipresent, as the epigram *"Putrefaction"* (*H-432*) bluntly states: "PUtrefaction is the end / Of all that Nature doth entend." Herrick's predilection for Latinisms stands him in good stead here, enabling him to present his observation with the succinctness of a scientific fact: every living thing (here *nature* has its seventeenth-century meaning of "life in general") eventually must decline, die, and go through a process of decomposition—all according to a plan. Depending on one's point of view, the speaker of the epigram is either cynical or merely realistic. However viewed, this is the persona of many of Herrick's epigrams—the truth teller, one who simply shows the way things are.

That such perceptions are often put forth with considerable if inconspicuous artistry should not, however, pass unnoticed. The genre of the epigram is an ancient and honorable one, and Herrick probably labored as diligently over these poems as he did over his lyrics and longer pieces. That, with Jonson, he regarded his epigrams as "the ripest of his studies"[5] is questionable, given his tendency in "*The Argument*" and elsewhere to present himself as a pastoral poet. Nevertheless, he wrote a great many epigrams and distributed them among his longer poems with care, making plausible Ann Coiro's theory that *Hesperides* is a kind of synthesis of pastoral collection and book of epigrams (1988, 30). In spite of the epigram's built-in limitations (and also because of them), the form had to have been a challenge to Herrick's powers of compression, to his ability to create an image and delineate a thought precisely, concisely, and poetically. The frequency of his success, then, is all the more remarkable.

In another epigram, "*All things decay and die*" (H-69), the theme of "*Putrefaction*" receives a somewhat more extended treatment:

> All *things decay with Time:* the Forrest sees
> The growth, and down-fall of her aged trees:
> That Timber tall, which three-score *lusters* stood
> The proud *Dictator* of the State-like wood:
> I meane (the Soveraigne of all Plants) the Oke
> Droops, dies, and falls without the cleavers stroke.
>
>   (ll. 1–6)

Appearing relatively early in *Hesperides,* this epigram indicates that the world of the book, "*Sacred Grove*" though it may be, is a world where natural law is not entirely suspended. The relevance of the fate of trees to the human condition is implied in the opening maxim, for people obviously must be included in the category of "all things." The remainder of the poem then can be read as an allegory as well as a description of a natural process. The personified forest consciously observes the life cycle of the individual trees that comprise it, just as a state monitors the lives and deaths of its citizens. The inevitability of atrophy is underscored by the fact that even the ruler of the state is subject to the laws of nature and "Droops, dies, and falls." Nor is the natural process the only threat: Herrick's reference to the "cleavers stroke" raises the possibility that the royal oak runs the risk of being laid low by a coup d'etat or revolution (as Charles I, in fact, would be in 1649). Herrick's attitude here is realistic and composed: he bemoans neither natural law nor the nature of *realpolitik*.

On a more speculative level, Herrick's allegory might be interpreted as another in a series of somewhat rueful, somewhat judgmental poems by various hands on the artistic deterioration of the proud dictator of the London literary scene, Ben Jonson. One of Jonson's collections of poems is entitled *The Forrest,* another is *Underwood,* and the compilation of his prose is called *Timber.* Although a member in good standing of the "Tribe of Ben" and a professed admirer of Jonson, Herrick must have been aware of his literary father's gradual decline from literary eminence: it was, after all, publicly commented on—for example, by another "Son of Ben," Thomas Carew, in "TO BEN. IOHNSON. *Upon occasion of his Ode of defiance annext to his play of the newe Inne.*" Herrick, then, might have seen Jonson's fate as an object lesson in the vanity of literary ambition (a lesson, however, he himself was not always able to take to heart).

The analogy between the cycles of nature and the patterns of human life hinted at in "*All things decay and die*" is made explicit in two of Herrick's frequently reprinted apostrophes, or poetic addresses—"*To Daffadills*" (H-316) and "*To Blossoms*" (H-467). The first poem expresses regret for the transiency of natural beauty that daffodils exhibit: "we weep to see / You haste away so soone" (ll. 1–2). It then calls on the flowers to wait "But to the Even-song; / And, having pray'd together, we / Will goe with you along" (ll. 8–10). Presenting the natural drooping of the heads of these flowers in the evening as a metaphor for prayer at once humanizes the natural world and naturalizes the human world. That the speaker will "go along" with the flowers into death prefigures another analogy between human beings and flowers that is explicitly drawn in stanza 2:

> 2. We have short time to stay, as you,
>   We have as short a Spring;
>   As quick a growth to meet Decay,
>   As you, or any thing.
>   (ll. 11–14)

From this recognition of the brevity of life, the fleeting nature of youth, and the rush to "putrefaction," the speaker passes on to a mood of philosophical acceptance of two profoundly simple facts—"We die" and we disappear, "Ne'r to be found again" (l. 20). This mood is in the spirit of the

injunction of the Greek philosopher Epicurus: "Accustom thyself to believe
that death is nothing to us, for good and evil imply [have their being in]
sentience [sensation], and death is the privation of all sentience."[6] That "*To
Daffadills,*" whose first stanza ends on an explicitly Christian note ("Evensong" means "vesper service"), should conclude on an implicitly philosophical note without alluding to the Christian consolation of life after death may
seem curious to the reader aware that Herrick is a poet-priest writing in an
intensely religious era. This poem, nevertheless, is only one of many that exhibit Herrick's Christian humanism (that is, his habit of thinking and feeling that leads him to interweave strands of classical Greek and Roman
culture and thought with traditional Christian doctrine and mythology
without making many qualitative distinctions between them).

The speaker in "*To Blossoms*" is unable initially to face the fact of transiency and its implications with the kind of equanimity displayed by the
persona in "*To Daffadills*":

> 1. FAire pledges of a fruitfull Tree,
>   Why do yee fall so fast?
>   Your date is not so past;
>   But you may stay yet here a while,
>   To blush and gently smile;
>   And go at last.

The answer to the speaker's question is implicit in its own phrasing: the
blossoms are the tree's "FAire pledges"—they promise fulfillment through
fruition, and they also serve by adding beauty to the world. At this early
point in the poem, however, these truths are lost upon the speaker, whose
feelings are emphasized by Herrick's meter: lines 2–3 are staccato, reflecting the speaker's surprise and concern, whereas lines 4–6 are largo, their
long vowels reflecting the extension of the blossoms' lives for which he is
pleading. Moreover, the manner in which the stanzas taper off suggests,
metrically and typographically, the blossoms' falling movement. (Herrick's
skillful manipulations of line length and meter always merit careful
attention.)

The irony implicit in the first stanza—that the beautiful and the good
are inevitably short-lived—is made painfully explicit in stanza 2:

> 2. What, were yee born to be
>   An houre or half's delight;
>   And so to bid goodnight?

> 'Twas pitie Nature brought yee forth
> Meerly to shew your worth,
> And lose you quite.

In *"To Daffadills,"* the tyranny of transiency is emphasized by dramatic foreshortening: while blossoms obviously bloom for more than 90 minutes, Herrick's compression of the natural cycle heightens the irony and makes the persona's charge of improvidence against nature seem more justifiable. Nevertheless, between stanzas 2 and 3 he achieves an insight:

> 3. But you are lovely Leaves where we
> May read how soon things have
> Their end, though n'er so brave:*
> And after they have shown their pride,
> Like you a while: They glide
> Into the Grave.

> *beauteous*

The conjunction "But" throws the emphasis of the first line on "lovely," which intensifies the ironic quality of the insight: even beauty has no power over destiny. That the blossoms are also "Leaves" from the "Book of the Creatures" is a serious pun, reminding the reader that there are lessons to be "read" from nature. Since neither the beauty and value of the blossoms nor human appeals can change the way things are, it follows that recriminations like those expressed by the persona in the first two stanzas are not only useless but inappropriate. The verb "glide," moreover, implies that the blossoms' falling to earth is as natural and easy as their flourishing; it also sets the tone of calm acceptance with which the poem ends.

By what is doubtless no coincidence, a trace of anxiety, rather than calm acceptance characterizes an epigram on man's fate *"Mans dying-place uncertaine"* (H-468), which Herrick inserts immediately after *"To Blossoms"'s* contemplation of the fate of flowers: "Man knowes where first he ships himselfe; but he / Never can tell, where shall his Landing be." Herrick's tendency to reinforce or qualify the thrust of a poem by juxtaposing it with another is also evident in the case of a work previously discussed: the philosophical generalizations of *"To Daffadills"* are concretely embodied in the next poem but one in Herrick's arrangement, *"Upon a Lady that dyed in child-bed, and left a daughter behind her"* (H-318). This miniature elegy repeats the theme of *"To Daffadills,"* the brevity of the lives of flowers and human beings, but adds the consolation of generation in the image of that "sweet Lady" who, to give her daughter life, "resign'd [her] own," but who will live on "in the pretty Lady-Flower" (ll. 9, 11).

"*To Blossoms*" and "*To Daffadills*" are, at one level, pleasingly melancholy lyrics, well suited to be set to music—as they have been.[7] At another level they are as much about states of mind as about plants. Both hint at a progression from naive idealism to mature neo-Stoicism, to a synthesis of a "modern" (that is, seventeenth-century) sensibility with a world view like that of the Stoic philosopher-king Marcus Aurelius:

Despise not death, but welcome it, for Nature wills it like all else. For dissolution is but one of the processes of Nature, associated with thy life's various seasons, such as to be young, to be old, to wax to our prime and to reach it, to grow teeth and beard and grey hairs, to beget, conceive, and bring forth. A man then that has reasoned the matter out should not take up towards death the attitude of indifference, eagerness or scorn, but await it as one of the processes of Nature.[8]

This sober theme will surface often in Herrick's secular verse, and there will be overtones of it in his devotional poetry as well.

Both "*To Blossoms*" and "*To Daffadills*" have been described as "meditation[s] on death."[9] A similarly formal contemplation of a serious subject that is also a lyric in Herrick's neo-Stoical vein is "*A Meditation for his Mistress*" (H-216). Here the poet carries his contemplation of transiency and death two steps further by particularizing their implications for both his lady love (whether real or imaginary) and himself. Rhetorically, "*A Meditation*" is a verse-compliment, with each of its seven triplet stanzas metaphorically comparing the speaker's mistress to a different thing of beauty. The metaphor of the first stanza and all but one of the others are based on Herrick's characteristic analogy between plants and people: "1. YOu are a *Tulip* seen to day, / But (Dearest) of so short a stay; / That where you grew, scarce man can say." Like the blooms of "*To Blossoms,*" the lady is, despite her beauty, a transitory thing, and because of that she is rare, even mysterious. Stanza 2 suggests her vulnerability, which her purity (stanza 3) can in no way shore up:

> 2. You are a lovely *July-flower,*
>   Yet one rude wind, or ruffling shower,
>   Will force you hence, (and in an houre.)

> 3. You are a sparkling *Rose* i'th'bud,
>   Yet lost, ere that chast flesh and blood
>   Can shew where you or grew, or stood.

The abstraction of *"Times trans-shifting"* is made concrete in the destructive winds and rains of raw nature, which can in an hour batter down a flower whose growth took weeks, just as other forces can doom youthful flesh and blood to oblivion. Transiency extends its tyranny, moreover, not only over beauty but also over beauty's corollary, love: "4. You are a full-spread faire-set Vine, / And can with Tendrills love intwine, / Yet dry'd, ere you distill your Wine." The eroticism of the mistress clinging to her lover—an eroticism Herrick reverses, with comic effect, in *"The Vine"* (*H*-41)—here intensifies the poignancy associated with a death that disallows even sexual fulfillment.

A similar notion is conveyed in the next stanza, although Herrick abandons the pattern of plant metaphors that helped unify the first half of his poem: "5. You are like Balme inclosed (well) / In *Amber,* or some *Chrystall* shell, / Yet lost ere you transfuse your smell." Not only is a metaphor here replaced by a simile, but the ground of the comparisons is lost: balm, although a natural product, is an extraction and is thus once removed from the class of flowers and vines. Conceptually, however, this stanza is a variation on the poem's central theme: as perfume, no matter how carefully preserved, eventually will lose its fragrance, so human life, regardless of how well it is protected, must also evaporate.

In stanza 6 Herrick returns to his metaphoric catalog: "You are a dainty *Violet,* / Yet wither'd, ere you can be set / Within the Virgins Coronet." It is a convention of pastoral poetry that rustic maids weave a crown of flowers for the shepherdess who rules over them. It can be inferred, therefore, that Herrick contemplates the possibility that his mistress, being a "dainty *Violet,*" cannot endure long enough to serve her lady (Flora, perhaps, goddess of flowers) and thus will be denied a form of social fulfillment. In the final stanza, however, she does at least receive a title of her own: "7. You are the *Queen* all flowers among, / But die you must (faire Maid) ere long, / As He, the maker of this Song." True to the conventions of the compliment and catalog forms, Herrick's poem ends with a climactic tribute to the lady. Embodying the beauty of all flowers, she is their queen, but not their goddess: goddesses are immortal, and she (she is reminded) is not. Like her poet-lover she comes under the indictment of nature. Neither beauty nor creativity (the capacity to make beauty) can be a stay against *"Times trans-shifting"*; yet the matter-of-factness of Herrick's second and third lines reflects the equanimity with which he confronts the lady's mortality, and his own. This "*Meditation*," which is also a song (an unusual combination of poetic forms), is at once a celebration of the lady and an assertion of the facts of life and death that qualify that celebration. Herrick achieves this dual effect by splitting his normally unitary triplet stanzas into one or sometimes two lines of conventional compliment followed by one or more lines of Stoical reflection on mortality. The unexpected allusion to the death of "the maker of this Song" that ends the poem nevertheless comes as something of a shock. It reverberates in the silence after the final stanza, reminding readers that they too share the fate of flowers, lovers, and poets.

In spite of the odd lapse in its figurative pattern, T. G. S. Cain maintains that

few poems in English convey so complete a sense of the brevity of all life as does ["*A Meditation for his Mistress*"]. It is a profoundly serious poem, not just in intent, but in realization. And yet the very grace and brevity which are the means of this realization make it difficult . . . to recognize it for what it is. (113)

The poem's implacable emphasis on life's brevity underscores life's values —such as glimpses of beauty, moments of love, and snatches of song—and therein lies a clue to the heart and mind of Robert Herrick as they find expression in his poetry.

This study so far has shown that Herrick's contemplation of the "Book of the Creatures"—the natural world—results in certain fundamental insights: that "*Times trans-shifting*" is a law of nature and, as a consequence, all living things decay, die, and undergo "putrefaction"; that since humans are denizens of nature's realm, they are not—despite their aspirations— exempted from this fatal cycle; and that the human condition, then, inevitably frustrates all attempts to achieve total fulfillment. In *Hesperides* these insights are transformed into themes to which Herrick turns again and again—not simply because he lacks invention, because he is merely following the lead of his classical models, nor even because, like others of his time, he is obsessed with death. A more comprehensive explanation for the preoccupation of Herrick and his contemporaries with transiency and its consequences is proposed by Douglas Bush:

The meditations on the brevity of life, so numerous and so rich throughout [English literature in the period between 1600 and 1660], are not the rhetorical funguses of an age of decay; they are the seventeenth-century version of the Dance of

Death, and they tell rather of immense vitality contemplating its inevitable extinction.[10]

Much of the poetry of the earlier seventeenth century, then, and Herrick's in particular, is vibrant with the tension between existence and extinction, between an awareness of death that is profound without being morbid and an equally profound, if not always solemn, sense of what Epicurus called "the desirableness of life" (653). This tension is the result of deeply knowing and feeling one's mortality and living in measured response to such a heightened awareness. According to Ernest Becker, most of us most of the time choose to "deny" our death, to live as if we will live forever.[11] Seventeenth-century writers like Herrick seem to have lived as if they would die tomorrow. Not all of them, however, react to the prospect of their imminent deaths in the same way. Some poets, like Herbert, respond by centering themselves in the life of the spirit and contemplating the Christian vision of life eternal. Others, like Donne in the *Holy Sonnets,* wish to do the same but vacillate between religious euphoria and depression. Secular poets like Lovelace escape into bravado or, like Suckling, into heedless hedonism. A few others, like Herrick, respond to mortality with a ringing, if qualified, affirmation of life. For Herrick such an affirmation takes the form of using poetry to explore and exploit life as he knows it but also to imagine life as he wishes it to be. In this sense, as a poet he is both critic and artist of life.

In poem after poem, then, Herrick confronts extinction by affirming existence—by exulting in and exalting such traditionally "Cavalier" values as friendship, hospitality, conviviality, love (of women, of king, and of country), and food and drink.[12] He also affirms, however, a combination of values that is more distinctively his own—such as kinship, achieving harmony with nature, the principle of moderation, what might be called "the aesthetics of living," the "religion" of poetry, and the rituals and ceremonies that sanctify all of these values. This is not to imply that *Hesperides* is a kind of neo-Epicurean/Christian-Stoic tract; it is, as advertised, a collection of poems. Nor am I suggesting that Herrick is, in essence, a kind of humanistic philospher: humanist he is, but he is above all a poet. Still, like the average person—and for all his genius there is much of the Everyman about him—Herrick has a reasonably well-defined identity; that is, the man reflected in the poetry demonstrates a good deal of consistency in his perceptions, feelings, attitudes, values, and beliefs. A fuller understanding and appreciation of *Hesperides* is possible, then, for the reader who is aware of the poet's fundamental concern that death inevitably frustrates self-fulfillment; of his basic assumption that life still has great value; and of his primary response to these ideas—that fulfillment must be attempted through a deliberate effort to seize life's values while one can. Playing off against these themes, perhaps even inspiring them in part, is a tough-minded criticism of flawed humanity and of an imperfect social order that emerges from *Hesperides'* hundreds of epigrams.

An awareness of Herrick's complex vision is helpful when examining individual poems, their relationships to each other, and Herrick's book as a whole; and it is toward helping the reader attain these ends that succeeding chapters are devoted.

Chapter Three
"The Country Life" and *"This Sacred Grove"*: Themes of the Good Life

Every age is "an age of transition," but some more so than others. Among historians it is generally agreed that what is thought of as the modern world was in effect born in Herrick's era, in the earlier seventeenth century, when various socioeconomic, political, and cultural trends that had begun in the late Middle Ages in England and accelerated during the sixteenth century began to crystallize. Douglas Bush has gone so far as to claim, "In 1600 the mind of the average educated Englishman was more than half medieval; by 1660 the mind of the average educated Englishman was more than half modern" (1). So sweeping a generalization has to be handled with care, but it is useful for putting in perspective the world in which Herrick lived and wrote. For all the changes taking place in that world, it must have seemed to him to be a relatively stable one, for until the Civil War finally broke out in 1642, his England managed somehow to weather both its external and its internal storms. A factor contributing to this relative national stability was a synthesis of spiritual and intellectual attitudes that had been inherited from the past, a synthesis that, as Bush has noted, significantly affected the literature of the age:

The working philosophy inherited by [English authors of the earlier seventeenth century] was the Christian humanism which during the Middle Ages and the Renaissance had fused Christian faith and pagan reason into a stable framework of religious, ethical, political, economic and cultural thought. That tradition, the main European tradition, comes from Plato and Cicero down through Erasmus and others to such men as Spenser, Hooker, Daniel, Chapman, and Jonson—and, though less obviously, Shakespeare. Its central religious and philosophical doctrine is order, order in the individual soul, in society, and in the cosmos. (35–36)

That this "working philosophy" and this "doctrine of order" are very much present in Herrick's poetry will become readily apparent.

The Sensuous Life

As chapter 7 will indicate, recent scholarship has shown that Herrick's *Hesperides,* so long regarded as a largely haphazard collection of miscellaneous poems, is, in fact, a book with considerably more than a semblance of artistic and thematic order. One aspect of that thematic order, discussed in chapter 2, is that *Hesperides* includes a significant number of poems in which death is resolutely confronted and ultimately accepted with equanimity. These may be labeled Herrick's "neo-Stoic" verses. Another aspect of this same thematic order derives from a series of poems that evolve in tone and attitude from a calm acceptance of human mortality to a determination to make an active response to that mortality. Such poems, like *"To enjoy the Time"* (*H-457*), fuse neo-Stoicism with neo-Epicureanism:

> WHile Fate permits us, let's be merry;
> Passe all we must the fatall Ferry:
> And this our life too whirles away,
> With the Rotation of the Day.

The most striking difference between this epigram and the poems treated in the previous chapter is the speaker's positive response to his confrontation with the grim reality of death. Unlike the persona of *"To Blossoms"* the speaker feels himself to be as much a part of the natural order as "the Rotation of the Day." His response to human mortality (which, he is careful to indicate, affects his readers as well as himself) is the Epicurean admonition "let's be merry."

That response is one with which Herrick is frequently associated, and with some justification. After all, his best-known poem begins "GAther ye Rose-buds while ye may." The point of view implicit in both these exhortations is succinctly summarized in Horace's phrase *carpe diem,* whose literal meaning—"seize the day"—is more effectively translated in the title of Herrick's epigram, *"enjoy the Time."* If so universal a theme can be assigned a source, it must be the poets of Rome's "Silver Age"—Horace, Tibullus, and Propertius. It is, therefore, no coincidence that "Roman" elements are conspicuous by their presence in Herrick's epigram. "While Fate permits" acknowledges that human life is governed by forces mysterious to human beings and over which they have no control. The only certainty is that eventually we all become passengers on Charon's "fatall Ferry" across the River Styx to the oblivion of Hades. Every rotation of the earth, moreover, "whirles" us closer to that destiny.

Herrick's response is, in the words of another epigram, *"To live Freely"* (*H-453*): "LEt's live in hast; use pleasure while we may: / Co'd life return, 'twod never lose a day." Readers only casually acquainted with the poet's work might assume that this hedonistic response sums up his philosophy; however, there are more things in that philosophy than casual readers have dreamt of, and certainly more than a simple affirmation of the pleasure principle. For the moment, though, it will be useful to consider a few more of those works that have advanced Herrick's reputation as a poet of the sensuous life—for example, the epigram *"Best to be merry"* (*H-231*):

> FOoles are they, who never know
> How the times away doe goe:
> But for us, who wisely see
> Where the bounds of black Death be:
> Let's live merrily, and thus
> Gratifie the *Genius*.

Behind this short poem lies a phase of literary history—Herrick is borrowing from Simonides, Persius, and Horace (*CW,* 521)—and a philosophical tradition. In its first four lines the speaker, like a good Stoic, unflinchingly confronts "black Death," with all its impediments to human fulfillment; however, like a satirist, he also mocks the folly of those who practice denial concerning the inexorable passage of time.

It was not only the Stoics who stressed death's place in the natural order of things and thus the futility of fearing it; so did the Greek philosopher Epicurus and his Roman disciple Lucretius. To the serious Epicurean, pain of any kind, including psychological suffering, was inimical to life's great purpose—the maximization of pleasure. Throughout intellectual history Epicureanism has been associated—somewhat unjustly, as will be seen below—with the pursuit of the kind of Dionysian pleasure that is recommended in the last two lines of *"Best to be merry."* Living merrily, Herrick's speaker implies, is merely acquiescing to the natural order, to the spirit or *"Genius"* of life here on earth. There is a difference, however, between "living merrily" and "living well," and the latter phrase more accurately represents the philosophy of Epicurus than the former. *"Best to be merry,"* therefore, is a neo-Epicurean poem more in the popular than the philosophical sense of the term.

The catch phrase "Eat, drink, and be merry, for tomorrow we die" is a popular modern version of *carpe diem,* but the self-conscious bravado evident in this exhortation has found its expression in poetry at least since the time of Anacreon, the legendary Greek lyrist of wine, women, and song. Herrick's imitations of the *Anacreontea*—like *"Anacreontike"* (*H*-450), *"Anacreontick Verse"* (*H*-996), and two poems entitled *"On himselfe"* (*H*-170, *H*-519)—reproduce the spirit of their originals and contribute to a Dionysian strain that lends periodic rambunctiousness to the overall mood of *Hesperides:* "Ile spend my comming houres, / Drinking wine, and crown'd with flowres" (*H*-519, 7–8). Less imitative and more ambitious affirmations of the sensuous life are two paired poems, *"His fare-well to Sack"* (*H*-128) and *"The Welcome to Sack"* (*H*-197)—works that on another level subvert themselves and satirize the Anacreontic temperament.

Although separated in the 1648 edition of *Hesperides* by 36 pages, these two poems must be regarded as companion pieces, as their parallel titles indicate. Herrick's purpose in separating them is for dramatic effect: the typographical "distance" is meant to suggest an interval in "real" time during which the poet has been on the wagon—or has at least abstained from drinking sack, a popular white wine. *"His fare-well"* establishes the controlling metaphor of both works, one that parodies conventional Renaissance love poetry: sack is presented as the speaker's goddesslike mistress, possessing "witching beauties" (l. 39) and beguiling looks (l. 46), dearer to him than "kindred, friend, man, wife" (l. 3). It gives life (l. 12) and takes away unhappiness, for it can control "That, which subverts whole nature, grief and care; / Vexation of the mind, and damn'd Despaire" (ll. 21–22). Sack is also essential to poetic inspiration: without it even Apollo, the god of poetry, and the nine muses are mute (ll. 23–30). Unfortunately, sack appears to be hazardous to the speaker's health: "Nature bids thee goe, not I" (l. 42). He must, therefore, forswear the inspiration of wine—"Let my Muse / Faile of thy former helps" (ll. 51–52)—and rely only on his talent. The result, he predicts, will be verses that "smell of the Lamp" (l. 54)—that is, the kind of pedantic poems that Herrick's mentor, Ben Jonson, was criticized for writing.

The extended hyperbole with which *"His fare-well"* celebrates sack establishes the poem as a comic case study in vinosity. Through his parody of a form of love poem favored by such seventeenth-century poets as Donne, the lovers' farewell, Herrick mocks his own addiction. An effect of this tour de force—and of *"The Welcome to Sack"*—is humorously to qualify his Anacreontics and perhaps those other poems in *Hesperides* that celebrate unbridled sensuousness.

If one reads straight through Herrick's book (as he intended), *"The Welcome"* (*H*-197) comes as a surprise, for *"His fare-well,"* in spite of its wit and humor, appears to express a firm decision to abstain from sack. The intervening 68 poems are meant to represent a period of time during which the poet did forswear his favorite drink. To justify his turnabout, he begins "*The Welcome*" with a sentimental simile comparing the resumption of his "affair" with sack to reunions in the natural world:

> SO soft streames meet, so springs with gladder smiles
> Meet after long divorcement by the Iles:
> When Love (the child of likeness) urgeth on
> Their Christal natures to an union.
>
> (ll. 1–4)

For Herrick, to resume drinking sack, it is implied, is as natural as the confluence of waters or (as he melodramatically continues) the reunions of "fierce Lovers" (l. 5): obviously he and sack are made for each other. Repetitions of metaphors and images from "*His fare-well*" remind the reader of the linkage between the two poems: addressed as "Divinest Soule!" (l. 19) in the first poem, sack here is saluted as "Soule of my life, and fame!" (l. 9). The conceit in "*His fare-well*"—that sack is the poet's divine mistress— here is made more explicit: "Welcome, O Welcome my illustrious Spouse" (l. 13); he then goes on to complain that their long separation has made his lover (like the typical "disdainful fair" of so many amatory verses) sullen toward him: "Why frowns my Sweet? Why won't my Saint confer / Favours on me, her fierce Idolater?" (ll. 25–26). Terms like "Saint" and "Idolater" call to mind the literary convention of "love's religion," one on which Herrick will frequently draw in his serious love poetry; here, however, he employs it comically for the purpose of keeping his ongoing burlesque properly overinflated. (This is the general tendency of Herrick's humor: veiled irony, subtle wit, and clever wordplay are less his style than is the comedy of the hyperbolic.)

The gentleman next protests (comically too much) that he will go to any lengths to seek forgiveness for his long "absence," and rhetorically denies that he was, during their separation, "unfaithful": "Have I divorc't thee onely to combine / In hot Adult'ry with another Wine?" (ll. 39–40). His excuse for his absence—that it was to make his heart grow fonder, "[to] double my affection on thee" (l. 43)—appears even more flimsy when the reader recalls that in "*His fare-well*" it was reasons of health that he said dictated his abstinence. Now he vows that never again will he and sack be separated: "When thou thy selfe dar'st say, thy Iles shall lack / Grapes, before *Herrick* leaves Canarie Sack" (ll. 47–48). By naming himself (as Ben Jonson also is wont to do), Herrick reinforces an autobiographical reading of the poem, breaking down the barrier between art and life that is one of poetry's usual conventions. Repeated elsewhere with some frequency— *Hesperides* includes 50 titles that begin with the personal possessive "his"— the effect is to imbue Herrick's collection with more of the illusion of verisimilitude than is sometimes recognized.

The poet's next tactic is the tried and true one of flattery. Sack, he says, makes him so light and lively that he becomes like the legendary Greek hero who "was so fleet of foot that he ran on the tops of growing grain in fields" (*CP*, 112): "Thou mak'st me ayrie, active to be born, / Like *Iphyclus*, upon the tops of Corn" (ll. 49–50). The drink, moreover, engenders love and (as "*His fare-well*" claims) poetic inspiration (ll. 53–56). With deliberate pedantry, Herrick turns to the authority of historical precedent for additional compliments: Cassius, who betrayed Julius Caesar, was a "weak Water-drinker," whereas "wise *Cato*," the Roman statesman (stigmatized by Herrick in *H-8* as "rigid *Cato*") approved of wine, and Hercules, "*Joves* son," drank wine to maintain his sexual prowess (ll. 61–67). On the strength of this last allusion, Herrick returns to his burlesque amatory refrain; ready at last to put his lips to the glass, he urges, "Come, come and kisse me; Love and lust commends / Thee, and thy beauties" (ll. 69–70), and then draws a comically inflated (yet lyrical) comparison to one of the most famous love affairs of all time:

> . . . or come thou unto me,
> As *Cleopatra* came to *Anthonie,*
> When her high carriage did at once present
> To the *Triumvir,* Love and Wonderment.
> (ll. 73–76)

In the poem's final movement Herrick reprises the conceit of "love's religion," melodramatically calling down mighty curses upon himself if he should ever "turn Apostate to [sack's] love" (l. 81). The most potent of these would be the curse of Apollo, the god of poetry; in the unlikely event that he should ever again abstain from the drink that has made him a poet, then, he cries,

> Call me *The sonne of Beer,* and then confine
> Me to the Tap, the Tost, the Turfe; Let Wine
> Ne'r shine upon me; May my Numbers all
> Run to a sudden Death, and Funerall.

And last, when thee (deare Spouse) I disavow,
Ne'r may Prophetique *Daphne* crown my Brow.
(ll. 87–92)

Beer, of course, is a plebian drink imbibed by the vulgar frequenters of such taverns as "the Tap, the Tost, the Turfe." Elsewhere in *Hesperides* (e.g., *"The Hock-cart"*) Herrick makes a class distinction on the basis of beverage preference, with wine identified as the drink of gentlemen. More importantly, however, here it is presented as the drink of poets, whose transcendent art ("Numbers") is symbolized by the laurel wreaths with which they have been crowned. To be deprived of such an honor because of a dearth of poetic inspiration is for the "foolish Herrick" of the sack poems—as it is for the "wise Herrick" of *Hesperides* generally—truly a fate worse than death.

Like *"His fare-well to Sack," "The Welcome to Sack"* can thus on one level be read as a burlesque of love poetry and on another as a satire on the extremism of the Anacreontic temper, a temper that tends to equate bibulousness and its corollaries with the good life. On yet another level both poems can be viewed as self-caricatures in which Herrick may be mocking one of his personal weaknesses (as his idol Ben Jonson does on occasion). Beneath the wit and humor of both poems, nevertheless, it is also possible to detect a healthy regard not only for strong drink but also for sex and love—and certainly for the poetry that celebrates such delights of the sensuous life. These Bacchanalian companion pieces, then, in their comic yet grandly poetical way, are poems of the good life even though they show that life carried to its alcoholic extreme.

The Urban Life

Pastoral poets historically have been urban and urbane people with an inclination to idealize the country—individuals who yearn in verse for a life close to nature but who tend to eke out their actual existence in the city. Herrick is different: although born and bred in London and educated in Cambridge, he experienced "the bucolic life" firsthand in his 32 years as a priest in a part of Devonshire that is to this day rural. The partial disenchantment that seems to have resulted from this experience, recorded in several poems about Devonshire, does not, however, seriously undermine his orientation toward the pastoral. Instead, his long and intimate encounter with English country living seems to have sharpened his awareness of the discrepancy between the traditional bucolic ideal and rural actuality and perhaps motivated his effort to bridge that gap with his own pastorals. An example of this tendency is a poem that may have been written about 1647 (although it appears early in *Hesperides*), when Herrick was expelled from his vicarage because of his royalist sympathies. The poem's irritable and long-winded title, "*To* Dean-bourn, *a rude River in* Devon, *by which sometimes he lived*" (*H*-86) signals this valediction's tone and its autobiographical content:

> DE*an-Bourn,* farewell; I never look to see
> *Deane,* or thy warty incivility.
> Thy rockie bottome, that doth teare thy streams,
> And makes them frantick, ev'n to all extreames;
> To my content, I never sho'd behold,
> Were thy streames silver, or thy rocks all gold.
>
> (ll. 1–5)

Implicit in Herrick's personification of the river is an analogy between humans and nature, poignantly employed in other poems to depict the transient beauty and rare worth of human life. Here, however, the emphasis is on the primitive in nature and in humanity. Conventional pastoral poetry is civilized to a fault—poetry without warts, in a manner of speaking. But "Dean-bourn" here stands for a world seemingly beyond domestication and civilization—a nature that defies the imposition of humanity's ameliorating vision and that is therefore rejected out of hand.

Pastoral poetry also traditionally exhibits "decorum" —a judicious blending of appropriate subject and proper style—avoiding extremes of either. Whereas the streams of conventional pastoral are silvery smooth, however, the surface of "Dean-bourn" (in what may be a metaphor for the realities of life in Devonshire) is agitated by the real, not the poetically golden, rocks it passes over. Since the qualities of order, harmony, and moderation that characterize the pastoral vision are implied to be utterly foreign to this river and the region it represents, the poet sarcastically denies that he could ever return to it. He seals this rejection with a third, a dismissal even of those who inhabit this primitive landscape:

> Rockie thou art; and rockie we discover
> Thy men; and rockie are thy wayes all over.
> O men, O manners; Now and ever knowne
> To be *A Rockie Generation!*
> A people currish; churlish as the seas;
> And rude (almost) as rudest Salvages

> With whom I did, and may re-sojourne when
> Rockes turn to Rivers, Rivers turn to Men.
>
> (ll. 7–14)

Herrick's Devonians are scarcely the gentle swains and sweet nymphs of the bucolic tradition: perceived as hardheaded and rough hewn in disposition and behavior, mean-spirited at best, these English primitives, depicted as being little more than savages, resemble pastoral's satyrs—half man, half goat—in their subhumanity. In other words, for the poet they are perfectly adapted to their hostile and unattractive environment, neither of which anything less than a total metamorphosis of nature, he claims, could ever make acceptable.

The historical fact that Robert Herrick actively sought to "re-sojourne" with Devonshire and its denizens (and succeeded in doing so) is less to the point here than the literary fact that, in his own book, *"To* Dean-Bourn" follows by only a few pages a brief lyric that defines the prevailing climate of pastoral poetry and celebrates it, *"The succession of the foure sweet months"* (*H*-70):

> First, *April,* she with mellow showrs
> Opens the way for early flowers;
> Then after her comes smiling *May*
> In a more rich and sweet array:
> Next enters *June,* and brings us more
> Jems, then those two, that went before:
> Then (lastly) *July* comes, and she
> More wealth brings in, than all those three.

Like figures in a seventeenth-century masque, the personified months of Herrick's poem enter and one by one remind us of the pastoral convention that bucolics are poetry of spring and summer—those seasons when nature is at her most benign and beautiful. The origin of the convention is likely the climate of the Mediterranean, where pastoral poetry has its roots. It is a convention even an English poet like Herrick does not tamper with much: the late fall and winter seasons are scarcely mentioned in *Hesperides.*

Preceding *"The succession"* by only five pages in the first edition of *Hesperides* is a meditative epigram whose title, *"Discontents in Devon"* (*H*-51), and first quatrain suggest antipastoral intentions. The complaint of lines 1–4, however, is subverted by the surprising admission of the second quatrain:

> MOre discontents I never had
>   Since I was born, then* here;
> Where I have been, and still am sad,
>   In this dull *Devon-shire:*
> Yet justly too I must confesse;
>   I ne'r invented such
> Ennobled numbers* for the Presse,
>   Then where I loath'd so much.

*than
*good poetry

The displaced Londoner, in a fit of depression and boredom, blames life in the West Country for his lack of contentment (a state Herrick specifically *associates* with rural life elsewhere). The bemused confession that follows raises an interesting point about creativity: it implies that Herrick is a paradoxical kind of fellow and suggests that in his own view his best work was written after 1630, when he was middle-aged, and with humor encourages the reader to take the poet's occasional antipastoral outbursts with a grain of salt.

Robert Deming has offered such poems as evidence against "labeling Herrick 'a pastoral poet,'"—one who upholds "the pastoral spirit" and has "the necessary commitment" to pastoral values. At the same time, Deming qualifies his claim with such statements as "Herrick is not a pastoral poet *in the conventional sense*" (143–44, my italics). What is meant here, however, is uncertain because Deming fails to offer an example of a "conventional" pastoralist; indeed, it might be difficult to do so, given the variety of ways in which Renaissance poets tested the limits of the tradition. Certainly Herrick's bucolics are seldom wholly "conventional," but neither is most pastoral poetry from the seventeenth century that is still read. Indeed, part of the poet's very unconventionality is that his *Hesperides* engages in a kind of dialogue about pastoral, celebrating it in the introductory poems and in important pieces throughout the volume but also qualifying and complicating pastoral's vision with his epigrams and occasionally with other antipastoral pieces like the well-known ode "*His returne to London*" (H-713).

This autobiographical work, however, is more of a panegyric to London than it is an anti-Devon, antipastoral poem like "*To Dean-Bourn*": its emphasis is upon hymning the capital as the poet's birthplace, his spiritual home, and as the very definition of all that is cosmopolitan:

FRom the dull confines of the drooping West,
To see the day spring from the pregnant East,
Ravisht in spirit, I come, nay more, I flie
To thee, blest place of my Nativitie!
Thus, thus with hallowed foot I touch the ground,
With thousand blessings by thy Fortune crown'd

(ll. 1–6)

"The drooping West" is, of course, the "dull *Devon-shire*" of "*Discontents in Devon*," a region that lies to the southwest of the capital. Herrick plays upon the traditional associations of west and east to sharpen the country-city contrast: it is in "the drooping West" that the sun goes down, whereas the new day receives its triumphant birth in the East. The West is traditionally associated with death, the East with birth (e.g., Christ's "Nativitie") and with resurrection. It is to the east that the fabled city of Rome lies. First implicitly, then explicitly, Herrick compliments London by comparing it to the city that claimed as its citizens those poets whom he most reveres and whom he most resembles in spirit:

O fruitfull Genius! that bestowest here
An everlasting plenty, yeere by yeere.
O *Place!* O *People!* Manners! fram'd to please
All *Nations, Customes, Kindreds, Languages.*

(ll. 7–10)

Like any other locale, London has its own "genius" or "spirit of the place," and considering the fact that in Herrick's lifetime London had been the home of Marlowe, Shakespeare, Jonson, Bacon, and the young Milton, among others, he is hardly guilty of exaggeration in calling the capital's genius "fruitfull." London is like a rich field that yields an abundance of literary crops. The odious comparison between city and country is underscored if the reader hears echoes of "*To* Dean-Bourn"'s exasperated "O men, O manners"—itself an allusion to Cicero's complaint (*o tempora o mores*) about what he saw as an age in decline. "The London life-style" would be a contemporary (if somewhat diluted) characterization of what Herrick is praising here—the city's embodiment of all the most positive associations of the word *urbane.*

With the seemingly natural, easy Latinizing that is so characteristic of him, Herrick now makes his Rome-London metaphor explicit in order to characterize himself as a city man:

I am a free-born *Roman;* suffer then,
That I amongst you live a Citizen.
London my home is: though by hard fate sent
Into a long and irksome banishment;
Yet since cal'd back; henceforth let me be,
O native countrey, repossest by thee!
For, rather than I'le to the West return,
I'le beg of thee first here to have mine Urn.
Weak I am grown, and must in short time fall;
Give thou my sacred Reliques Buriall.

The metaphor of the speaker as Roman citizen contributes more than classical decor and imagistic unity to the poem: by recalling the tradition that exile from the capital was to "a free-born *Roman*" the supreme penalty, more feared than death (represented by the funeral urn), Herrick's trope melodramatically expresses the pull that London, the lodestone metropolis of English life, could exert on the imaginations of those separated from her.

Although it is true that "Roman" Herrick actually did "to the West return," that he lived, not for a "short time," but for more than another quarter century, and that his "Reliques" would receive their burial in the small churchyard at Dean Prior, such facts are less relevant to the question of how Herrick may be most profitably approached as a poet than the fact that this implicitly antipastoral work is followed (only two short poems later) by one of his more conventional pastorals, "*A Beucolick, or discourse of Neatherds*" (*H*-716), and two pages after that, in the first edition, by one of his most original and personal "Englished" pastorals, "*His Grange, or private wealth*" (*H*-724). It seems ingenuous, then, to reject Herrick's own characterization of his muse and his usual practice on the grounds that *Hesperides* does not always adhere to a textbook definition of a pastoral collection. It is the very fact that his poetry transcends such definitions that Herrick is clearly *not* "a pastoral poet in the conventional sense" and that he continues to be read with pleasure today, whereas a William Browne, say, is not. Devonshire and London are only geographical locations; "*This Sacred Grove*" constitutes a world of its own, one that receives its main outlines from a vision of the good life that so many of Herrick's poems explore.

The Rural Life

Herrick occasionally is capable of writing idealized versions of rural life that are mannered and self-consciously artificial, for example, the lyrical dialogue "*A Bucolick betwixt Two: Lacon and Thyrsis*" (H-984), a conventionalized anticipation of Andrew Marvell's "The Nymph Complaining for the Death of her Faun." Most of his "Bucolicks," nevertheless, are recognizable by (1) their distinctively English mode or their synthesis of native and classical pastoral elements; (2) their relatively realistic depictions of rural life and landscapes; (3) their awareness of socioeconomic and political aspects of country existence; and (4) their insights into the psychology of the rural way of life.

A poem that is at first glance mainly a charming description of an annual country parish festival, "*The Wake*" (H-761), serves as a convenient example of the complexity of Herrick's pastoralism. It begins with the speaker's extending an invitation to a lady who presumably is, like himself, not a simple rustic:

> COme Anthea let us two
> Go to Feast, as others do.
> Tarts and Custards, Creams and Cakes,
> Are the Junketts* still at Wakes:
> Unto which the Tribes resort,
> Where the business is the sport.
>
> (ll. 1–6)
>
> *desserts

Although the lady's name is more Roman than English, the sweets itemized in lines 3–4 establish the native British setting and in their concreteness create a strong illusion of reality. There may also be a slight condescension in the distinction that the speaker makes between "us two" and "the others" and in his imputation of primitiveness to the latter, who make up "Tribes." The implication that he and Anthea are socially superior to the revelers persists as he catalogs the festival's various entertainments—"Morris-dancers," a Robin Hood pageant, and plays put on by a troop of ragged itinerant actors:

> Players there will be, and those
> Base in action as in clothes:
> Yet with strutting they will please
> The incurious Villages.
>
> (ll. 11–14)

That the speaker and his addressee themselves would not be as pleased by
such vulgar diversions as the country folk is self-evident. His attitude toward his social inferiors, however, is more patronizing than critical: neither
their roughness nor their drunkenness receives outright condemnation:

> Neer the dying of the day,
> There will be a *Cudgell*-Play,
> Where a *Coxcomb* will be broke,
> Ere a good *word* can be spoke:
> But the anger ends all here,
> Drencht in Ale, or drown'd in Beere.
>   (ll. 15–20)

Bemusedly, the speaker expects that the "*Cudgell*-Play," an athletic contest
involving the use of wooden clubs, may lead to an injury or two, but all will
be forgiven in the general alcoholic haze. This thought leads him to ponder,
by way of conclusion, a difference in sensibility that seems for him to be
based upon social class:

> Happy Rusticks, best content
> With the cheapest Merriment:
> And possess no other feare,
> Then to want the Wake next Yeare.
>   (ll. 21–24)

Condescension, ironically, is subverted here by a touch of envy. The country
folk are able to find happiness in the kind of simple pleasures the wake offers, and their only concern is that this annual festival could be cancelled.
For the more sophisticated speaker, contentment may not be so easily won
nor anxiety so easily assuaged. The rustics' ignorance is their bliss; the
speaker's heightened sensibility is his curse. His awareness that there are
more and superior pleasures to be wrung from life comes at a considerable
cost—the knowledge that there is more to lose than the rustics are ever
likely to realize.

Although "*The Wake*" can legitimately be classified as a pastoral poem
because it illustrates some of the simple pleasures of country life, it is hardly
a conventional bucolic. It is not set in some perfect mythical Arcadia but in
the real English countryside; its cast of characters includes no nymphs or satyrs but authentic English country folk and no Pans or Floras but an English
gentleman and his lady. The poem affirms the good life to be had in the

country while acknowledging the limitations of such a life: a "rockie" Devonshire resists easy transformation into a "*Sacred Grove.*" "*The Wake,*" moreover, offers an insight pertinent to any vision of life—that the burdens as well as the blessings of life increase in direct proportion to the level of one's awareness. Also present in this poem (as it is in "*To* Dean-Bourn," for example) is what Ann Coiro refers to as Herrick's "social ambivalence," in which his "uneasy sense of his own status" (uneasy because technically he is a commoner though he mixes with gentry and nobility) expresses itself "by debasing those of whose inferiority to himself he can be reasonably certain" (1988, 158). While *debasing* may be a bit strong to describe Herrick's tendency to patronize his social inferiors, Coiro is very much to the point in her observation that the poet's stance in poems like "*The Wake*" qualifies "the critical argument that Herrick's art is devoted to ceremony as a way of defeating transiency," for the very reason that he has such reservations about "the simple happiness and cyclical sense of surety such ceremonies can give" (1988, 160).

Another poem exhibiting this kind of ambivalence is the widely anthologized address "*The Hock-cart, or Harvest home*" (H-250), another example of Herrick's "Englishing" of the pastoral tradition. Its subject is the holiday upon which farm workers celebrate the completion of the annual harvest, but it is dedicated (and in part addressed) to a titled landholder, "*the Right Honourable,* Mildmay, Earl of Westmorland." The hock cart, a wagon in which the last load of crops from the fields is brought in, is the central symbol of the ceremony. In addition to describing this ceremony, Herrick's poem is itself a kind of ritual, for it consists of two public exhortations to the rustics that frame an invitation to the lord of the manor. These speeches are not only ceremonial, but also partly didactic, attempting to reinforce certain socioeconomic principles. These principles are derived from two philosophical concepts which serve as the poem's main thematic strains: one involves the relationship between humans and nature, the other involves relationships in the social hierarchy, and both are implicit in the opening couplet, "COme Sons of Summer, by whose toile, / We are the Lords of Wine and Oile." The epithet "Sons of Summer" idealizes the farm laborers being addressed, but the couplet itself pointedly distinguishes between them and the higher social class to which Herrick assigns himself. By the poem's conclusion this distinction and its implications will have been made abundantly clear.

"Sons of Summer" also suggests that the rustics are creatures of the season, just as the land they work is. This relationship, however, is only partly harmonious, for it is these natural men "By whose tough labours, and rough

hands, / We rip up first, then reap our lands" (ll. 3–4). Both the sounds
and the images here suggest a near rape of nature, although one that eventually results in fruition and celebration: "Crown'd with the eares of corn,
now come, / And to the Pipe, sing Harvest home" (ll. 5–6). The ceremony
sanctifies the harvest and the acts that led up to it and symbolically draws
humans and nature together: the swains are crowned as victors, but they
have literally and figuratively stooped to conquer, for their crowns are woven
of the stalks of grain they themselves have gathered.

In the poem's next passage Herrick, who may be envisioned as standing
before the entrance to Mildmay Fane's country house, turns and offers a
peroration inviting the earl outside to observe the festivities: "Come forth,
my Lord, and see the Cart / Drest up with all the Country Art" (ll. 7–8).
Whether or not "Like Jonson, Herrick aspired to be the poet of the privileged classes" (Coiro, 1988, 156), here he presents himself as a kind of
chaplain to Westmorland, or even a member of the latter's social class, "The
Lords of Wine and Oile." Implied as well is that he and the earl share a superior sensibility, one that can discriminate between "Country" and more sophisticated Art. (Fane himself was a poet and, in fact, a distinctly
"Herrickean" one.) As he calls the earl's attention to the sights and sounds
of the festival, however, Herrick's appreciation and approval of these rural
pastimes are evident:

> See, here a Maukin,* there a sheet,
> As spotless pure, as it is sweet:
> The Horses, Mares, and frisking Fillies,
> (Clad all, in Linnen, white as Lillies.)
> The Harvest Swaines, and Wenches bound
> For joy, to see the *Hock-cart* crown'd.
> About the Cart, heare, how the Rout
> Of Rurall Younglings raise the shout;
> Pressing before, some coming after,
> Those with a shout, and these with laughter.
>
> (ll. 9–18)

scarecrow

Through language like "frisking," "bound," "Rout," and "shout," the poem
suggests the tension between sanctification and uninhibited celebration, a
tension that is as endemic to such rituals as the varied pleasures they offer
the eye and ear.

At the same time Herrick can find amusement in the country people's simple pantheism, one that confuses symbols for what they stand for—a benign and bountiful nature: "Some blesse the Cart; some kiss the sheaves; / Some prank them up with Oaken leaves" (ll. 19–20). In these people Christianity and the worship of nature come together with no sense of strain: "Some cross the Fill-horse; some with great / Devotion stroak the home-borne wheat" (ll. 21–22). While the act of making the sign of the cross over a horse is not necessarily condemned here, the hint of amusingly misplaced piety broadens into jocularity at the expense of the least re-strained revelers: "While other Rusticks, lesse attent / To Prayers then to Merryment, / Run after with their breeches rent" (ll. 23–25). The ritual collapses from its own weight into slapstick comedy. In an attempt to ensure that the serious significance of the holiday is not irretrievably lost, Herrick turns from addressing Westmorland to speak directly to the "Harvest Swaines and Wenches" once more.

Their attention is called to the custom which helps make the event such a special one—that of making the earl's hearth and home theirs for a day. By doing so, however, Herrick again reinforces the distinction between the working and the leisured classes:

> Well, on, brave boyes, to your Lords Hearth,
> Glit'tring with fire; where, for your mirth,
> Ye shall see first the large and cheefe
> Foundation of your Feast, fat Beefe:
> With Upper Stories, Mutton, Veale
> And Bacon, (which makes full the meale).
>
> (ll. 26–31)

The rustics are officially invited to come into the great hall (from which pro-tocol would normally exclude them), and there they are to partake of the feast laid on by Westmorland, one that ranges from a veritable palace of roast meat to (as succeeding lines note) a choice of desserts. Though the "brave boyes" may not be offered the beverage of their betters—"smirking Wine"—they will be able to make "merry cheere" with "that, which drowns all care, stout Beere" (l. 37). Even beer drinking, however, must on this day proceed with all due ceremony, specifically with a series of toasts arranged in prioritized order:

> . . . freely drink to your Lords health,
> Then to your Plough, (the Common-wealth)
> Next to your Flailes, your Fanes,* your Fatts;**

Then to the Maids with Wheaten Hats:
To the rough Sickle, and the crookt Sythe,
Drink frollick boyes, till all be blythe.

(ll. 38–43)

*fans for winnowing grain
**storage vats

Westmorland comes first in the toasts, not only because it is his generosity that supplies the feast but also because he represents the sociopolitical hierarchy to which the country folk owe their ultimate allegiance. The plough likewise is toasted both for itself and as a symbol of agriculture: in Herrick's multilevel pun, agriculture is the "Common-wealth," England itself (because it is the nation's chief industry), as well as the "realm" over which farm workers directly "reign," and finally, the common source of sustenance and income for master and servants alike. The rest of the farm equipment, being also of symbolic as well as practical value, and the straw-hatted girls who aid in the work likewise have their places in the ritual of the toast.

With this reminder of the swains' ceremonial obligations off his chest, Herrick concludes his address on the poem's most serious note, reverting from his role of master of the revels to that of chaplain. So that the ultimate significance of the festival will not be lost upon the merrymakers, he draws from the day's rituals some pointed socioeconomic inferences:

Feed, and grow fat; and as ye eat,
Be mindfull, that the lab'ring Neat*
(As you) may have their fill of meat.
And know, besides, ye must revoke*
The patient Oxe unto the Yoke,
And all goe back unto the Plough
And Harrow, (though they'r hang'd up now.)
And, you must know, your Lords word's true,
Feed him ye must, whose food fils you.
And that this pleasure is like raine,
Not sent ye for to drowne your paine,
But for to make it spring againe.

(ll. 44–55)

*cattle
*return

While literally urging his auditors to enjoy themselves, by using terms like "feeding" and "growing fat" Herrick figuratively reduces them to the status of animals, a reduction reinforced by his comparing them specifically to cattle. These rustics are in a sense "owned" by Westmorland, and for them the holiday is only a temporary respite from the cycle of seasonal labor that is the foundation of English country life: humans as well as beasts must eventually return to the plow.

The last five lines of the poem aphoristically express its two main themes. The first is that of the mutual dependency of masters and servants in the socioeconomic hierarchy. The second, having to do with the purpose of "this pleasure" (the holiday), involves a double meaning. If the word "paine" is understood in its common seventeenth-century sense of "work"—here specifically the rustics' capacity for hard physical labor—and if "spring" is taken as a verb, then Herrick's final triplet can be paraphrased as follows: "This holiday is being celebrated, not to inhibit your capacity for labor, but to revitalize it." On the other hand, if "spring" is read as a noun, then "paine" refers to the act of harvesting, thereby ringing in the concept of natural flux, of the death and rebirth of nature: "This holiday serves not to conclude the fruitful cycle so much as to signal its continuance." In the light of the dual themes of the poem, both interpretations apply, with the first suggesting the economic realities behind the holiday ritual and the second reflecting the real and symbolic relationships between humans and nature that the holiday is intended to celebrate. Feudal though such thinking may appear today, it accurately represents widespread conservative attitudes of Herrick's age and possibly, as Coiro claims, "Herrick's social prejudices" as well (1988, 156).

The critical attention that *"The Hock-cart"* has received and the critical controversy it has aroused[1] indicate that Herrick's pastoralism on occasion can be complex, serious, and subtle. Like *"The Wake"* this poem's vision of the good life is ironic and relativistic, implicitly acknowledging both the values and the limitations of living in the actual English countryside. From both poems, however, it can be inferred that for the happy few—lords and ladies of the manor, country squires, gentlemen farmers, and the like—a reasonable approximation of the pastoral ideal is attainable—and in England, not Arcadia. This is the argument Herrick makes in an address to his lifelong friend John Wicks (see Coiro, 1988, 145).

The work's complete title, *"A Paranaeticall, or Advisive Verse, to his friend,* Master John Wicks" (*H-670*), announces that this is to be more of a philosophical than a descriptive poem. Herrick's role will be that of sage rather than priest (Wicks is also a clergyman) and, because he is addressing one of his peers, he will advise rather than sermonize. The ethical principle on which his advice will be grounded, that of moderation, is apparent from the opening lines:

> IS this a life, to break thy sleep?
> To rise as soon as day doth peep?
> To tire thy patient Oxe or Asse
> By noone, and let thy good dayes passe,
> Not knowing This, that *Jove* decrees
> Some mirth, t'adulce* mans miseries?
>
> (ll. 1–6)

*sweeten

Bishop Wicks, it would seem, has been acting more like "the Sons of Summer" in *"The Hock-cart"* than its "Lords of Wine and Oile." Not for Herrick is the Puritan ethos that work is virtue and pleasure is sin. While he does not go so far as to fall back on Genesis and depict physical labor as punishment, he indicates that even though work may be a tiresome necessity, there is also real value in leisure—an assumption that has always been a part of the pastoral ethos. Moderation, it can be inferred, constitutes a basic principle of the human condition (decreed by *"Jove"*): misery may be man's lot, but it is to be balanced by mirth. The answer to the poem's opening rhetorical question, then, is that Wicks has not in fact been living the good bucolic life:

> No; 'tis a life, to have thine oyle,
> Without extortion, from thy soyle:
> Thy faithfull fields to yeeld thee Graine,
> Although with some, yet little paine.
>
> (ll. 7–10)

The human condition may require that people live by the sweat of their brows, but the demands of Nature are moderate: her bounty need not be taken by force, for she "yeeld[s]" it. Implicit here is the "pathetic fallacy" so crucial to the pastoral vision—the sense that nature is inherently benign, even to the point of being responsive to humanity's needs, desirous of acting as a faithful servant.

Herrick continues his depiction of the country life as the good life by demonstrating that, once work has been put in perspective and sustenance

obtained, it is possible to have peace of mind and, moreover, the contentment afforded by wedded love:

> To have thy mind, and nuptiall bed
> With feares, and cares uncumbered:
> A Pleasing Wife, that by thy side
> Lies softly panting like a Bride.
> This is to live, and to endeere
> Those minutes, Time has lent us here.
>
> (ll. 11–16)

Herrick's version of pastoral here is remote from the idylls of the tradition,
with their romantic liaisons between swains and shepherdesses, and far more
realistic: while English country life and marriage may not be the stuff of
which "Cold Pastoral" is constituted, they afford security and happiness.
Even with time's winged chariot always hurrying near, a "Pleasing Wife"
who is also a coy mistress—a "softly . . . panting Bride"—makes existential
melodrama superfluous.

The principle of *carpe diem*—take advantage of the time—so often associated with Dionysian excess, is here set forth (as it usually is in *Hesperides*)
as a reasonable response to life's brevity and as a way to enjoy liberty, if not
license:

> Then, while Fates suffer, live thou free,
> (As is that ayre that circles thee)
> And crown thy temples too, and let
> Thy servant, not thy own self, sweat,
> To strut* thy barnes with sheafs of Wheat.
>
> (ll. 17–20)

*fill

Bluntly undemocratic as these lines are, they remind us that democracy was
not perceived as a socioeconomic and political ideal by conservatives like
Herrick nor, generally speaking, by his age. For him, to be a member of the
leisure class, or at least to be able to avoid laboring by the sweat of his brow,
means to be as free as one can possibly be, under sentence of death from fate
as we are. Neither past moments nor friends who have passed away can be
brought back:

> *No sound recalls the houres once fled*
> *Or Roses, being withered*
> Nor us (my Friend) when we are lost,
> Like to a Deaw, or melted Frost.
>   (ll. 24–27)

Since this is a poem of advice, it is appropriate that some of that advice be
presented epigrammatically, in the form of aphorisms inserted into the middle of Herrick's exhortation. Even while the italicized lines underscore the
inevitability of human fate, however, their images suggest its naturalness.
The specific application of these words of wisdom to both the poet and
Wicks is eased by the parenthetical "my Friend" and enhances the whole
passage's tone of lyrical Stoicism.

After having criticized the quality of his friend's present life, having
shown him the possibilities for a good life in the country, and having demonstrated the urgent need for obtaining it, Herrick is ready to advise Wicks
as to the best means to that end:

> Then live we mirthfull, while we should,
> And turn the iron Age to Gold.
> Let's feast, and frolick, sing and play,
> And thus lesse last, then live our Day.
> *Whose life with care, is overcast,*
> *That man's not said to live, but last:*
> *Nor is't a life, seven yeares to tell,**
> *But for to live that half seven well:*
> And that wee'll do; as men, who know,
> Some few sands spent, we hence must go
> Both to be blended in the Urn,
> From whence there's never a return.
>   (ll. 28–39)

*count

To live the good life is to recapitulate the legendary Golden Age (typically
envisioned as a bucolic era), when the world and humanity were young; it is
to live rather than merely to exist. Thus, this Church of England priest, in
the manner of an Epicurean philosopher, not only affirms to a fellow priest
the value of sensuous pleasure but also of the state of mind we think of as
"carefree." What today we would call "quality of life" rather than longevity
is what counts for Herrick because no pleasures await after death: the "Urn"

is the end. To the saints and martyrs of this world such an ethos can—in spite of the gnomic seriousness of the poet's mode of utterance—seem frivolous, but its combining of Stoic and Epicurean strains places it in a long and honorable tradition of moral philosophy.

A variation upon this ethos appears in *"A Country life: to his Brother, Master Tho: Herrick"* (*H*-106). "Placed very early in the book," Ann Coiro notes, this poem "is important to the pastoral mood of *Hesperides'* beginning, while the many epigrammatic *sententiae* embedded within it suggest the shape of the volume as a whole." It may also be one of the poet's earlier pieces, written, according to Coiro, on the occasion of Herrick's older brother's "leaving London about 1610 to become a gentleman farmer" (1988, 152). So ambitious and impressive is this poem, however, that it is difficult to imagine its published version, at least, as being written by a 16-year-old, even a precocious one. A striking example of the eclecticism and elusiveness of Herrick's art, *"A Country life,"* like Ben Jonson's panegyric or public compliment *"To Sir Robert Wroth,"* has been associated with the genre of the "country-house poem" and has been shown to contain echoes of English writers ranging from Shakespeare to Robert Burton and of classical authors from Virgil to Horace.[2]

Herrick employs conventional pastoral diction to create an image of the world in which Thomas lives: it is a "Rural Sanctuary" and an "Elizium," a paradise of "Damaskt medowes," "peebly streames," and "Purling springs, groves, birds, and well-weav'd Bowrs, / With fields enameled with flowers" (ll. 45–46). At the same time, however, Herrick's references to "Nettles, Colworts, Beets," the "singing Crickits by [the] fire," a "brisk Mouse," and a "green-ey'd Kitling [kitten]" lend a homely, familiar, quite English quality to this bucolic world. Moreover, although the poem is more of a tribute to his brother than versified advice, here too the poet adopts the role of pastoral sage, beginning by affectionately commending his spiritual as well as natural brother for his judiciousness:

> THrice and above, blest (my soules halfe) art thou,
> In both thy Last, and Better Vow:
> Could'st leave the City, for exchange to see
> The Countries sweet simplicity:
> And it to know, and practice. . . .
>
> (ll. 1–5)

The tension between urban and rural life so basic to pastoral becomes in this poem the foundation on which Herrick erects a complex ethical theory. It is well, he claims, that Thomas has determined to forsake the city for the country because, by imitating the simple rural ways, he will "growe the sooner innocent." Innocence here is not ignorance but rather that state which prelapsarian Adam and Eve enjoyed in the Garden of Eden (the original "*Sacred Grove*"), a state in which the knowledge of the good and the practice of it were one. By choosing the country life, Thomas can approach the condition of the parents of the race—able to live according to nature and reason:

> Led by thy conscience; to give
> Justice to soon-pleas'd nature; and to show
>   Wisdome and she together goe,
> And keep one Centre. . . .
>   (ll. 12–15)

By centering his life upon naturalness and right reason, Thomas will learn moderation, "to confine [his] desires," and he will come to know that "riches have their proper stint [limit], / In the contented mind, not mint" (ll. 16–18). These aphorisms once more reveal Herrick's kinship with the Stoics (for whom moderation is a cardinal virtue) and Epicurus (for whom moderation follows inevitably from prudence). Thus Herrick can compliment his brother for being able "To keep cheap Nature even, and upright; / To coole, not cocker [stimulate] Appetite" (ll. 25–26), to control his own sensuous nature. It is as Epicurus said, "To habituate one's self . . . to simple food and inexpensive diet supplies all that is needful for health" (10.128, 651).

Herrick goes on to indicate that the same principle of moderation is relevant to sexual appetite. Once again he portrays love, which in traditional pastoral is often mere sexuality or sentimentality, as at its best a golden mean between those two extremes, a blessed state attainable through the sanctification of marriage:

> But that, which most makes sweet thy country life,
>   Is, the fruition of a wife:
> Whom (Stars consenting with thy Fate) thou hast
>   Got, not so beautifull, as chast:
> By whose warme side thou dost securely sleep
>   (While Love the Centinell doth keep).
>   (ll. 31–36)

To the modern reader these lines may seem clumsy (as for Herrick they are) and undiplomatic. A seventeenth-century reader, however, would understand that the poet is wrestling with the antifeminist cliché that, as the cynical persona of Donne's "Song" puts it, "Nowhere / Lives a woman true, and fair." Thomas Herrick is fortunate, his younger brother is trying to say, to have a wife who is even more faithful than she is beautiful. The pair enjoy the "cleanly-*Wantonnesse*" alluded to in "*The Argument of his Book*"—that combination of sensuality and virtue Herrick perfectly captures in two lines: "But still thy wife, by chast intentions led, / Gives thee each night a Maidenhead" (ll. 41–42). He goes on to conjure up a classical pastoral landscape, complete with protective Roman deities, which makes the couple's sleep "sound" and "sweet," and then morning devotions, which also have a "pagan" cast, concluding with a Latinate piety: "*Jove for our labour all things sells us*" (l. 62). With this sententia what may be regarded as the poem's first movement comes to an end.

Having complimented his brother for the latter's choice of a country life and for his temperance, his marriage, and his piety, Herrick proceeds to contrast the agricultural life Thomas has chosen with the life of commerce:

> Nor are thy daily and devout affaires
>   Attended with those desp'rate cares,
> Th'industrious Merchant has; who for to find
>   Gold, runneth to the Westerne Inde,
> And back again, (tortur'd with feares) doth fly
>   Untaught, to suffer Poverty.
>
>   (ll. 63–68)

Implicit in this passage is an ongoing debate of the period as to whether happiness is best attained by living the "active life" in the mainstream of worldly affairs or the "contemplative life" of quiet retirement. Because the former way of life is associated with the city and the latter with the country, this debate bears on the fundamental tensions of the pastoral mode. Naturally, the poet of "*This Sacred Grove*" portrays the Active Man—here represented by a merchant—as a driven, anxiety-ridden, pitiable creature who, in the words of the Epicurean Lucretius, "struggles to flee from himself" but finds only frustration (x.131, 657). Thomas, however, is described, according to the convention, as sitting in his country house, doing his traveling—always perilous in the seventeenth century—safely and inexpensively simply by perusing maps.

In pastoral literature the royal court can sometimes substitute for the city

in the city/country opposition, and sometimes, as in the third movement of
"*A Country Life*," it represents the epitome of decadent urban existence:

> And when thou hear'st by that too-true-Report
>   Vice rules the Most, or All at Court:
> Thy pious wishes are, (though thou not there)
>   Vertue had, and mov'd her Sphere.
>
>   (ll. 89–92)

Although Thomas is far removed from the sinful court, as a dutiful and devout subject it is natural for him to desire that that powerful body be governed by ethics (as his own country life is) rather than by evil. For all its
bluntness, such criticism is conventional, based on the dubious assumption
that there can be a world of moral difference between the monarch and his
court.

Unlike most courtiers, Thomas is said to live without fear, his face never
showing whether his present fortune is good or bad,

> But with thy equall thoughts, prepar'd dost stand,
>   To take her by the either hand:
> Nor car'st which comes the first, the foule or faire:
>   *A wise man ev'ry way lies square.*
>
>   (ll. 95–98)

The portrait painted here is that of the "Compleat Stoic," a man unmoved
by life's vicissitudes, accepting whatever it has to offer—a man of philosophical and psychological "poise." The storms of life, Herrick goes on to
say, only strengthen such a man, as the "*Oke*" is strengthened by the winds
that buffet it. Surprisingly, however, this noble portrait turns out not to be
of Thomas as he presently is, but as his younger brother wishes him to be:
"Be so, bold spirit; Stand Center-like, unmov'd; / And be not only
thought, but prov'd / To be what I report thee" (ll. 101–3). Herrick idealizes his subject, as his mentor Ben Jonson often does, in order to foster inspiration and aspiration.

In the next movement, however, Herrick acknowledges that his brother is
already a good Epicurean, one whose life illustrates that philosopher's
maxim, "The greatest fruit of self-sufficiency is freedom" (Fragment 77).
Because Thomas's needs are so modest, he is free from want, content with
whatever his "private *Larr*," or household god, may provide and undesirous
of haute cuisine—"fare, / Which Art, not Nature, makes so rare" (ll. 111–

12). As another of Herrick's aphorisms sums it up: "*Content makes all ambrosia*" (l. 116)—whatever satisifies is good to one who follows the "Theame" of moderation, "To shun the first, and last extreame" (l. 132). Ever judicious, Thomas knows his limitations, never exceeding his "Tether's reach," preferring to "live round, and close" within his own compass, so as to be "wisely true / To thine owne selfe: and knowne to few" (ll. 135–36). Herrick's phrasing here recalls Polonius's parting advice to his son, but although he spouts almost as many maxims as Shakespeare's fatuous character does, the poet presents himself as a social critic and sage. He is a pastoralist, too, one who commends a way of life—"Thus let thy Rurall Sanctuary be / *Elizium* to thy wife and thee" (ll. 137–38)—because it exemplifies moderation, the principle of the "golden mean." Finally, Herrick is also a priest who echoes the language of the marriage service in his concluding blessing:

> Live, and live blest; thrice happy Paire; let Breath,
>   But lost to one, be th'others death.
> And as there is one Love, one Faith, one Troth,
>   Be so one Death, one Grave to both.
> Till when, in such assurance live, ye may
>   Nor feare, or wish your dying day.
>   (ll. 141–46)

Having lived and loved so well, Thomas Herrick and his Elizabeth will be able to say with Epicurus, "Death . . . is nothing to us" (10.125, 651). Only life without the other could seem fearful or endless.

Somewhat rambling and occasionally clumsy, "*A Country Life*" is nonetheless an ambitious work; except for his two marriage poems, it is Herrick's longest. It seeks through a personal tribute to portray the ideal man and an idea of the good life and to suggest the philosophical bases for each. In some ways it is the most thoroughly philosophical poem of *Hesperides*. As such it helps demonstrate that Herrick is more than a lightweight lyrist and that in the earlier seventeenth century the metaphysical poets had no monopoly on cerebration. Herrick's poem is a repository of ethical values espoused by the Sons of Ben, as Earl Miner has shown, and is, in addition, "an evocation of that greenest and loveliest of English counties, Herrickshire" (151–53, 278–80). Ann Coiro observes that "'*A Country Life*' stands near the entrance of *Hesperides* as a testament to Stoic virtue and pastoral happiness." She adds that—like the next poem to be examined here, "*The Country Life, to the honoured Master* Endimion Porter, *Groome of the Bed-Chamber to his Majesty*" (*H-662*)—"*A Country Life*" in effect "embodies the cultural program current in the Stuart reign" (1988, 152).

That program, begun by James I and supported by his successor, involved urging the English nobility to leave the royal court and return to their landholdings, the better to supervise them and the people living on them (Coiro, 1988, 147). In the 1620s Endymion Porter held the important title of Groom of the Bedchamber (under the office of the Lord Chamberlain) and could therefore be regarded as one who was thoroughly familiar with the vice-ridden court attacked in "*A Country Life.*" Herrick, of course, diplomatically declines to raise such issues in his poem to Porter and, as a consequence, "*The Country Life*" focuses more upon the bucolic vision of the good life. Its opening movement is reminiscent of the pastoral to Thomas Herrick: the poet contrasts the freedom of the "SWeet Country life" to the unhappy bondage of serving others rather than oneself, a kind of bondage endemic to "Courts and Cities"; he again decries the Active Man who must plow "the Oceans foame" to bring back "rough Pepper" and the "scorched Clove"—allusions to the dangerous spice trade (ll. 5–8). He then directly addresses Porter, ascribing to him a sincerely bucolic spirit: "thy Ambition's Master-Piece / Flies no thought higher then a fleece" (ll. 11–12). Given the Renaissance belief that ambition, far from being a virtue, posed a threat to the divinely ordained sociopolitical order, it is a compliment to the courtier Porter to portray him as one who desires only to raise his sheep and to pay off his debts—"cleere / All scores; and so to end the year" (ll. 13–14). Also implied is an affirmation of the Stuart policy of returning to the land.

The next 31 lines of this ostensibly unfinished poem offer an idealized description of and panegyric to the country life as Porter supposedly lives it, presented in the form of a familiar rural ritual—the lord of the manor's tour of inspection about his estate. Portrayed in both conventional pastoral and distinctively English images, Porter's world is one whose equivalent is today to be found in British travel posters—a world not quite as idyllic as presented. The concluding 30 lines of this commendatory poem offer an account of other country rituals, the holidays and pastimes of rustic folk. The inclusion of these activities may have political as well as artistic significance, for the Stuarts encouraged such "lawfull Recreation[s]" as morale builders (Marcus, 3).

Together, these 61 lines also constitute a kind of tour of Herrick's poetic techniques. For example, he juxtaposes a tribute to Porter's temperance with an appropriate aphorism:

> [Thou] walk'st about thine own dear bounds,
> Not envying others larger grounds:
> For well thou know'st, *'tis not th'extent*
> *Of Land makes life, but sweet content.*
>
> (ll. 15–18)

Vignettes of English country life and images from traditional pastoral literature are combined with sententiae and "pagan" thought:

> There at the Plough thou find'st thy Teame,
> With a Hind* whistling there to them:
> And cheer'st them up, by singing how
> The Kingdoms portion** *is the Plow.*
> This done, then to th'enameld Meads
> Thou go'st; and as thy foot there treads
> Thou seest a present God-like Power
> Imprinted in each Herbe and Flower.
>
> (ll. 25–32)

> **rustic*
> ***source of wealth*

The image of the plowman whistling to his oxen as they move along the fur-
rows comes from the poet's observation of actual English farm life, while
"enameld Meads" is a cliché of pastoral rhetoric. The sententia of l. 28 may
be Herrick's borrowing from himself (l. 39 of *"The Hock-cart"*), but the
pantheism of ll. 30–32 can be traced through the bucolic tradition at least
as far back as Virgil's *Georgics*. Added to these and other juxtapositions are
lush descriptions of grazing livestock ("great-ey'd Kine"); another nearly anthropological catalog of rural holidays and diversion, whose idyllicism is
qualified (as in *"The Wake"*) by the country folk's limited awareness—"O
happy life! if that their good / The Husbandmen but understood!" (ll. 70–
71); and an allusion to poaching that could also be a satiric comment on
court politics—Herrick's sly observation that Porter sets traps to catch
"pilfring Birds, not Men" (l. 69).

   Although the poet adds his own note to the effect that *"The Country
Life"* is an unfinished work, his poem makes a major contribution to his
general pastoral vision of the good life. That vision is presented from the
perspective of one less loftily positioned in society than Endymion Porter or
the Earl of Westmorland (but of a station superior to that of "Husband-

men") in two of Herrick's autobiographical poems, "*His content in the Country*" (*H-552*) and "*His Grange, or private wealth*" (*H-724*).

The title of the former poem recalls a gnomic line from "*A Country life*"—"*Content makes all ambrosia.*" The neo-Stoic, neo-Epicurean cast of his poem to his brother is also present here, Herrick practicing what Herrick preaches. Thus he and his maid, Prudence Baldwin, find contentment in mere sufficiency:

> HEre, here I live with what my Board,
> Can with the smallest cost afford.
> Though ne'r so mean the Viands* be,
> They well content my *Prew* and me.
> Or Pea, or Bean, or Wort,* or Beet,
> What ever comes, content makes sweet.
>
> (ll. 1–6)

> **ordinary victuals*
> *for making beer

Herrick's list of common, garden-variety vegetables and herbs illustrates the Epicurean principle of modest living proclaimed in the first two couplets. His casual reference to his maid more than personalizes the pastoral: it deritualizes, even depoeticizes it. We seem to be reading a letter from one who knows us well enough to be certain that we will know who "*Prew*" is. Both of Herrick's techniques here help to transform the convention-ridden pastoral tradition into a distinctively English, highly original, and quite realistic poetic mode—one that can also lend itself to social criticism:

> Here we rejoyce, because no Rent
> We pay for our poore Tenement:
> Wherein we rest, and never feare
> The Landlord or the Usurer.
>
> (ll. 7–10)

As vicar, Herrick lived rent-free in the parsonage across the lane from his church—a house that even today, although enlarged and improved since the seventeenth century, is still far from pretentious. Unlike many Englishmen, then, he did not have to be anxious about borrowing money to pay the rent. (In this vein, it is worth noting that, before Herrick, references to "filthy lucre" are rare in bucolic literature. Subsistence generally is not an issue in idylls, but Herrick makes it one in his version of pastoral.)

Ann Coiro's opinion that "Like Jonson, Herrick aspired to be a poet of the privileged classes" (1988, 156) may be well founded; however, in *"His content"* the well-to-do come in for sharp criticism:

> We eate our own, and batten* more,
> Because we feed on no mans score*:
> But pitie those, whose flanks grow great,
> Swel'd with the Lard of others meat.
>
> (ll. 13–16)

> **thrive*
> **indebtedness*

The contrast between the poet raising his own food and his image of the wealthy, bloated parasite makes the point that self-sufficiency has social ramifications: one's survival need not be at others' expense. This is not to suggest that Herrick is a democrat at heart; nevertheless, the kind of social criticism he offers here plus the fact that his use of "we" pointedly includes his servant (very likely an illiterate country woman) in his portrayal of his way of life both indicate that Herrick cannot readily be written off as a mere sycophant of the English establishment.

Indeed, the poet's quiet life is an implied rebuke of the highly visible public life associated with courts and cities:

> We blesse our Fortunes, when we see
> Our owne beloved privacie:
> And like our living, where w'are known
> To very few, or else to none.
>
> (ll. 17–20)

Although Herrick's desire for fame and glory finds frequent expression in *Hesperides,* it is a literary not a political reputation he seeks. Even the young Milton had to acknowledge a similar yearning, though he sees it (in *Lycidas*) as "That last infirmity of noble mind." Thus it is Herrick the neo-Stoic pastoralist whose voice we hear in *"His content in the Country"* more than Herrick the Cavalier poet or Son of Ben. This is also the case with another uniquely Herrickean pastoral closer to the end of *Hesperides,*[3] *"His Grange, or private wealth"* (*H*-724).

Both of these poems have in effect the same subject, the poet's way of life, and the same theme—"Where care / None is, slight things do lightly please" (ll. 31–32); but as poetry "*His Grange*" (the title refers to a country home) is radically different from "*His content in the Country.*" The latter's typically Herrickean couplets (in iambic tetrameter) give way to the highly complex metrics of "*His Grange*"—a series of eight quatrains with an *abab* rhyme scheme, whose first and third verses are iambic monometer and whose second and fourth verses are iambic tetrameter:

> THough Clock,
> To tell how night drawes hence, I've none,
> A Cock,
> I have, to sing how day drawes on.
> (ll. 1–4)

The contrast between mechanical and natural methods of telling time (and between night and day) hint at the opposition between urban and country life. From this point on, Herrick catalogs those "toyes," or pleasant trifles, that contribute to his version of the good life, including a fertile hen, a goose that acts as a watchdog, an orphaned lamb, a spaniel named "*Trasy,*" and the faithful Prudence Baldwin:

> I have
> A maid (my *Prew*) by good luck sent,
> To save
> That little, Fates me gave or lent.
> (ll. 5–8)

The Stoic note sounded in this quatrain is by now familiar. What is intriguing about these lines is their literary-historical interest: they are one of several instances where Herrick refers to his maid by name—making him possibly the only important English poet up to this time (and perhaps since) to do anything of the sort. And not only does he allude to her but he credits Prudence with being as good as her name: her housewifery keeps the poor parson's head above water. It is doubtful, moreover, that there has ever been a canonical English poet who mentions his pet dog by name in a poem that clearly has some pretensions to be a serious (if not solemn) effort.

It is clear enough that Herrick had a strong autobiographical impulse: more so than most English poets up to his time he specifically invites readers to read some of his poems, among them several of his most important, autobiographically. Certainly allusions to a "*Prew*" or a "*Trasy*" have the effect of grounding a poem in the poet's personal reality. Critics have remarked on Herrick's sense of poetic language as magic and as incantation, preserving and giving a heightened reality to the thing named. But present in *Hesperides* as well may be a prefiguration of what we think of as the modern sensibility—one that is capable of perceiving the ordinary as extraordinary, that can attribute importance to the familiar and the commonplace, and that can allow that there is nothing so mundane that it is not worthy of being presented, even celebrated, in art. Poet of decorum though Herrick is, he also tests traditional notions of decorum, notions that modernism eventually exploded.

In any case, *"His Grange,"* together with Herrick's other country-life poems, constitute a vision of the good life that, for all of its idealization, is grounded in English reality, that is, a world where animals have names, personalities, and histories; where people fall into various social classes, from the most privileged to the least; where there is work to do and bills to be paid; and where danger can lurk. But this world can also be a *"Sacred Grove,"* sanctified by its closeness to nature, by the natural beauty of its flora and fauna, by the sweet simplicity and radical innocence that often characterize its inhabitants, and by the art that gives expression to all of these. Herrick offers readers a "possible pastoral"—the good life that is within the reach of simple country folk, who live for holidays; within the reach of the nobility, whose position enables them vicariously to enjoy rural existence without its hardships; and within the reach of those who, like Parson Herrick, can find contentment in an existence whose peace and security adequately compensate for its modesty.

The Rules of Life

It may seem a non sequitur to turn from the well-known and important country-life poems of *Hesperides* to its little regarded if largest class of poems, the epigrams. Yet, as we have seen, Herrick sometimes "embeds" epigrams in his pastorals to make explicit those principles of the good life that are otherwise implicit in his celebrations of rural existence. Moreover, in individual epigrams like *"Change common to all"* (H-583)—"All things subjected are to Fate; / Whom this Morne sees most fortunate, / The Ev'ning sees in poor estate"—Herrick reiterates themes taken up in his longer pastorals.

As poetic modes, of course, epigrams and pastorals differ from each other in significant ways: epigrams are brief, pithy works with a minimum of description, whereas pastorals are typically extended and visual poems that are only occasionally cerebral. Yet both types loom large in *Hesperides,* which

suggests that Herrick himself did not perceive them as incompatible. Moreover, thanks to recent efforts by several scholars, we are beginning to get a
better sense of the nature and functions of these epigrams and their relationships to other poems in Herrick's collection. Such matters are taken up
more generally in chapter 7; here our attention is confined to those epigrams
that reinforce and expand the poet's vision of the good life.

Over the years the epigrams of *Hesperides* have posed more problems to
Herrick's readers, and even to his editors, than the rest of his works combined. For example, a nineteenth-century editor, A. W. Pollard, apparently
out of deference to his gentler readers, relegated the epigrams to a separate
appendix. Other editors, in compiling selected editions or anthology collections, often omit the epigrams almost entirely. The result is a distorted view
of Herrick and his *Hesperides*. It must be assumed, after all, that the poet
had reasons for including even the ugliest of his epigrams in his collection,
that they were a part of the total artistic effect he wished his poetry to have
on his reader. Readers, he understood, were not as delicate as they might
pretend to be:

> To read my Booke the Virgin shie
> May blush, (while *Brutus* standeth by:)
> But when He's gone, read through what's writ,
> And never staine a cheek for it.
> *(Another* [H-4])

Moreover, another of Herrick's editors, L. C. Martin, has theorized that

Herrick's own explanation [for the presence of the "ugly" epigrams amid the "beauties" of his book] would probably have been on the lines of his epigram on love:
"Love's of it self, too sweet; the best of all / Is, when loves hony has a dash of
gall"—and the apparent disorder of the poems in *Hesperides* may well have been
calculated, so that each poem might be a foil to its immediate neighbors. (*CW,*
xx.n1)

Martin's theory has been supported and expanded by Richard J. Ross, for
whom Herrick's epigrams are demonstrations of the poet's adherence to the
principle of "Art above Nature."[4] In Ross's view, a "gross" epigram like
"*Upon a free Maid, with a foule breath*" (H-588)—"YOu say you'l kiss me,
and I thanke you for it: / But stinking breath, I do as hell abhorre it"—
serves to display human nature in the raw, unimproved by Art. "Art," in this

case, includes the art of proper living, the imposition of "manners," civility," and "vertue" upon social behavior (1958, 93).

Ross's theory can be illustrated by a series of epigrams on a subject that frequently figured in seventeenth-century catalogs of female charms—teeth. For example, in the epigram *"Upon one who said she was always young"* (H-462) the speaker treats his subject with brutal frankness: "YOu say y'are young; but when your Teeth are told / To be but three, Black-ey'd, wee'l thinke y'are old." Decorum aside, the humor has a satiric point. Taking his title into account—something it is always well to do in reading Herrick—it is evident that his persona is exposing a sham, denying one's age. The poet's adroit word choice makes his mockery of this form of hypocrisy especially devastating: to "tell" someone's teeth is to count them as one would do with a horse, to determine age, and the fact that there are only three, each dark and decayed at the center, makes the task easy, however unpleasant. The lady lacks tact as well as taste and thus falls short in both truthfulness and beauty.

In this and other epigrams in a similar vein Herrick shows his kinship with the Elizabethan formal verse satirists. Like them he is concerned with reforming human nature. Like them he tries to do so by holding human deficiencies up to ridicule, even if it calls for the plainest kind of speaking, for the most naturalistic imagery, and sometimes for the treatment of apparently trivial subjects: as one scholar has observed, "to the Neo-Stoic moralist nothing reprehensible was trivial."[5] Furthermore, human beings are such that they sometimes respond more readily to the familiarly trivial than the distantly significant: for example, the lady addressed so bluntly in *"Upon one who said she was always young"* might well attend better to an epigram than to a lecture on truth and beauty.

Beauty, however, is also taken up by Herrick in such epigrams as *"Upon Lucie"* (H-649): "SOund Teeth has *Lucie,* pure as Pearl, and small, / With mellow Lips, and luscious there withall." Part of Lucy's attractiveness is due to the soundness of her teeth as well as to their size and color: beauty has its origin in good health, in what is natural. When the natural is aesthetically inadequate, however, art—or at least artfullness—can improve on it:

> CLose keep your lips, if that you meane
> To be accounted inside cleane:
> For if you cleave* them, we shall see
> There in your teeth much Leprosie.

*expose

Entitled, with painful explicitness, *"To women, to hide their teeth, if they be rotten or rusty"* (*H*-738), this epigram is more advisive than satiric, concerned with appearances (which are, after all, important in approaching life as an art form). Given the Renaissance conception of the poet as one who improves on nature, as in pastoral, Herrick is being consistent when he recommends that ladies do the same thing. Indeed, he is quite explicit about this in another epigram, *"Painting sometimes permitted"* (*H*-641): "IF Nature do deny / Colours, let Art supply." Our own century, in which "painting" or the application of cosmetics begins before puberty and ends only with interment, has certainly embraced Herrick's principle—and is not self-evidently the worse for having done so.

As an example of the way in which Herrick has arranged his poems in his book so that they "comment" on one another, the epigram *"To women to hide their teeth"* is immediately followed by another, *"In praise of women"* (*H*-739):

> O *Jupiter,* should I speak ill
> Of woman-kind, first die I will;
> Since that I know, 'mong all the rest
> Of creatures, woman is the best.

Although proclaiming his vow to Jupiter makes Herrick's seriousness suspect, that the antifeminism of his age was less deeply engrained in him than in some of his peers is apparent throughout *Hesperides.* Women, after all, figure importantly in his vision of the good life, and in more than merely decorative or sexual ways. Although the poet himself never married, he would scarcely say of his *"Sacred Grove"* what Andrew Marvell says (in "The Garden") of Eden: "Such was that happy garden-state, / Where man there walked without a mate."

Since *Hesperides* demonstrates that ugliness in appearance and behavior can be found in the city as well as in the country, the observation of J. Press that Herrick may have printed his "gross" epigrams "to display his unruffled acceptance of life as he had found it among the rude and churlish savages of Devonshire" (9) is an oversimplification. Richard Ross is closer to the truth with his comment that these poems reveal Herrick's "ambivalence toward nature, relishing its proper 'wildness' yet deprecating its 'incivility'" (1958, 93). Whether manifested in nature, where it may exemplify nature's infinite variety and vitality, or in human nature, where it may be a consequence of decadence, ugliness is something few artists are able to ignore, although some are willing to do so. Because his vision of the good life is aesthetic as well as ethical and social, in his "ugly" epigrams Herrick is able to employ a variation on the Renaissance theme of "poetry as delight and instruction"—poetry as repulsion and instruction.

More straightforward "instruction" in living well is to be found in Herrick's "philosophical" epigrams, poems that may deal with some figuratively ugly aspects of the human condition, yet gratify with their presentation of an attitude or stratagem for coping with such matters. One example is an epigram that appears early in *Hesperides, "Sorrowes succeed"* (H-49): "WHen one is past, another care we have, / *Thus Woe suceeds a Woe; as wave a Wave.*" The alliteration and parallelism of the second line communicate a sense of an infinite succession of waves beating dully against a shore, evoking that feeling of weariness and futility that Matthew Arnold would capture centuries later in his poem, "Dover Beach." At the same time, however, the image of the wave and the matter-of-fact tone of the epigram suggest that woe is natural in the human condition and thus needs to be accepted. The melancholy of this epigram's mood and the grimness of its perspective are qualities not often associated with Herrick, yet (as chapter 1 suggests) the attentive reader of *Hesperides* comes to recognize that they are almost as characteristic of his persona as is the theme for which he is best known, *carpe diem.*

That theme is advanced in such epigrams as *"To live Freely"* (H-453): "LEt's live in hast; use pleasure while we may: / Co'd life return, 'twod never lose a day." This abbreviated version of the *carpe diem* philosophy, re-iterated in other epigrams like *"An end decreed"* (H-639), *"To be merry"* (H-806), and *"To Youth"* (H-655)—"DRinke Wine, and live here blithefull, while ye may: / *The morrowes life too late is, Live to day"*—is of course a popular reduction of Epicureanism to a primitive Dionysianism. As long as human beings are motivated by the pleasure principle such exhortations can exert a strong appeal. But Herrick is too much of a realist to maintain that unbridled sensuousness alone is sufficient to sustain human life and human society. His practice in *Hesperides* is to follow the Jonsonian precept that poetry, in addition to giving readers pleasure, must offer them "a certain rule and pattern of living well, and happily, disposing [them] to all civil offices of society" (*BJ,* 83). For Herrick as for Jonson, then, poetry serves the pleasure principle in that it can act as a guide to "living . . . happily." But it can also serve as a guide to the moral life—"living well" (i.e., virtuously)—and to the ethical life, to the performance of those duties—"civil offices"—required of the good citizen. Thus it is that a moralizing epigram like *"On himself"* (H-1088), which concludes, *"He lives, who lives to virtue: men who cast / Their ends for Pleasure, do not live, but last,"* while it qualifies the *carpe diem* motif of *Hesperides*, does not necessarily contradict it—or vice versa. Time and time again Herrick presents his readers with opposing viewpoints, trusting to their intelligence and common sense to mediate between them.

Although recent scholarship has argued that *Hesperides* wages a covert campaign against the Puritans,[6] some of Herrick's rules for life, like those expressed in the epigram "*Vertue*" (*H*-298), read as if they had been written by a versifying John Bunyan: "Each must, in vertue, strive for to excell; / *That man lives twice, that lives the first life well.*" Striking a seemingly Puritanical note as well is the moralizing epigram, "*Choose for the best*" (*H*-936) —"GIve house-roome to the best; '*Tis never known / Vertue and pleasure, both to dwell in one*"—a point of view that would seem to exclude "cleanly-*Wantonnesse,*" for example. Less extreme is "*Pleasures Pernicious*" (*H*-1088): "WHere Pleasures rule a Kingdome, never there / Is sober virtue, seen to move her sphere." This epigram could be taken as an attack on the hedonism of the Stuart courts or as a more general observation about the ethos of a citizenry. In any case Herrick's point is not so much that pleasure in itself is pernicious but that a nation controlled by the pleasure principle is in trouble. Although an individual may "seize the day," a state, which is also subject to transiency, must look to its past and to its future.

From one perspective those epigrams of Herrick's that offer "rules" and "patterns" for the good life constitute a mass of contradictions, from another a comprehensive world view. Contributing to this problem is the fact that there are so many of these poems and they are scattered throughout *Hesperides*. In responding to them the readers's own beliefs and values inevitably come into play. In fact, Herrick's collection is so vast and varied that it readily lends itself to being used to reinforce one's own preconceptions. Reading *Hesperides,* it is not difficult to come to the conclusion that whether one's orientation is Dionysian, Apollonian, or something in between, it can be readily accommodated by the "Herrickean" point of view. This indeed may be part of the genius of *Hesperides:* it is so highly "polyvalent" that it offers many—though clearly not all—readers the possibility of reading themselves into Herrick's poetry, of imaginatively transforming themselves into Herrick and Herrick into themselves.

With that caveat, the theory advanced here is that Herrick's philosophical epigrams in the aggregate synthesize a vision of life that strikes a balance between extremes. If this is the case, it is consistent with a tendency that pervades *Hesperides* and Herrick's pastoralism in particular—a tendency to hew to the *via media,* the "middle way," the path of moderation. This orientation, which is both Stoic and Epicurean, is expressed in an ethical epigram, *"Excess"* (*H*-1109), placed near the end of the collection: "EXcesse is sluttish: keep the meane; for why? / Vertue's clean Conclave is sobriety." Following "the golden mean" through behavior that avoids extremes is the way to the house of virtue. Here virtue is personified as a tidy homemaker, whereas excess is a messy one. The metaphor is not inappropriate: if the Dionysian temperament is guilty of an excess of sensuousness, the Puritanical temperament (as satirists of the age like Jonson were fond of pointing out) is guilty of an excess of religious zeal, and both violate the principle of decorum—doing the right thing in the right place at the right time.

Keeping to the mean does not, in Herrick's view (nor in the views of Epicurus or Aristotle), mean straddling ethical fences or settling for mediocrity; rather, it involves seeking out what is most beneficial, relative to the general order of things. Because one lives amid both the order of society and the order of nature, whatever is best for oneself can never be that which is bad for the common good or subversive of natural order. Moderation then, as Herrick announces in *"The Meane"* (*H*-812), is essential to order and harmony: "*IMparitie doth ever discord bring: / The Mean the Musique makes in every thing.*" Herrick's music metaphor is apt for his musical age, one that heard a kind of music in the natural, cosmic, and divine spheres that the discordant human sphere very much needed to emulate. Moderation, then, begins to look very much like a universal principle, for without it discord and chaos return.

Although Robert Herrick's *Hesperides* has in the past sometimes been regarded as a chaotic and discordant collection, the evidence accumulated by scholars in recent years suggests that its disorder is more apparent than real. Among its several significant ordering elements, one of the most important is the complex, ultimately subtle, even profound vision of the good life it embodies in a wide range of poetic forms and modes.

Chapter Four

"Cleanly-*Wantonnesse*" and "*This Sacred Grove*": Themes of Love

For many readers Robert Herrick's name is synonymous with love poetry, with graceful lyrics celebrating a score of pretty women (or celebrating one pretty woman under a score of names). But although some of his most widely known and most admired works have been his love poems, they have also brought Herrick his share of criticism. They have been condemned as being amorous without intensity or as being idealistic without elevation. The poet has even been criticized because there appears to be no instance of sexual consummation in the love poetry of his *Hesperides*[1]—as if that were unusual for published seventeenth-century verse. Herrick also has been charged with being, at best, a voyeur in poetry, one who obtains gratification from spying on women, or, at worst, a fetishist, more enamored of female garments than the females wearing them. It even has been implied that he is no true Cavalier poet, full of gallantry and passion, but a mere sentimentalist who is more in love with love than with women.

Some of this criticism seems to depend on which of *Hesperides'* scores of love poems the critic has examined. Moreover, because critical *evaluation* sometimes can suggest more about the evaluator than the work being evaluated, the critical evaluation of poems dealing with such highly sensitive subjects as sex and love is particularly likely to reflect the critic's own deep-seated wishes, anxieties, conflicts, and frustrations at least as much as the poet's.

That said, this consideration of Robert Herrick, the love poet, will begin with the claim that, for all the criticism of his amatory verses, in "*To* Anthea, *who may command him any thing*" (*H-267*) he has written a love lyric that is as successful as any such poem composed by Ben Jonson or his other "sons":

> 1. BId me to live, and I will live
>   Thy Protestant to be:
>   Or bid me love, and I will give
>   A loving heart to thee.

2. A heart as soft, a heart as kind,
    A heart as sound and free,
  As in the whole world thou canst find,
    That heart Ile give to thee.

3. Bid that heart stay, and it will stay,
    To honour thy Decree:
  Or bid it languish quite away,
    And't shall doe so for thee.

4. Bid me to weep, and I will weep,
    While I have eyes to see:
  And having none, yet I will keep
    A heart to weep for thee.

5. Bid me despaire, and Ile despaire
    Under that *Cypresse* tree:
  Or bid me die, and I will dare,
    E'en Death, to die for thee.

6. Thou art my life, my love, my heart,
    The very eyes of me:
  And hast command of every part,
    To live and die for thee.

The effectiveness of this poem does not begin with its originality (a quality little esteemed in Renaissance aesthetics), although it has some original touches, such as its use of the word "Protestant" (l. 2). J. Max Patrick explains that here the term means "a suitor; one who solemnly declares [makes protestations of] his love" (*CP*, 150), but the word's reverberations are wider. "Protestant" is an imaginative way of establishing the convention of "the religion of love" as the poem's controlling metaphor: her lover perceives Anthea as a goddess. Herrick's usage is also daring, because only a century or so after the Reformation the word still could call up memories of bitter struggle, spiritual crisis, and psychic stress: Sir Thomas Browne, in the opening passage of his *Religio Medici* (1643), could say of "Protestant," "I am of that reformed new-cast Religion, wherein I mislike nothing but the name."[2] The word then lends a higher seriousness to the speaker's protestations, resulting in a transcendence of the poem's conventional form, a series of commands that the lady may issue and her lover vows to obey.

Although the sentiments the lyric expresses are commonplace, they are expressed in language that is unembellished to the point of spareness: of the poem's 152 (mainly Anglo-Saxon) words, all but 14 are monosyllabic. The purpose of such carefully wrought simplicity appears to be to create an impression of sincerity. That the speaker will even dare death for Anthea, then, seems not especially melodramatic. Herrick's understatement heightens the poem's intensity even as it conceals its conventionality, confirming Leigh DeNeef's point that the concision and control that mark Cavalier poetry are not necessarily symptomatic of a lack of strong feeling (86–7). The symmetry of "*To* Anthea," with its last stanza both summarizing the motifs of the other five and coming full circle to the language and the thesis of the first, foreshadows the mathematical passion of some of Andrew Marvell's most admired love poems.

"*To* Anthea, *who may command him any thing*" is not one of Herrick's most anthologized works. His critics (admirers as well as detractors) do not always seem to be mindful that he wrote more poems than any other important seventeenth-century poet, many of them love poems, and that therefore generalizations about his poetry, even those not based on limited or skewed samples, are always tricky and inevitably tentative (including, of course, the generalizations offered in this study).

Any consideration of Herrick's love poetry does well to take note of the poet's own pronouncements in "*The Argument of his Book*." It is worth noting, for example, that his first reference to love celebrates it ("I sing") in the context of marriage (l. 4); only after three specific allusions to the sacrament of marriage does he announce that his book will also treat ("I write") the traditional subjects of "*Youth*" and "*Love*" and celebrate ("I sing" again) what is apparently his love ethos, suggested by the seeming oxymoron of "cleanly-*Wantonnesse*." The balance implied here between what Freud would have viewed as the superego or conscience and the id or the passions also follows logically from Herrick's neo-Epicureanism, from the principle of moderation that is central to that philosophy, and from his aesthetic. The truth of "cleanly-*Wantonnesse*," which he expresses in so many of his love poems, is that love is a matter of both Nature and Art: it involves one's physical being, with its "wanton" demands, but also the capacity and compulsion to manage and ameliorate one's physicality, to make it "cleanly." At its best, then, love hews to the golden mean and thus attains a maximum of pleasure with a minimum of pain. It is a "wilde civility," sanctioned by religion, philosophy, and art.

The Rituals of Love

Although the only ritual of love referred to in *"The Argument of his Book"* is the wedding service, other poems in *Hesperides* treat the varied stages and events of the love relationship, informal as well as formal, from first attraction to a lover's death. A good example is one of Herrick's best known poems, *"Upon Julia's Clothes"* (*H-779*), a mere six lines—two stanzas, that are, however, rarely absent from any anthology of poetry and about which considerable critical ink has been spilled.[3] The discussion that follows is indebted to several ingenious explications of this poem, but chiefly to that of Louis H. Leiter.[4] Leiter suggests that this poem derives its structure and its subtle wit from a "submerged metaphor" having to do with the sport of fishing.

Although Herrick's title seems to signal that his subject will be fashion rather than a particular female, rather more is involved. The poem opens with a lover's impression:

> WHen as in silks my *Julia* goes,
> Then, then, methinks, how sweetly flowes
> That liquefaction of her clothes.

The impression described apparently is evoked specifically when Julia wears a silk gown—that is, very likely on special occasions. The speaker calls her "my" Julia, but upon what his proprietary sense is based cannot be determined from the poem itself. "My" could be an expression of love that is not in fact returned. However, Herrick wrote 77 poems about Julia, far more than about any of his other poetic mistresses,[5] and many of them precede this one in the order of the text. For the assiduous reader of *Hesperides,* then, this will be a poem about one aspect of a complex, on-going love relationship.

The attention-getting word of this triplet stanza is, of course, "liquefaction," here meaning the apparent reduction of a solid object (Julia's flowing silk dress) to liquid. The speaker is entranced (the repetition of "then" suggests strong feeling) by an illusion ("me thinks"): when Julia walks, her body movements seem to transform her silk gown into shimmering rivulets of water. The eye of her beholder has been fooled into a perception that, as Julia goes by, she is walking in water.

The fact that water is associated with fish is the basis for Herrick's further development of his submerged metaphor in stanza two:

> Next, when I cast mine eyes and see
> That brave vibration each way free;
> O how that glittering taketh me!

Like a fisherman casting his line, the speaker casts his eyes in the direction of "That brave [splendid] vibration," the movement of Julia's silk-sheathed body, presumably, as well as the movement of the dress itself. But his prey fails to rise to the bait of his obvious admiration. Instead, a comic reversal takes place, and it is the fisherman, not the fish, who gets hooked: he is bedazzled by the "glittering" sight and so Julia is able to "take" him as a fisherman uses a net to take a caught fish.

"*Upon Julia's Clothes*" is a small triumph of Herrick's art—two triplet stanzas, six lines, 39 words—that has been widely admired. It has been suggested that the poem is about aesthetics or about Art and Nature[6]—and it is both—but it is unlikely that its broad appeal derives from such abstract and abstruse themes. Ordinary readers, and even some critics, probably appreciate the poem because it wittily treats a familiar but still mysterious aspect of sexual aesthetics—not fetishism (as has been suggested) but the fact that a person can be especially appealing to us when they dress in a certain way—and because it describes a familiar phenomenon of sexual negotiations: in seeking to snare the female, the male is himself ensnared by the very attractiveness that drew him to her in the first place. It is, then, a poem that wittily treats human susceptibility and thus is one to which susceptible humans can readily relate.

Herrick's model for this poem might have been John Donne's "The Baite," which employs a similar metaphor to describe a similar experience. But whereas "*Upon Julia's Clothes*" is a witty vignette on the psychology of sexual attraction, Donne's poem is a piscatory variation on the traditional invitation-to-love form. Like many poets of the period, Herrick also tried his hand at this genre. But his "*To* Phillis *to love, and live with him*" (H-521), for example, is a more ambitious effort than most. By its elaboration, indeed its foregrounding, of the pastoral setting that is one of this genre's conventions, the poem becomes an invitation to participate not only in love but in a bucolic vision—the "*Sacred Grove*" of nature improved by art.

The invitation extended in the poem's first couplet, "LIve, live with me, and thou shalt see / The pleasures Ile prepare for thee," is followed by a catalog of idealized pastoral delights considerably more extensive than that in Christopher Marlowe's classic of the genre, "Come live with me and be my love":

What sweets the Country can afford
Shall blesse thy Bed, and blesse thy Board.
The soft sweet Mosse shall be thy bed,
With crawling Woodbine over-spread:
By which the silver-shedding streames
Shall gently melt thee into dreames.
Thy clothing next, shall be a Gowne
Made of the Fleeces purest Downe.
The tongues of Kids shall be thy meate;
Their Milke thy drinke; and thou shalt eate
The Paste of Filberts for thy bread
With Cream of Cowslips buttered.

                                        (ll. 3–14)

The "Country" pleasures enumerated are seductive in themselves but are made more so by Herrick's manipulation of the sounds of sensuous long vowels and sibilants. The catalog itself implies that, by accepting the invitation, Phillis will be doing what comes naturally: by allowing nature to feed, clothe, and shelter her, she becomes one with the pastoral world. By accepting her admirer's love, then, she gains the good life everyone seeks.

In Herrick's pastoral version of the good life, nature is humankind's servant:

Thy Feasting-Tables shall be Hills
With *Daisies* spread, and *Daffadils*
Where thou shalt sit, and *Red-brest* by,
For meat, shall give thee melody.

                                        (ll. 15–18)

Normally a poetic convention and an illusion, here the pathetic fallacy seems almost realistic: in her new way of life Phillis will be able to enjoy picnics and, with a little bribery, birdsong. Relatively realistic as well are the modest gifts offered to her:

ILe give thee Chaines and Carkanets
Of *Primroses* and *Violets*.
A Bag and Bottle thou shalt have;
That richly wrought, and This as brave;

> So that as either shall expresse
> The Wearer's no meane* Shepheardesse.
>   (ll. 19–24)

*humble

Like the heroine of a seventeenth-century pastoral drama, Phillis will be revealed to be more than an ordinary Arcadian: subsequent lines (25–32) promise that she will be the toast of each country holiday and finally be crowned "The *Queen of Roses* for that yeere," a living symbol of love and beauty. To her, dutiful subjects will bring offerings from nature's treasury like "the blushing Apple, bashfull Peare," Herrick's personifications implying that as humankind draws closer to nature, nature becomes more like humankind.

Having presumably entranced Phillis with his vision of her glorification, her admirer now begins to speak more directly of love. In the tradition of the amorous shepherd, he vows to carve her name in every tree that is as "straight and smooth-skin[ned]" as she. And, with the same kind of witty reversal that the persona of "*Upon* Julia's *Clothes*" acknowledged, he promises,

> To thee a Sheep-hook I will send,
> Be-pranckt with Ribbands, to this end,
> This, this alluring Hook might be
> Lesse for to catch a sheep, then me.
>   (ll. 43–46)

But Phillis's lover has moved a step beyond the admirer of Julia in her silks: he *anticipates* being "hooked" by his lady-love.

As the tempo of the seduction builds, the pastoral world fades into the background, to be replaced by an indoors world, situated "neer the glitt'ring Hearth" (l. 50). Here more fashionable, more intimate, and more urbane gifts are promised—"Gloves, Garters, Stockings, Shooes, and Strings"—which, Phillis's lover claims, "shall move / Others to Lust, but me to Love" (ll. 53–54). The very juxtaposition of love and lust brings "cleanly-*Wantonnesse*" to mind: although the speaker protests against lust, readers are probably justified in suspecting that he protests too much. That this is the case is further suggested by the just perceptible note of urgency in the poem's concluding couplet: "These (nay) and more, thine own shal be, / If thou wilt love, and live with me" (ll. 55–56). Nonetheless, if a lady is to be seduced by a poem, it is doubtful that this one is it. Like most invitations to love, *"To* Phillis" is an exercise in a convention, more a demonstration of the poet's wit and imagination than of his passion. In their comic mode, poems of this type tend to become near parodies of the ritual of seduction, illustrating the extremes to which the amorous male will go. On the other hand, when the theme of *carpe diem* is introduced, the genre can begin to approach high seriousness. Herrick, as shall be seen below, is more than capable of writing in a more serious vein, but here he seems as interested in charming the reader with a pastoral jeu d'esprit as he is in charming some real or imaginary Phillis. To expect passionate intensity in such poems is to misunderstand their nature and functions.

Although Herrick demonstrates in another compliment poem, *"The Eye"* (*H*-133), that he can also write love poetry in the metaphysical manner, that he can, like John Donne, explore and exploit a conceit (his lady's eye as a microcosm of the heavens), his artistic temper is essentially "classical." That is, he is a poet who relies heavily on design, the careful structuring and patterning of a poem; on decorum, selecting a poetic form that is appropriate to his chosen subject and theme and developing both through an appropriate diction and style; and on imitation, modeling his verses on English, Latin, or Greek originals. These qualities are well represented in a pastoral entitled *"Mistresse* Elizabeth Wheeler, *under the name of the lost Shepardesse"* (*H*-263), in which Herrick treats a later and more serious stage of love than those illustrated in the two poems just considered.

That Mrs. Wheeler was actually Herrick's cousin and that his title assigns her a role in what sounds like a pastoral tragicomedy call attention to the artifice of the poem, one that turns out to combine compliment verse and the love complaint, all within the bucolic mode. As he did in *"To* Phillis," the poet takes up the role of pastoral swain, but here he plays a forsaken shepherd engaged in a lovesick dialogue with Cupid:

> AMong the Mirtles, as I walkt
> Love and my sighs thus intertalkt:
> Tell me, said I, in deep distresse,
> Where I may find my Shepardesse.
> (ll. 1–4)

The incipient sentimentality of the moment is broken by Cupid's rude rejoinder: he calls Herrick a fool because he doesn't know that his lost shepherdess is "in every thing that's sweet" (l. 6). The little god of love then goes on to catalog her beauties as they find their embodiment in nature's blossoms:

> In yond' *Carnation* goe and seek,
> There thou shalt find her lip and cheek:
> In that ennamedl'd *Pansie* by,
> There thou shalt have her curious eye:
> In bloom of *Peach,* and *Roses* bud,
> There waves the streamer of her blood.
>
> (ll. 7–12)

Like a pastoral goddess, Elizabeth Wheeler has left an imprint of herself on the natural landscape. But as the reference to her blood reminds us, this goddess is subject to time, as blossoms are. Seeking to weave a garland of these blooms—"I went to pluck them one by one, / To make of parts an union"—the speaker is frustrated by their abrupt fading: "But on a sudden all were gone" (ll. 14–16). Ironically, in attempting to hold fast to beauty, he loses it. The meaning of this mystery for the swain is explicated by Cupid:

> these be
> The true resemblances of thee;
> For as these flowers, thy joyes must die,
> And in the turning of an eye;
> And all thy hopes of her must wither,
> Like those short sweets, ere knit together.
>
> (ll. 17–22)

If life and joy are fleeting, it follows that love, or even the hope of it, is also doomed to be short-lived. It is unusual for a pastoral compliment to end on so grim a note—particularly one addressed to a real person—for pastoral is typically life affirming; and even the Renaissance love complaint is somewhat more likely to conclude in frustration than in doom and despair. By ringing in the themes of star-crossed lovers and transiency Herrick broadens and deepens the tone and mood of this conventional genre. The poem also links Herrick, the Cavalier, to the more pessimistic love poetry of John Donne and to the near nihilism of Andrew Marvell's "The Definition of Love" and "To his Coy Mistress."

T. G. S. Cain's analysis of "Elizabeth Wheeler" invokes the name of yet another well-known contemporary, George Herbert. Calling attention to this pastoral's meditative tone and structure, Cain sees it as a "secular par-

ody" of devotional poems like Herbert's variation on the theme of transiency, "Life" (125). Herrick's vision, however, lacks even an implied consolation: traditional romantic sentiments to the contrary, it offers no hope that
love affords transcendence of nature's laws. Such skepticism—or realism
—in evidence throughout *Hesperides*, lends a particular depth and seriousness to Herrick's amatory strain, counterbalancing his equally important
but lighter and more idealistic love lyrics.

The Implications of Love

Something of the rich variety of Herrick's love poetry may be indicated
by the fact that in two not unrepresentative pages of *Hesperides* are juxtaposed *"Upon Cupid"* (*H*-229), a fanciful epigram on the unremitting
human sexual drive; a sensual but at the same time humorously pedantic
epigram, *"Upon* Julia's *breasts"* (*H*-230); a serious admonitory love poem,
"The Changes to Corinna" (*H*-232); a scurrilous epigram whose point is anticipated in its title, *"No Lock against Letcherie"* (*H*-233); and a satiric jibe
against marriage, *"Upon himselfe"* (*H*-235). As this sampling suggests,
Herrick's erotic and comic love poems through sheer weight of numbers
clamor for attention somewhat more loudly than his more serious and often
more ambitious efforts—like *"The Changes to* Corinna."

"The Changes" seems so unrelievedly grim as to hardly pass for a love
poem at all, but it is in fact a perfectly structured and powerful example of
an amatory subgenre, the admonition of a disdainful lady. Corinna's suitor,
who apparently feels that she has rejected him out of foolish pride alone, addresses her peremptorily: "BE not proud, but now encline / Your soft eare
to Discipline." Here "Discipline" is to be understood as "instruction." Like a
schoolmaster he will read her a lecture in mortality, first drawing on contemporary physics: "You have changes in your life, / Sometimes peace, and
sometimes strife" (ll. 3–4). The kind of precarious and shifting balance that
exists among the four elements of earth, air, fire, and water characterizes her
existence as well. Flux is as endemic to human life as it is to nature, and the
changes in her state of health are reflected in her face, as the phases of the
moon can be seen in the cycles of the tides: "You have ebbes of face and
flowes, / As your health or comes, or goes" (ll. 5–6). Corinna's psychological state is likewise subject to cycles, as she responds emotionally to life's vicissitudes: "You have hopes, and doubts, and feares, / Numberlesse, as are
your haires" (ll. 7–8). Finally, her very sexuality fluctuates (as the speaker
apparently has reason to know): "You have Pulses that doe beat / High,
and passions lesse of heate" (ll. 9–10).

To a mature woman such admonishments would be gratuitous; but Corinna, the speaker implies, has fallen prey to the self-delusion of youth—that age cannot wither her:

> You are young, but must be old,
> And to these, ye must be told,
> Time, ere long, will come and plow
> Loathed Furrowes in your brow:
> And the dimnesse of your eye
> Will no other thing imply,
>   But you must die
>   As well as I.
>   (ll. 11–18)

Such frankness approaches the brutal; what makes the passage unusual for poems of this type is the fact that the speaker forces himself as well as his proud fair to confront the *memento mori* of disfiguring wrinkles and a lackluster eye, the face's intimations of mortality. There is a kind of grim Stoical acceptance of the flux of human life in the terseness of the final dimeter couplet. As Leigh DeNeef has noted, Herrick does not allow Corinna, the reader, or himself the relief of returning to the love relationship once his admonition has been registered: we are left to contemplate the ravages of time without hint or hope of consolation (99). We are not even granted the bravado of a *carpe diem* conclusion to assuage our pessimism.

"*The Changes to* Corinna," then, contrasts starkly with those "seize the day" poems with which Herrick is popularly associated, "*Corinna's going a Maying*" and "*To the Virgins, to make much of time.*" Basic to such works is the claim that though love (read *sex*) cannot halt the momentum of time's winged chariot, it is at least capable of making life's fleeting moments pleasurable. In such works Herrick's Stoic premise leads him to an Epicurean conclusion, as one of his less well-known poems, "*To* Sappho" (*H-*691), illustrates:

> LEt us now take time, and play,
> Love, and live here while we may;
> Drink rich wine; and make good cheere,
> While we have our being here:
> For, once dead, and laid i'th grave,
> No return from thence we have.

This, of course, is Herrick in his Anacreontic vein, affirming the validity of a Dionysian response to the reality of human mortality. But the fleshly frivolousness that some readers might find in the poem's first three lines is qualified by the philosophical abstractness of the transitional fourth line, then justified by the spare final couplet, as serious and laconic (if not as vividly witty) as Andrew Marvell's "The Grave's a fine and private place, / But none, I think, do there embrace."

While it is only Herrick's *"Corinna's going a Maying"* that can appropriately be compared with Marvell's "To his Coy Mistress," it is the older poet's *"To the Virgins, to make much of Time"* (*H*-208) that has fixed the concept of *carpe diem* in the popular imagination forever. Scholarly investigation has revealed that Herrick is heavily indebted to a variety of sources—some classical, some English—in this poem (*CP*, 118n; *PW*, 517–19), but his synthesizing is so artful that the lyric's derivativeness is hardly noticeable. Not in the least pedantic, this poem has been so popular that its opening line has become proverbial:

> 1. GAther ye Rose-buds while ye may,
>   Old Time is still a flying:
>   And this same flower that smiles today,
>   To morrow will be dying.
>
> (ll. 1–4)

The admonition of the title and the image of time in flight convey some sense of urgency. However, even gathered, rosebuds are beautiful, and the personification, "Old Time," suggests a genial greybeard more than a grim reaper. The fact that this ancient is "a flying" almost makes him seem more comic than ominous. But then the ironically foreshortened image of the flower dying amid its smile manifestly darkens the mood even as it hints at the analogy between maidens and blossoms. That mood is intensified in the second stanza by an image which suggests that transiency is inherent in the cosmos as well as in sublunary nature:

> 2. The glorious Lamp of Heaven, the Sun,
>   The higher he's a getting;
>   The sooner will his Race be run,
>   And neerer he's to Setting.
>
> (ll. 5–8)

The metaphoric first line of the stanza is pretentiously poetic compared to the colloquial character of stanza 1. Herrick's purpose is to inflate the eminence of the sun so that its decline, taken up in the last two lines, may seem even more swift and precipitous. It begins to appear that irony is a law of nature: in the comos as in a rose garden, the nearer things are to their apogee, the closer they approach the slide down to their perigee.

The object lesson to be drawn for the virgins from such natural phenomena is outlined in argumentative fashion in the two remaining stanzas. First, the girls are presented with a twofold proposition:

> 3. That Age is best, which is the first,
>   When Youth and Blood are warmer;
>   But being spent, the worse, and worst
>   Times, still succeed the former.
>   (ll. 9–12)

Since human beings are subject to the law of atrophy—"*All things decay and die*"—youth, when growth is still taking place, has to be the optimum time of life. The grand illusion of youth, however, is that it is forever, an illusion the virgins' lecturer curtly dispels with his image of adolescent heat soon giving way to the chill of age. His conclusion, then, becomes almost self-evident:

> 4. Then be not coy, but use your time;
>   And while ye may, goe marry:
>   For having lost but once your prime,
>   You may for ever tarry.
>   (ll. 13–16)

This last stanza makes it clear enough that to the speaker young women are coy by nurture rather than by nature. Their receptivity to love is under their control. The delaying tactics that social custom prescribes for them are self-defeating, threatening to waste life's most precious commodities—time, youth, and love. "Goe marry" can be taken merely as a euphemistic imperative to seek sexual liberation, but given the magisterial posture of the speaker a literal interpretation is the more likely one: the virgins are encouraged to lose their virginity without delay but to lose it in an act of love that is socially sanctioned.

Slightly earlier in *Hesperides,* Herrick is preoccupied with all these themes and more in "Corinna's *going a Maying*" (*H*-178); like "*To the Vir-*

gins," it is a somewhat derivative poem but one that is commonly viewed as his supreme achievement. It has received considerable attention from such critics as Cleanth Brooks, Robert Deming, Leigh DeNeef, and Leah S. Marcus,[7] to all of whom the following comments are indebted. For example, Brooks has observed that "Corinna" is a "traditional" poem in the sense that its form and much of its content have precedents in poetry of the past, such as the invitation to love or song of seduction, and the pastoral, a poem (as we have seen) set against a rustic background that assumes both a deep sympathy between humankind and nature and a marked tension between rural and urban life.

"Corinna" is also a "ceremonial" poem, for not only does it celebrate the traditional holiday of May Day and the folk and religious rituals that undergird it, but it is also in a sense a part of those rituals, a lover's plea on a day dedicated to love. (Marcus calls it Herrick's "most sacramental poem—in the sense of its sanctification of life—though not a religious one" [158].)

Finally, Herrick's masterpiece can from one perspective be viewed as a "metaphysical" poem—that is, a witty, argumentative, and dramatic work, through "conceits" simultaneously expressing strong feeling and significant ideas. All of these elements are contained within a highly formal design. The poem's metrical scheme, for example, is elaborately symmetrical: each of its five 14-line stanzas consists of seven couplets, the first, fourth, and seventh of which are in iambic pentameter, with the second, third, fifth, and sixth in iambic tetrameter. This complex patterning controls and contains the onrushing tempo of the poem and the welling of its emotion. Longer and more ambitious than the majority of the poems in *Hesperides,* "Corinna" nonetheless exemplifies the philosophical and emotional poise and the artistic balance that are so characteristic of that collection generally.

The poem's dramatic quality is apparent from the start, for it begins in medias res, as if the reader had stumbled upon a lovers' quarrel, and it begins, moreover, with the kind of colloquial exhortation one is accustomed to encountering in metaphysical love poems like Donne's *"The Sunne Rising"*:

> GEt up, get up for shame, the Blooming Morne
> Upon her wings presents the god unshorne.
> > See how *Aurora* throwes her faire
> > Fresh-quilted colours through the aire:
> > Get up, sweet Slug-a-bed, and see
> > The Dew-bespangling Herbe and Tree.
> Each Flower has wept, and bow'd toward the East,
> Above an houre since; yet you not drest,

> Nay! not so much as out of bed?
> When all the Birds have Mattens seyd,
> And sung their thankfull Hymnes: 'tis sin,
> Nay, profanation to keep in,
> When as a thousand Virgins on this day,
> Spring, sooner then the Lark, to fetch in May.
>
> (ll. 1–14)

The originality of this stanza, like the originality of the entire poem, resides in Herrick's unique synthesis of traditional elements with characteristic touches of his own. Juxtaposed, for example, with the comic realism of "GEt up, get up for shame," are a delicately idealized personification of "the Blooming Morne"; an untraditionally phrased traditional identification of the sun with Apollo, the young, golden-haired god whose arrival the budding goddess of the morning signals with the spreading of her wings; and a folksy comparison of the dawn sky to the colors of an English quilt. Here Herrick has done more than merely set a scene: he has endowed an ordinary event, the advent of day, with so many dimensions—the vernacular, the painterly, the mythic, and the dramatic—that daybreak seems to take on a transcendent beauty and significance.

Reversing the usual pattern of the invitation-to-love poem, this one has the speaker trying to get his lady-love *out* of bed rather than into it. His aim, however, is to induce her to participate in a day sacred to fertility and traditionally associated with sexual license. Consequently, Corinna's would-be lover adopts a tone that is both amusingly familiar, calling her "sweet-Slug-abed," and formal, with overtones of sacred ritual. Thus, the flowers are like penitents at an early morning service, and the birds as chorus have sung the morning hymns. The implication is that if natural creatures can perform human offices, then humans, like the "thousand" dutiful virgins who have begun the day right, can perform natural offices. Thus, for Corinna to remain in bed is to "sin" against the "religion" of nature and against her own nature, because between nature and human nature a profound sympathy exists.

Words like "sin" and "profanation," although they primarily demonstrate the speaker's talent for witty cajolery, contribute to a muted and ambiguous religious motif that runs through the poem. Still, the predominantly playful tone established in the first stanza continues in the second, as Corinna's lover takes another tack in order to persuade her to get up:

> Rise; and put on your Foliage, and be seene
> To come forth, like the Spring-time, fresh and greene;
>   For Jewels for your Gowne, or Haire:
>   Feare not; the leaves will strew
>   Gemms in abundance upon you:
> Besides, the childhood of the Day has kept,
> Against you come, some *Orient Pearls* unwept:
>   Come, and receive them while the light
>   Hangs on the Dew-locks of the night:
>   And *Titan* on the Eastern hill
>   Retires himselfe, or else stands still
> Till you come forth. Wash, dress, be briefe in praying:
> Few Beads are best, when once we goe a Maying.
>
> (ll. 15–28)

The sympathy between nature and human nature, established in stanza 1, is here amplified through her lover's representation of Corinna herself. She will become another Flora, he avers, another blooming and beautiful goddess of the spring, wearing her dress like "Foliage." Her costume needs no jewels for its enhancement, only the pearl-like dewdrops nature has been saving for her. Nature's god, the sun himself, violates natural law by waiting for this new goddess to appear. On so special a day, the speaker claims, convention can be peremptorily dismissed: prolonged prayers and drawn-out devotions with the rosary should give way to more natural forms of worship.

Traditional religion itself, however, has not been banished from this scene; in fact, it will be reaffirmed in a succeeding stanza. What Herrick is dealing with in this poem is, in a sense, accommodation—the accommodation of the natural to the human and the human to the natural (as in stanza 1), of traditional religion to nature's religion, and, as stanza 3 demonstrates, of country to town and town to country:

> Come, my *Corinna,* come; and comming, marke
> How each field turns a street; each street a Parke
>   Made green, and trimm'd with trees: see how
>   Devotion gives each House a Bough,
>   Or Branch: Each Porch, each doore, ere this,
>   An Arke a Tabernacle is
> Made up of white-thorn neatly enterwove;
> As if here were those cooler shades of love.
>   Can such delights be in the street,

And open fields, and we not see't?
Come, we'll abroad; and let's obay
The Proclamation made for May:
And sin no more, as we have done, by staying;
But my *Corinna,* come, let's goe a Maying.

(ll. 29–42)

The accommodation that Corinna is being urged to make has already been
accomplished in the world beyond her bedchamber. Town and country have
in a sense switched places and become one: so many villagers have made
their way into the fields that the latter begin to look like the streets of the
town, while the streets themselves have taken on the appearance of park-
land, so green are they with foliage brought back by the celebrants for May
Day decorations. Festooned as they are with boughs, the houses begin to resemble the woodland groves that are the tabernacles of nature's religion.
The "religion of love" also figures in here, for these same "*Sacred Groves*" are
also the cool haunts of lovers seeking privacy. Corinna's lassitude is not only
causing her to miss a rare sight but the opportunity to become a part of the
picture herself. This is a "sin" as well as a "crime" of omission: both natural
religion and natural law proclaim that to every thing there is a season, and
May Day represents the season of generation and regeneration.[8]

"Love's religion" also has its rituals, and according to her lover, these too
are being scanted by Corinna:

There's not a budding Boy, or Girle, this day,
But is got up, and gone to bring in May.
A deale of Youth, ere this, is come
Back, and with *White-Thorn* laden home.
Some have dispatch'd their Cakes and Creame,
Before that we have left to dream.

(ll. 43–48)

Like Corinna in her "foliage," the young people of the village are "fresh and
greene," "budding," and thus ripe for love. Unlike her, however, they have
obeyed the proclamation of the season (of the year, of their lives) and performed the rituals prescribed for May Day. Some have even "wept, and
woo'd, and plighted Troth, / And chose their Priest, ere we can cast off
sloth" (ll. 49–50). The compression of what are normally months or even
years of courtship rituals into one couplet and a morning may give the impression that they have been performed hastily, even perfunctorily. But one

of the traditions of May 1st is that it is a day for lovers to announce their en-
gagements. Moreover, these lovers, however impassioned they may be, do
seek the church's sanctification of their desires, its ability to make "cleanly"
what was "wanton."

And "wantonnesse" has been rampant:

> Many a green-gowne has been given;
> Many a kisse, both odde and even:
> Many a glance too has been sent
> From out of the eye, Loves Firmament:
> Many a jest told of the Keyes betraying
> This night, and Locks pickt, yet w'are not a Maying.
>
> (ll. 51–56)

May Day has witnessed a range of amorous behaviors, from flirtatious looks
to kissing to lovemaking on the greensward. Some lovers may have even
rushed the season, with bold girls contriving to provide their lovers with
keys to their rooms, and with bold lads, lacking such conveniences, simply
picking bedchamber locks. Despite the fact that society might normally
condemn such actions, on May Day, the speaker's humorous tone suggests,
anything goes *if* one takes advantage of the time—seizes the day.

They have not seized this particular day, however, which seems to bother
Corinna's lover more than anything else. We do not, after all, know where
he is located when he addresses Corinna: he could be outside her window or
her door, but his use of *we*—particularly in the line "Before that we have left
to dream"—makes it possible that he could also be in her room or even in
her bed. Thus, it may be that the urgency he feels is as much metaphysical
as sexual: he and Corinna have not taken advantage of a time that comes
but once a year:

> Come, let us goe, while we are in our prime;
> And take the harmless follie of the time.
> We shall grow old apace, and die
> Before we know our liberty.
> Our life is short; and our dayes run
> As fast away as do's the Sunne:
> And as a vapour, or a drop of raine
> Once lost, can ne'r be found againe:
> So when or you or I are made
> A fable, song, or fleeting shade;

> All love, all liking, all delight
> Lies drown'd with us in endlesse night.
> Then while time serves, and we are but decaying;
> Come, my *Corinna,* come, let's goe a Maying.
>
> (ll. 57–70)

Time more than love is the ultimate concern here, as is reflected in this stanza's serious tone. Love, sex, and the May Day rituals are only "harmlesse follie" when all is said and done. What counts is that Corinna and her lover—although now in their prime, when time seems to serve them—are "decaying"; all too soon they will be mastered by time, permanently. Old age comes "apace," far sooner than youth expect, and the "liberty" that comes from being young and vital and capable of living life to the fullest is irretrievably lost.

At this climactic moment in the poem it becomes apparent that establishing Corinna to be a creature of nature has been essential to her lover's argument: natural creatures bloom but also fade away and die. They are all children of the sun, and their fates, like their days, are linked to the sun's natural motions. Annihilation is as natural as generation: like mist, like raindrops, we simply disappear, leaving no trace. Even though a few lovers, unlike other creatures of nature, can become "immortalized" in legends or lyrics or possibly in some ghostly existence after life, eternity is essentially emptiness, "endless night." Sex, affection, pleasure in any form—holidays, for example—are for the here and now only. Hymns, prayers, and priests are all well and good, but the hereafter is nowhere, nothing.

"Corinna's *going a Maying,*" then, appears to be as much an invitation-to-live poem as an invitation-to-love poem. Life it certainly does affirm: nature, society, rituals, love and sex, religion—all are accommodated within the speaker's vision, all are valorized. Given the dramatic situation and the relationship between her lover and Corinna, sex may seem to loom largest here, but the final stanza leaves us aware that without *carpe diem* there can be no *carpe amorem* or anything else. As he did in *"To the Virgins, to make much of Time,"* Herrick here implies that while love is "delight" and an important form of natural fulfillment as well as a pleasure, it offers no transcendence of time, death, or even pain, despite what other poets may say. This is a measure of Herrick's realism: here as elsewhere in *Hesperides* he acknowledges that love is a means of easing, not resolving, the tension between existence and extinction.

The Varieties of Love

The poems examined thus far in this chapter could give the impression that Herrick's amatory verse concerns itself more with *"Wantonnesse,"* with sensuality, than with *"Wantonnesse"* made "cleanly," refined and sanctified by culture. Yet Herrick's conception of love, or at least his awareness of the diverse traditions of love poetry, enables him to range widely over other aspects of amatory experience besides the physical. He can, for example, write in the spirit and manner of the Elizabethan versifiers who attempted to capture in English the bittersweet sense of love that was Petrarch's. To their stock situations, images, and language, however, he brings a capacity to inform such clichés as the disdainful fair and the doting lover with fresh dramatic and emotional intensity. A case in point is the lyric *"The Teare sent to her* [Mrs. Dorothy Keneday] *from* Stanes" (*H*-123). This poem is the second of a pair of love complaints, the first of which, *"His parting"* (*H*-122), expresses a lover's bewilderment at the lady's coolness on the occasion of their recent separation. In its companion piece he has come to recognize that he has been rejected, but the wit, the dialectic, and the emotional development of the poem transform what might otherwise be a conventional complaint into one that combines the strengths of the neo-Petrarchan and the metaphysical amatory modes.

The poem takes the form of an apostrophe to the river Thames, on whose bank Staines is situated:

> 1. GLide gentle streams, and beare
>   Along with you my teare
>   To that coy Girle;
>   Who smiles, yet slayes
>   Me with delayes;
>   And strings my teares as Pearle.
>   (ll. 1–6)

The situation is ripe for sentimentality: a lover weeps at his rejection, one tear falls into the river, and hyperbolically, he begs the currents to carry it to his beloved. What saves the stanza from cheap emotion is Herrick's wit, displayed in his image of the lady making a necklace of his tears. This is a cruel fair to reckon with, one who wears her lover's pain as evidence of her charms. However, when we actually see her in the second stanza she appears considerably more innocent, weaving her own necklace of flowers. Still, her admirer persists in requesting the river to carry his tear to her, with this further instruction:

> 3. Then say, I've sent her one more
>   Jem to enrich her store;
>   And that is all
>   Which I can send,
>   Or vainly spend,
>   For teares no more will fall.
>   (ll. 13–18)

Herrick's use of such terms as "enrich," "store," and "spend" lends a kind of mercantile quality to the proceedings, a convention of the period's love poetry that may say a good deal about the reality behind romance in the seventeenth century. This submerged metaphor becomes the basis for the imagery of the rest of the poem, where Herrick's wit and ingenuity push the convention to its limits.

In stanza 4 the lover refuses to develop a new "supply" of tears because it is all he can do to protect the source of that supply, his eyes. If, he continues in the fifth stanza, the lady should demand that he "surrender" his eyes, focus only upon her, then he would have to cry his eyes out, thus becoming blind to her beauty. Otherwise he must also lose his "poore, yet loving heart," which would go out to her. But his resolve lapses almost immediately:

> 6. Say too, She wo'd have this;
>   She shall: Then my hope is,
>   That when I'm poore,
>   And nothing have
>   To send, or save;
>   I'm sure she'll ask no more.

If he lets her have tears, eyes, heart, all, he will be emotionally bankrupt, and then, he hopes, she can make no more demands on him. Being one who only receives love but never gives it, she will have no more use for him. And he will be bereft of feelings but free of the pain that loving this lady brings.

Several things set Herrick's poem apart from the hundreds of love complaints of the period. Its wit is mirrored in its technical virtuosity: each of its six six-line stanzas begins with an iambic trimeter couplet, followed by three iambic dimeter lines, whose second and third constitute a couplet but whose first (line 3) rhymes with the final iambic trimeter line. Yet the poem's diction, the carrier of all this technical and semantic complexity, is simplicity itself—another characteristic of Herrick's. The tear-pearl simile and the mercantile metaphors are conventional, but using proper names to ground a fanciful lyric in an actual native setting is much less so. *"The Teare sent to her from* Stanes" hardly qualifies as a metaphysical poem, but it is more than an imitation of Petrarchanism. *Jonsonian* may in fact be the best term to describe it, if by that term we mean the kind of love poem whose art does not conceal its art.

His love poetry is not usually counted as one of Ben Jonson's most impressive literary achievements. He does not "specialize" in it, as do Herrick and other Sons of Ben like Carew, Suckling, and Lovelace. In fact, the number of his extant love poems is quite small. And yet no poetic mode is more associated with Cavalier poetry, whose source and fountain Jonson is, than the love lyric. As Earl Miner puts it, "I cannot believe that Cavalier love poetry comprises the fullest and greatest canon on that most human of subjects. But . . . it seems to me to have assisted the seventeenth century in making its profoundly important step forward in understanding the human psyche" (248–49). Miner's point, so easily lost when the Cavaliers are stereotyped as Royalist gentlemen who wrote with ease, is well taken in Herrick's case. Although *"The Tear sent to her from* Stanes" may seem more than anything else like a showcase for the poet's talents, his addressing it to a real lady, the unknown Mistress Keneday, and personalizing it by identifying the place of its composition can make the reader imagine a twinge of felt pain—and perhaps a surge of hostility—beneath the tour de force. Herrick's poem well illustrates Miner's point that "Cavalier love poetry, like all important poetic canons on that subject, combines real experience and numerous conventions for transforming the real into art" (249). Although none of the Cavaliers may have possessed more true (if underutilized) genius than Carew and none may have been more truly intelligent than Suckling, his love poetry alone demonstrates that Herrick too has his share of genius (but also energy) and of intelligence (but also learning). And none of Ben's sons nor even Ben himself can touch him for poetic range and craftsmanship.

When he chooses to do so, Herrick can write amatory verse that is as cynical as Suckling's—see, for example, *"Upon some women"* (*H*-195) and *"No fault in women"* (*H*-291); as sensual as Carew's—see *"Upon* Julia's *unlacing her self"* (*H*-414); or as romantic as Lovelace's—*"The Tear sent to her from* Stanes," for example. Lovelace is sometimes held up as the quintessential Cavalier Poet, but more, one suspects, for his character than for his talent, for as a poet he is as careless about sense as he is about structure. The difference between his capacities and Herrick's becomes apparent if their efforts on a similar subject are compared. In *To Amarantha, that she would dishevel her Hair* and *Upon Julia's haire, bundled up in a golden net* (H-881), Lovelace and Herrick are dealing in a conventional romantic subject and conventional romantic attitudes. But Herrick's poem is more witty, more compressed, and more artfully structured. For example, it begins with a compliment that is also a criticism:

> TEll me, what needs those rich deceits,
> These golden Toyles, and Trammel-nets,*
> To take thine haires when they are knowne
> Already tame, and all thy own?
>
>   (ll. 1–4)
>
> *fishnets

Julia is accused of gilding the lily, for a decorative net both controls and gives body to ladies' hair and her crowning glory is implied to need neither. Her coiffure, then, entails both a delusion and a snare. In just four lines Herrick has set up a whole series of bipolar oppositions—truth-falsehood, rare-common, bondage-freedom, tame-wild, natural-artificial—on which the wit and the tension of the rest of the poem will be based.

By way of answering his own question, Julia's admirer goes on to claim: "'Tis I am wild, and more then haires / Deserve these Mashes [meshes] and those snares" (ll. 5–6). "Wild" can suggest his passion for Julia but it also implies "free," "not in bondage." "Deserve" also generates a dual meaning: either the speaker is a wild creature (note the pun on "haires") who should be netted and tamed, or he is so enamored of Julia that he desires nothing more than to tangle himself up in her hair. These readings are not, of course, incompatible: the speaker can be a free spirit who both needs and desires Julia's domestication. This being the case, his conclusion is foregone—Julia should liberate her hair and incarcerate her admirer:

> Set free thy Tresses, let them flow
> As aires doe breathe, or winds doe blow:
> And let such curious Net-works be
> Lesse set for them, then spred for me.
>
>   (ll. 7–10)

In addition to constituting a romantic gambit in the guise of a plea for natural hair styles, these lines, like others throughout *Hesperides,* implicitly express the Herrickean esthetic of nature improved by but not imposed upon by art. It is a principle that Herrick applies to fashion, to female beauty, and to poetry. Lovelace's lyric, by comparison, proceeds charmingly for four stanzas to plead for an unfettered hairdo, then inexplicably shifts into an erotic pastoral fantasy for two stanzas, followed by a grammatically unintelligible single stanza on transiency.

For a poet with a reputation for lucidity and simplicity, Herrick has generated his share of controversies, one of which concerns the imagery of another erotic fantasia, "Julia's *Petticoat*" (*H*-175).[9] Here, through the exercise of his wit and imagination, Herrick takes his slightly risqué subject and comically inflates it into a symbol for the phenomena of sexual attraction and sexual desire. This process begins almost at once, as the speaker, addressing Julia, launches into a fanciful description of her petticoat:

> THy Azure Robe, I did behold,
> As ayrie as the leaves of gold;
> Which erring here, and wandering there,
> Pleas'd with transgression ev'ry where.
>
> (ll. 1–4)

The image is one of Herrick's most painterly—or, more appropriately, given its sense of movement, "cinematic": Julia's blue and gold petticoat resembles an autumn sky seen through a shower of autumn leaves, and it moves with the lightness and randomness of such leaves. Leaves do not, of course, fall in some prescribed order; hence, they "err" here and "wander" there. Nonetheless such randomness, "transgression," is visually pleasing. The sight of Julia's petticoat is similarly pleasing, particularly if, in the fashion of the time, such undergarments were not supposed to be seen but were contrived to show only on occasion. Such a "transgression" (literally a "moving across," figuratively a "sin") is titillating. However, this is titillation without guilt or with only enough guilt to give an edge to the experience.

In the next four lines the sensual character of this experience becomes even more explicit:

> Sometimes 'two'd pant, and sigh, and heave,
> As if to stir it scarce had leave:

> But having got it; thereupon
> 'Two'd make a brave expansion.
>
> (ll. 5–8)

On the literal level her admirer is merely describing the billowing and con-
traction of the petticoat as Julia moves, but quite obviously a lover too can
"pant, and sigh, and heave" in the throes of passion, particularly unsanc-
tioned passion, that does not "have leave" to express itself. Once a lover receives such leave, it could lead to "a brave [showy] expansion"—such as,
perhaps, an erection in the case of a male lover, a pregnancy in the case of a
female one.

At this point Herrick momentarily retards his poem's development into
artful bawdry by shifting his imagery from the sensual to the celestial, recalling the sky imagery of the opening verses: "And pounc't with Stars, it
shew'd to me / Like a *Celestiall Canopie*" (ll. 9–10). Now the autumnal sky
of lines 1–2 has become a night sky and the "leaves of gold" that "pounce"
or decorate the petticoat have become stars. Night is, of course, a time for
lovers, so the romantic mood of the poem is retained, but it is also restrained
by the vaguely religious connotations of "*Celestiall*."

Herrick next brings in yet another figure of speech to complement the
sky simile and the submerged but inexorably surfacing sexual metaphor:

> Sometimes 'two'd blaze, and then abate,
> Like to a flame growne moderate:
> Sometimes away 'two'd wildly fling;
> Then to thy thighs so closely cling,
> That some conceit did melt me downe,
> As lovers fall into a swoone
> And all confus'd, I there did lie
> Drown'd in Delights; but co'd not die.
>
> (ll. 11–18)

Like a fire burning blue and gold, Julia's petticoat inflames her admirer,
and when it outlines her thighs (doubtless a rare sight in a long-skirted age),
his imagination paints him such a picture or "conceit"—perhaps of Julia's
genitals, according to the logic of the imagery here—that he dissolves in
bliss, as lovers are prone to do. He too is prone, having collapsed into a picturesque faint, but Julia has moved on and so, although he is sexually
aroused he cannot "die"—in seventeenth-century usage, achieve an orgasm.
Were this not a poem about a petticoat and playful from the start, it might

be possible to take all this as serious sensuality, but Herrick's voyeuristic premise keeps it at the level of clever farce.

The farce turns into burlesque in the poem's conclusion: Herrick returns once more to his vein of petticoat-sky-heaven imagery, this time compounded with an Old Testament allusion that would be blasphemous were its intent not so clearly comic:

> That Leading Cloud, I follow'd still,
> Hoping t'ave seen of it my fill;
> But ah! I co'd not: sho'd it move
> To Life Eternal, I co'd love.
>
> (ll. 19–22)

The billowing petticoat has now become like the "pillar of cloud" in which Jehovah led the children of Israel out of Egypt (Exodus 13:21). Now, however, the Promised Land presumably is Julia's sexual favor. Her admirer, Love's Moses, even loses sight of it—and we recall that Moses, never entered the Promised Land.

"Julia's *Petticoat*" can only be described as a tour de force, a sex comedy whose main aim seems to be the witty exposure of the folly to which doting lovers can stoop. But the poem is not quite a satire: it is more like the kind of love-poetry game John Donne so often plays (see, for example, Donne's very different but equally silly exercise entitled "*The Indifferent*"). Conceivably Herrick's poem could have been intended as a comic compliment to a lady; however, it is really not so much about her or even about her petticoat as it is about the imagination and the libido of her admirer. It is a male (and bachelor) poet's expression of amusement and bemusement about sexual attraction, and about the contribution of the imagination and sexual esthetics to such attraction.

That a priest in good standing of the Church of England could compose such a poem as "Julia's *Petticoat*," much less publish it, would raise more than few eyebrows were Herrick writing today. That he would print so blatantly bawdy a poem as "*The Vine*" (*H*-41) suggests that Puritan rectitude and ambivalence regarding human sexuality may not have figured as importantly in the seventeenth-century sensibility as they sometimes seem to in our own. In spite of some modern critics' nervousness about the sexuality expressed in *Hesperides,* Herrick himself seems relatively unself-conscious about it. Thus, "*The Vine*," far from being buried somewhere deep within *Hesperides,* appears on page 14 of the original edition. Its form is that of a dream vision, but one that today seems more Freudian than medieval:

> I Dream'd this mortal part of mine
> Was Metamorphoz'd to a Vine;
> Which crawling one and every way,
> Enthrall'd my dainty *Lucia*.
>
> (ll. 1–4)

One might initially surmise "this mortal part" to be a reference to the speaker's body generally, which literally and figuratively captivates the lady in an all-encompassing embrace; or one might suspect—correctly, as it will turn out—that the phrase refers to the speaker's penis.

The catalog of beauties of traditional love poetry, in Herrick's hands, becomes an enumeration of those "parts" of Lucia enwrapped by the speaker's "vine"—"her long small legs and thighs," "Her Belly, Buttocks, and her Waste," and even "her temples," "her neck," and her "armes and hands." Lucia has become his "prisoner of love." At this point in the poem what psychoanalysis calls the manifest or literal dream and the latent or actual wish-fulfillment dream become almost one in the bawdily humorous conclusion of the work. As is so often the case in such poetic catalogs, last to be itemized are the lady's genitals:

> But when I crept with leaves to hide
> Those parts, which maids keep unespy'd,
> Such fleeting pleasures there I took,
> That with the fancie I awook;
> And found (Ah me!) this flesh of mine
> More like a *Stock,* then like a *Vine.*
>
> (ll. 18–23)

Like a poetic joke, *"The Vine"* ends with a sure-fire punchline. The conclusion is also psychologically authentic: dreamers often repress threatening dream materials by wakening before they become too literally expressed.

How much of a ladies' man Herrick actually was has been a subject of considerable (if relatively pointless) discussion. He never married, and we have no factual knowledge of romantic relationships with eligible women. A contemporary allegation that when he was in his forties he fathered an illegitimate child has never been confirmed or refuted and thus must be relegated to the category of literary gossip (*PW*, xvii). In the world of his poetry, however, women and love loom very large indeed. By Ann Coiro's count 158 poems by this bachelor priest deal with his "mistresses," and this figure does not include those poems that name no lady or deal with love generally

(1987, 67). Some readers have accepted all of Herrick's ladies as real, while others, suspecting that such a proliferation of amours smacks of overkill, have concluded that none of them was. Allegations of obsessiveness, voyeurism, and even fetishism in the poetry have given rise to such psychoanalytic diagnoses of the man as that of Gordon Braden:

The emphasis on foreplay and nongenital, especially oral, gratifications, the fixation on affects (smells, textures) and details (Julia's leg), and the general voyeuristic preference of perception to action . . . are all intelligible as a wide diffusion of erotic energy denied specifically orgiastic focus and release. (223)

In the absence of the kind of biographical information about Herrick that might help validate such an analysis, the items Braden enumerates are also intelligible as a love poet's originality and his unique strategy of decorum. On the other hand, it is likely that a bachelor priest living in a tiny rural village would have few opportunities for sexually gratifying dalliance, and in the annals of psychoanalysis there is ample warrant for speculating that such a man might sublimate his libido in erotic poetry. But that this kind of poetry comes to be regarded as seriously problematic says more about Herrick's critics than about the man and his poetry. Braden observes, "What is missing in the *Hesperides* is aggressive, genital, in other words, 'adult' sexuality. The retreat from intercourse is pervasive, and especially notable in a poet whose concerns are so often explicitly sexual" (223). But the seventeenth century is not, finally, the twentieth, and the "retreat from intercourse" in love poetry is in general a characteristic of the age. John Donne, another Anglican priest, is the only other notable poet of the era who wrote as much love poetry as Herrick; rarely is that poetry sexually explicit, and if it represents the poetry of "adult sexuality" of which Braden seems to approve, then "adult sexuality" often seems seriously afflicted by insecurity, misogyny, self-loathing, guilt, and morbidity.

The point is that any unease that may be felt about Herrick's love poetry is inherently a problem in the reader, not in the poetry or the poet. To make judgments about the poetry and the poet based on assessments of sexual "normalcy" muddles the distinction between art and life. As we have seen, when Herrick himself waxes philosophical about sex and love he is inclined to think in terms of balance, and moderation—"cleanly-*Wantonnesse*." As the proverbial "*Love me little, love me long*" (*H*-143) indicates, the *via media* is the way of love as well as the way of life:

> YOu say, to me-wards your affection's strong;
> Pray love me little, so you love me long.
> Slowly goes farre: The meane is best: Desire
> Grown violent, do's either die, or tire.

Plain-dealing of this sort bespeaks the era's distrust of what Robert Burton called "heroicall love,"[10] the kind of grand passion much admired by romantics. But this epigram is also a typically Herrickean antidote to the extremes of his own love poetry. In fact, "*Love me little*" is bracketed in *Hesperides* by a piece of comic erotica entitled "*The Vision*" (*H*-142) and a romantic epigram in imitation of Jonson's "Song To Celia" ("Drink to me only with thine eyes"), "*Upon a Virgin kissing a Rose*" (*H*-144). "*The Vision*" begins like a conventional pastoral love complaint, with the unhappy suitor weeping beside "a Silver-shedding Brook" (l. 2). Also conventionally, he falls asleep, and the poem becomes a dream vision of a "glorious forme" who could be Diana, virgin goddess of the hunt. But as the dreamer's catalog of her beauties arrives at "the happy dawning of her thigh" (l. 16), the poem modulates into sexual farce. The dreamer attempts "To kisse that tempting nakedness" (l. 18) but is halted in his tracks by "Diana's" mirtle wand and her rebuke: "Hence, Remove, / *Herrick*, thou art too coarse to love" (l. 22). Coming as it does in the last line of what appears to be a deliberately artificial poem, the poet's own name startles, and is bound to make the reader wonder if "*The Vision*" might be based on an actual incident or dream. In any case the portrait of Herrick as lecher offered here leads (as noted above) into Herrick as love's Epicurean in "*Love me little*" and then to Herrick as neo-Petrarchan in "*Upon a Virgin kissing a Rose*," where the lady's breath miraculously transforms a single rose into a wreath.

His very arrangement of this set of poems, then, illustrates the kind of amatory poise Herrick advocates in "*Love me little*" and in another epigram, "*Moderation*" (*H*-1038): "LEt moderation on thy passions waite / Who loves too much, too much the lov'd will hate." However, the most cogent expression of the poet's amatory neo-Epicureanism is a sententious passage (ll. 20–25) from "Connubii Flores, *or the well-wishes at Weddings*" (*H*-633), in which a chorus of old men give a bridal couple some sage advice:

> Love is a thing most nice;* and must be fed
> To such a hight; but never surfeited.
> What is beyond the mean is ever ill:
> '*Tis best to feed Love; but not over-fill:*

> Go then discreetly to the Bed of pleasure;
> And this remember, *Vertue keepes the measure*.

*particular

It is the kind of advice Polonious might give—or Ben Jonson—sounding pretentious but eminently sensible, and most likely to be ignored in spite of the common sense it displays. Indeed all three—Shakespeare's character, Jonson, and his "son"—are realists of a sort. Although Herrick is sometimes depicted as a libertine poet and occasionally can be, certainly he is enough of a realist to recognize that marriage is probably the most workable long-term arrangement for maximizing the pleasure and minimizing the pain of love. It is, then, no coincidence that the lines quoted above come from marriage verse. Variations on it reappear in other of Herrick's nuptial pieces, poems that are among the most admired of the genre in English and that lend a special priestly emphasis to the *Hesperides'* amatory vein.

The Ideal of Love

One of the most memorable passages of *Paradise Lost* is where Milton celebrates prelapsarian sexuality (5.750 ff.). It begins:

> Hail wedded Love, mysterious Law, true source
> Of human offspring, sole propriety
> In Paradise of all things common else.

Almost 50 years before these lines were published, Robert Herrick had anticipated them in "*An Epithalamie to Sir* Thomas Southwell *and his Ladie*" (*H*-149A) and in "*A Nuptiall Song, or Epithalamie, on Sir* Clipseby Crew *and his Lady*" (*H*-283). These two poems in a sense qualify but also cap *Hesperides'* rich vein of love poetry. They are that collection's longest and in some ways its most ambitious works. Although both are occasional poems, written in celebration of two actual weddings, they too are grounded in the principle of "cleanly-*Wantonnesse*."

As is the case with most of the poetic forms with which Herrick works, the epithalamion—a lyrical ode in honor of a bridal couple—has a long history. "The Song of Solomon" is one of the earliest and most familiar examples of the genre. There can be little doubt that Herrick was also aware of *Carmina* 61, 62, and 64 of Catullus as well as Edmund Spenser's "Epithalamium" and "Prothalamium" and Jonson's *Hymenaei*, which in-

cludes an epithalamion (*CP*, 510–12). But sources are one thing; performance is another. Since Herrick's poems were occasional pieces meant to
honor and please the powerful (doubtless with a hope of receiving some
consideration in return), his learning is far less an issue than his artistry. And
when it comes to artistry the consensus is that Herrick does not disappoint.

Like most epithalamia, Herrick's are lyric sequences composed of linked
stanzas. In "*A Nuptiall Song*" the form of the stanzas themselves is unusual:
each consists of an iambic pentameter couplet, followed by a more typical
iambic tetrameter couplet, and then a single dimeter line rhyming with a
much longer pentameter line; here a full stop usually halts the stanza before
it moves on to a new pattern, consisting of a single tetrameter line rhymed
with a single pentameter line, and finally, a single trimeter line rhyming
with a single tetrameter line. The nonpoet's mind boggles, for this almost
grotesquely difficult scheme must be made to seem vivacious and spontane-
ous, as befits the happy occasion—and it does. The apparent irregularity in
the metrics lends a sense of nervous excitement to the lyric, which is then
tempered and controlled by the rhymes and the very repetitions of the stanzaic patterns. On the grounds of prosody alone, then, "*A Nuptiall Song*"
strikingly exhibits that unity in variety, that *discordia concors,* for which
Herrick often strives.

To a somewhat lesser degree "*An Epithalamie*" exhibits the same quality,
but in neither poem is it realized through witty prosody alone: both also exhibit a fundamental unity of structure that is based on the events they
celebrate—the rituals of the wedding day. Herrick further unifies these
poems by focusing these rituals on the actions and reactions of the bride and
by filtering his descriptions through a speaker who is both a fascinated observer of and a participant in the ceremonies. Finally, the poet carefully inte-
grates his images and symbols to create visual patterns that lend a high
degree of consistency to the textures of each poem. Limitations of space
make it necessary that these qualities be demonstrated in "*A Nuptiall Song*"
only.

This wedding poem opens as the narrator, peering off into the distance,
sights the approaching bride. Gallantly he asks, is this truly she or are we
being blessed by a vision?

> 1. WHat's that we see from far? the spring of Day
> Bloom'd from the East, or faire Injewl'd May
>   Blowne out of April; or some New-
>   Star fill'd with glory to our view,
>   Reaching at heaven,

To adde a nobler Planet to the seven?
Say, or doe we not descrie
Some Goddesse, in a cloud of Tiffanie
To move, or rather the
Emergent Venus from the Sea?

(ll. 1–10)

Answering his own question with a series of questions (advanced in order of increasing importance), the narrator compliments the bride by implicitly elevating her to a goddess: she is likened to the dawn, to May, the season of rebirth, to a heavenly body adding luster to the cosmos, and, since the planets are named after gods and this is a ceremony of love, to the goddess of love herself—Venus.

In stanza 2 the narrator is able to give a definitive answer to the question he raised in stanza 1 because the bridal procession has moved closer to him:

2. 'Tis she! 'tis she! or else some more Divine
Enlightned substance; mark how from the Shrine
Of holy Saints she paces on,
Treading upon *Vermilion*
And *Amber;* Spice-
ing the Chafte* Aire with fumes of Paradise.
Then come on, come on, and yeeld
A savour like unto a blessed field,
When the bedabled Morne
Washes the golden eares of corne.

(ll. 11–20)

*warmed

Now it is clear that the bride is not the mythical Venus but a truly divine being associated with the saints whose temple she has just left. Her vaguely Christian aura is complicated by Herrick's characteristic olfactory images, which simultaneously link her spiritually to the incense of an Anglican service and sensually, through the allusion to Paradise, to prelapsarian Eve and to a nature deity like Ceres, usually associated with fields of grain.

Exotic and erotic olfactory images also dominate the next stanza:

3. See where she comes; and smell how all the street
Breathes Vine-yards and Pomgranats: O how sweet!
As a fir'd Altar, is each stone,

> Perspiring pounded Cynamon.
>   The Phenix nest,
> Built up of odours, burneth in her breast.
>   Who therein wo'd not consume
> His soule to Ash-heaps in that rich perfume?
>   Bestroaking Fate the while
>   He burnes to Embers on the Pile.
>
> (ll. 21–30)

As the wedding procession moves along the street, each paving block the bride treads hyperbolically becomes an altar from which arises the incense of her fragrance, a blend of fruitlike smells appropriate for a nature goddess. Compounding the conceit, she herself becomes an altar as, phoenix-like, she burns in the fires of her own passion but is not consumed. Here the narrator amusingly opines that any male spectator would willingly sacrifice himself on the altar of her breast, to be consumed by the heat of her sensuality and the perfume of her body. (Typical of Herrick's witty arrangement of his works, the poem immediately preceding "A *Nuptiall Song*" is "On a perfum'd Lady" whose scent, unlike Lady Crew's, is artificial, and intended to conceal.)

The building "*Wantonnesse*" of the poem's mood is momentarily (but only momentarily) checked in the fourth stanza, as the narrator prays that now the Roman god of marriage may also sanctify the occasion with his presence:

> 4. *Himen, O Himen!* Tread the sacred ground;
> Shew thy white feet, and head with Marjoram crown'd:
>   Mount up thy flames, and let thy Torch
>   Display the Bridegroom in the porch,
>   In his desires
> More towring, more disparkling then thy fires:
>   Shew her how his eyes do turne
> And roule about, and in their motions burne
>   Their balls to Cindars: haste,
>   Or else to ashes he will waste.
>
> (ll. 31–40)

Hymen is traditionally represented as bearing his symbolically phallic torch, the flames of which illuminate the bridegroom, whose own passion burns even more fiercely. Building on the comic vein of the previous stanza, the Roman deity is asked to tell the bride, whose eyes are probably modestly downcast, to look at her groom before his own eyes, enflamed at the sight of her, burn up, and the rest of him with them.

By now the bride has arrived at the spot where the narrator waits. From here on until the final stanza he will accompany the pair through the various stages of the nuptial rites, apparently as an honored guest. In stanza 5 he uses nature imagery to direct the bride's progress: in her long gown with its train she is like a stream gliding between "banks of Virgins" lining the road to bestrew her with "Shewers of Roses" and four-leaf clovers (ll. 41–42). From a balcony above, a "cloud" of white-robed children sing, while the crowd tosses rice, compliments, and homilies (like *"Blest is the Bride, on whom the Sun doth shine,"* l. 48). Finally, in a comically clumsy extension of the stream metaphor (ll. 49–50), the well-intending masses "gladly wish / [her] multiply, as doth a Fish" (a traditional wedding motif to which Herrick will return).

Adopting a somewhat avuncular tone, the speaker compliments the bride for her traditional show of modesty and coyness, but gently warns her not to carry such fastidiousness too far and thus "turne *Apostate*" to love's religion (l. 57). He has his own homily to offer her: "Love will / Part of the way be met; or sit stone-still" (ll. 57–58). At this point in the narrative the bride actually crosses the threshold of her new home, giving the speaker an opportunity to have some sport with his social inferiors, the household staff. All of them are eager to see their new mistress: "the Codled [overheated] Cook / runs from his *Torrid Zone*," the steamy kitchen; old servants bless their new young mistress; and "the smirk Butler" feels obliged to offer witty commentary—each of them "striving to devise / Some gin [trap or means] wherewith to catch [the bride's] eyes" (ll. 69–70).

Now bride and groom are at last reunited (after the earlier marriage service) and the speaker-priest urges them,

> 8. To bed, to bed, kind Turtles,* now and write
> This the short'st day, and this the longest night;
> >   But yet too short for you: 'tis we
> >   Who count this night as long as three
> > > Lying alone,
> Telling the Clock strike Ten, Eleven, Twelve, One.
> >   >   (ll. 71–76)

*turtle doves

Although he plays wittily upon the relativity of time to lovers, a distinctly
poignant note is sounded when the speaker contrasts the short night to be
enjoyed by the newlyweds with the long night that he and similarly solitary
souls must spend as they sleeplessly listen to the chimes marking the tedious
passage of time. But the speaker soon recovers his celebratory mood and
urges the pair to complete the public ceremony by distributing small items
of their wedding costumes such as garters and laces for souvenirs. In the
next stanza (9) he warns the wedding guests not to allow any unpleasant-
ness to arise as they compete for these prizes, for that would "divide" the
just-united pair.

In stanza 10 the speaker again employs nature imagery, this time to inau-
gurate the ritual of preparing the bride for bed. Addressing her attendants
he urges, "Strip her of Spring-time," the flower-bedecked bridal gown that
symbolizes her youthful innocence, for "Now *Autumne's* come," the season
of her coming-of-age, which can no longer be put off (ll. 91–93). With traditional male posturing the speaker warns that if the bridesmaids will not
"strip her," "unto her / Let him come, who dares undo her," the stereotypi-
cally lusty bridegroom (ll. 99–100). Providing the background music to all
of this, stanza 11 tells us, and elevating the occasion into a sacred moment,
are the music of the spheres and an angelic chorus. Juxtaposed with these
are deities from the pagan pantheon (like Hymen), "a thousand *Cupids*"
who are fancifully imagined as lighting their hymeneal torches "at the
Brides bright eye" (l. 108). Symbolizing the sanctified course of human affection, these little gods of love have abandoned their bows and arrows to
become gods of marriage.

To build toward his poem's sensual and romantic climax, in stanza 12
Herrick focuses on the marriage bed, which is described in nature images
reminiscent of those of stanza 5. With the innuendoes concerning pregnancy that seem obligatory to nuptial rhetoric, the "Plumpe bed" is compared to a "swelling" cloud, then to a bird associated with romance, the
swan, and then, because swans swim as well as fly, to a stream, into whose
"white Pride" the speaker humorously urges the couple to throw themselves
(ll. 111–20). In the next stanza the vein of humor becomes even more
pointed and more "wanton" as the bed is described as a maze at whose end
lies the mystery of consummated love. As a mystery must be unraveled to
be understood, so must sex. Lovers must learn its lessons, must employ their
imaginations to transform this physical act into an art form—"and some
way teach / Nature and Art, one more / Play, then they ever knew before"
(ll. 128–30)—an erotic application of Herrick's esthetic of "*Art above
Nature.*"

Since the time for the couple to put all the speaker's sage advice into practice is rapidly drawing near, in stanza 14 he indicates that the ceremonies, like Corinna's beads and prayers, can be quickly dispensed with: "If needs we must for Ceremonies-sake, / Blesse a *Sack-posset* [beverage]; Luck go with it; take / The Night-Charme [to ward off evil] quickly" (ll. 131–33). Since spells and magic can be associated with the devil and the devil with hell and hell with fire, the speaker makes another attempt at mildly bawdy humor: the lovers will have to pass through the "hell" of passionate lovemaking, but so agreeable a hell is it that no one would complain about residing in it forever. Recalling the phoenix image of stanza 3, he comically urges the pair to "Frie / and consume, and grow again to die"—achieve orgasm—"And live, and in that case, / Love the confusion of the place" (ll. 137–40). Although they will "expire" from bliss, they will continue to live "and grow." Such a state might well be one of "confusion," but it is desirable because, in the Latinate origin of the term, such "confusion" arises out of the "pouring together" of their nuptial union.

From such verbal jokes the speaker turns his attention in stanza 15 to a practical joke—the traditional one of sewing the bride up in a sheet so as to provide still another obstacle to the eager groom. Here Herrick has an opportunity to flatter Sir Clipseby who will, the speaker claims, be no more deterred by this obstacle than Jove was by the brass tower that imprisoned the object of his lust, Danae. As Jane Pulteney was implied to be a goddess in the opening passage of the poem, so her husband here appears almost godlike (although the comparison is amusingly of great things to small): "like a / Bold bolt of thunder he will make his way, / And rend the cloud [the sewn sheet]" (ll. 147–49).

In the discreet silence between stanza 15 and the final stanza the other wedding guests have retired, and either the couple has been left alone with their honored guest or from his own chamber he mentally addresses them. The mood has changed: "All now is husht in silence." Only the "*Midwife-moone*" and her "*Owle-ey'd* issue," the moonbeams—another allusion to the fertility associated with the wedding ceremony—share the bedchamber with them (ll. 151–53). Here Herrick departs from the tradition that Artemis, the moon deity, is a virgin goddess; rather, to prefigure his final theme, he emphasizes her function as the deity who presides over childbirth. Her benign influence and that of other "Planetary bodies," the speaker prays, will result in a union blessed by many children, female as well as male, from whose two lines "Two Nations" will spring that will immortalize "the vertue" of Sir Clipseby and Lady Crewe (ll. 158–60).

Herrick's 160-line epithalamion thus ends with its occasion transcended by the sweep of futurity. It is a grand, if conventional kind of climax. None-theless, and in spite of its low comedy and lower bawdry, the poem works as celebration and as poetry that conveys yet transcends compliment. It exem-plifies the principle of "cleanly-*Wantonnesse*" and proclaims that principle's relevance to human pleasure, to the good life, and to mankind's future. (It is recorded that Lady Crewe died "in her thirtieth year" and that in his will her husband "desired to be buried near his wife," *PW*, 523–24.)

The Religion of Love

The dynamics of "*A Nuptiall Song*" and Herrick's other wedding poems are generated by the tension between religion and human sexuality, tension apparent in the sacred as well as the profane literature of the seventeenth century. The common Renaissance practice of using religious language to treat love and of using the language of love to treat religious experience sug-gests as much, as does the idea of "love's religion."

Although the concept of a "religion of love" was a familiar one in the Elizabethan poetry that Herrick must have read, he himself employs the term "*Loves Religion*" only once (but early on) in *Hesperides,* in "*To his Mistresse objecting to him neither Toying or Talking*" (*H*-38). The poem's premise is indicated by its title; its theme is expressed in the speaker's oath: "By *Loves Religion,* I must here confesse it, / The most I love, when I the least expresse it" (ll. 5–6). The lady is guilty of the false assumption that the extent to which a lover is demonstrative and articulate is a measure of the depth of his feelings. Nevertheless, her complaint raises questions with which both lovers and poets have to wrestle: where to find language intense and inventive enough to express human love in all its breadth and depth. For the Renaissance the "religion of love"—as an imaginative construct, of course, rather than as an actual religious practice—provided one answer. Al-though not a new poetic trope when Herrick came to employ it, in his hands it distinctly enhances his love poetry, especially since, classicist that he is, he is capable of drawing upon "pagan" as well as Christian religion for his im-agery. A case in point is "*To* Julia, *the* Flaminica Dialis, *or* Queen-Priest" (*H*-539), in which an invitation to love is submerged beneath an elaborate and quasi-Roman ceremony of love's religion.

Although Robert Deming offers an extensive account of Herrick's ex-ploitation of the trappings of Roman state religion in this poem, he quite properly concludes that this elaborately titled work "is a very elegant com-pliment" to its true subject, Julia, and in the end "a bit of learned foolery"

(90–92). The poem begins with the speaker instructing Julia who, as the title indicates, seems to be some kind of Roman high priestess:

> THou know'st, my *Julia,* that it is thy turne
> This Mornings Incense to prepare and burne.
> The Chaplet,* and *Inarculum*** here be
> With the white Vestures, all attending Thee.
> (ll. 1–4)

> *wreath
> **A twig of Pomgranat, which the queen-priest
> did use to weare on her head at sacrificing
> [Herrick's note].

What, one wonders, was a seventeenth-century reader to make of all this? The tone is grave and the lines are stately, but if the title may look just a bit pedantic, that sense is increased by the presence of the poet's learned foot-note and the proliferation of ceremonial terms. Is this supposed to be a seri-ous English imitation of a Roman poem, or is Herrick playing some kind of game? His speaker's explanation to Julia suggests the answer:

> This day, the *Queen-Priest,* thou are made t'appease
> Love for our very-many Trespasses.
> One chiefe transgression is among the rest,
> Because with Flowers her Temple was not drest:
> The next, because her Altars did not shine
> With daily Fyers: The last, neglect of Wine:
> For which, her wrath is gone forth to consume
> Us all, unlesse preserv'd by thy Perfume.
> (ll. 5–12)

Now the reader understands that Herrick's ostentatious scholarship has been in the service of building an elaborate metaphor, with Julia as a priest-ess of the long defunct worship of Venus and the speaker a priest: in other words, they are lovers. If the rituals enumerated represent sexuality's varied pleasures, Julia's lover may be mock-complaining that they have neglected lovemaking itself, and it is this that has aroused Venus's ire. The comic note here is accented by the elaborate flattery that attributes the power to deflect a goddess to Julia's perfume.

This being the case, the poem's conclusion can be read as a metaphorical invitation to love: Julia's lover urges the *"Pious-Priestresse"* to put fire in her censer (a womb-shaped vessel) and thus pacify Venus, who has decreed their deaths. Since he apparently is only too willing to undertake the venereal rites, the rest is up to her: *"Redemption comes by Thee"* (l. 16). Such a line, deliberately playing as it does on Christian doctrine, would in an age of faith be blasphemous were it not in the fanciful context of love's religion.

A more serious employment by Herrick of the notion of the religion of love is to be found in another Julia poem, *"The Transfiguration"* (*H*-819). Although a love lyric and a panegyric to Julia, from its title on it draws heavily upon Christian rhetoric. As Ann Coiro has noted, *"The Transfiguration"* is "one of the few poems in *Hesperides* that more or less explicitly anticipates *His Noble Numbers"* (1987, 79), the collection of Herrick's devotional poetry:

> IMmortal clothing I put on,
> So soon as *Julia* I am gon
> To mine eternall Mansion.
>
> Thou, thou art here, to humane sight
> Cloth'd all with incorrupted light;
> But yet how more admirably bright
>
> Wilt thou appear, when thou art set
> In thy refulgent Thronelet,
> That shinest thus in thy counterfeit?

The compliment to Julia is based upon the premise that the speaker, like other ordinary mortals, will put on incorruption, will be transfigured, only at death, whereas Julia in life is "Cloth'd all with incorrupted light"—an elegant substitute for the lover's conventional term of endearment, *angel*. Even so, when this angel becomes a saint in heaven—that is, after her own death—her present luminosity will seem a "counterfeit," an inferior physical representation of the idea and ideal of Julia.

In *"The Transfiguration"* Herrick combines orthodox Christianity, Neoplatonism, and the religion of love to create a poem that, although a far cry from his Cavalierly erotic verses, can be seen as an interesting example of his cleanly-wanton synthesis. Although it seems far more "cleanly" than "wanton," *"The Transfiguration"* is still a poem in praise of a mistress who is earthly and—to judge from some of Herrick's other Julia poems—earthy. (Ann Coiro has noted that in the very next lyric to Julia in *Hesperides,* "To Julia, *in her Dawn, or Day-breake"* [*H*-824], separated from *"The Transfig-*

uration" by only four short poems, her admirer imagines her "as smooth, and nak't, as she that was / The prime of *Paradice*" [1987, 79–80].)

Although Herrick is not that much of a neo-Petrarchan and even less a Neoplatonist, some of his epigrams about love have an abstract and idealistic cast to them. For example, very early in *Hesperides*, in "*Love what it is*" (*H*-30), he offers this abstruse definition: "LOve is a circle that doth restlesse move / In the same sweet eternity of love." Although the epigram is as cryptic as its title is straightforward, some things about it are decipherable. The circle, of course, is the perfect figure, and true love is supposed to perfect life. On the metaphysical level, the circle is also an emblem for God, who is from all eternity and who is love; out of love he created the circle of the universe. If these inferences are valid, then Herrick's learned couplet claims that love makes not only the world go round but also the universe and even eternity itself. Such an interpretation receives some support from a comment of Robert Burton's that was likely the source not only of this epigram, but of a slight variation on it, entitled "*Upon* Love" (*H*-839): "LOve is a Circle, and an Endless Sphere; / From good to good, revolving here, and there." In Burton's definition love is "*Circulus a bono in bonum,* a round circle still from good to good; for love is the beginner and end of all our actions, the efficient and instrumental cause, as our poets in their symbols . . . shadow unto us" (*Anatomy,* 3.1.1.2).

It is worth noting that Herrick's two abstract definitions of love in a sense bracket *Hesperides,* one coming quite early in the collection, the other relatively late, almost as if to establish a symbolic consistency, however limited, amid all his many variations on the theme of love. Nevertheless, what appears to be Herrick's last word on the subject comes just six poems from the end of *Hesperides,* in another epigram "*On Himselfe*" (*H*-1124):

> Ile write no more of Love; but now repent
> Of all those times that I have in it spent.
> Ile write no more of life; but wish twas ended,
> And that my dust was to the earth commended.

This epigram was probably written late to serve as a transition to *His Noble Numbers.* Its mode is that of the retraction, in which Christian poets at least as early as Chaucer have endeavored to apologize to readers who disapproved of their profane verse. At the same time a retraction functions as a kind of ritual of self-absolution in which the poet psychologically defends against his own guilt for writing profane verse by publicly disavowing it. But Herrick, of course, like Chaucer, far from burning his love poems, preserved them. Moreover, he points to them with pride in "*The Argument of his Book*." And with regard to his "confession" that he has been in love many times and repents that as well, its validity too may be called into question by the epigram that concludes *Hesperides*: "To his Book's end this last line he'd have plac't, / *Jocond his Muse was; but his Life was chast*" (H-1130). Both Ben Jonson and Milton believed that only a good person could write good poetry. One suspects that Herrick may have been a bit less idealistic. In any case, his concluding epigram allows him to cover himself, insisting upon a distinction between art and life (that his poetry itself often—and deliberately—blurs) and valorizing both his art and his life. Moreover, the epigram allows this unashamedly self-conscious artist to bridge meaningfully the gap between *Hesperides* and *His Noble Numbers*, preparing his dutiful reader for a volume quickened by divine love after a volume vibrant with "cleanly-*Wantonnesse*."

Chapter Five
"The White Island" and *"This Sacred Grove"*: Themes of Faith

The subtitle of *Hesperides* is THE WORKS *Both Humane and Divine of Robert Herrick.* The "humane" works begin on a confident note. As we have already seen, *"The Argument of his Book"* (*H*-1) boldly announces the poet's subjects, themes, and poetic modes, as well as his personal confidence as a Christian. Even before this, his volume's prefatory poem to the Prince of Wales, while crediting young Charles with being the poet's inspiration, also announces, "Full is my Book of Glories" (l. 9). But the beginning of Herrick's "divine" works, *HIS Noble Numbers: or, His pious Pieces,* sounds a different note:

> *His Confession.* (*N*-1)
> LOok how our foule Dayes do exceed our faire;
> And as our bad, more then our good Works are:
> Ev'n so those Lines, pen'd by my wanton Wit,
> Treble the number of these good I've writ
> Things precious are least num'rous: Men are prone
> To do ten Bad, for one Good Action.

Here the novelty and freshness of *"The Argument"* give way to a pious convention, a ritual poem consisting merely of a series of aphorisms strung together. Although it is personalized—Herrick identifies himself as a poet—there is no personality in it. This is not a promising opening, especially for the modern reader who recognizes that the poet is confessing to the "sin" of writing the very poems for which he would become best known and most loved.

In the second of the series of nine introductory pieces to this collection (paralleling the eight poems that introduce the poet's "humane" works) Herrick the penitent proceeds to the next redemptive ritual and offers *"His Prayer for Absolution"* (*N*-2). Here he asks that his "unbaptized Rhimes," indeed "every sentence, clause, and word, / That's not inlaid" with God, be razed from his book (ll. 1–6). They were not, of course, even though

Herrick, who supervised the printing of his volume, had the opportunity to do so. Thus the relationship between the poet's sacred and profane verse, somewhat confused from the start—is *"The Argument of his Book"* (*H*-1) meant to introduce *Noble Numbers* as well as the secular poetry?—grows more confusing the more one examines it.

Herrick even gets his arithmetic wrong: *"His Confession"* claims that he has written three times as many secular as devotional poems, but as J. Max Patrick has observed, *"Hesperides* contains more than four times as many poems as *Noble Numbers* and more than five times as many lines." Patrick adds that "many of the poems in *Hesperides* could be classified as 'pious Pieces,'" a point to be taken up below (*CP*, 450n.).

Nonetheless, readers are to be forgiven if they are confused by *Noble Numbers,* for even its separate title page is problematical. First of all, since *"The Argument of his Book"* seems to proclaim that what follows will indeed contain devotional poetry—"I write of *Hell;* I sing . . . / Of *Heaven"*—why a separate title for *His Pious Pieces* at all? And why should *His Noble Numbers* be dated 1647 while the title page of *Hesperides,* which precedes *Noble Numbers* in the published volume, is dated 1648? Patrick's theory is that "Herrick may have originally intended to have *Noble Numbers* precede *Hesperides,"* but by the time the latter's title page was set up 1648 had arrived; the poet then changed his mind and ordered *Hesperides* put first without bothering to synchronize the publication dates" (*CP*, 449). If this theory is correct, however, *"His Confession"* and *"His Prayer for Absolution"* were likely written at the eleventh hour to provide a transition between the secular and the devotional collections, a transition that would not have been needed had *Noble Numbers* been printed first in the book. Indeed, it will only be as transitional devices—attempts to bridge the gap between one complex of subject area, tone, and mood to another—that these two poems will be acceptable to some modern readers. On their face, after all, they seem to present Herrick as at worst a hypocrite, parading his lines of "wanton Wit" even as he guiltily prays God to expunge them, or at best merely a tired traditionalist, wed to the medieval convention of the retraction. Today it may be difficult to understand that the poet, living in an age in which it was still possible to feel that he should devote his life and talent to God, could truly regret writing secular poetry, even though he must have known how well he did it. Metaphysical poets like John Donne and Cavaliers like Thomas Carew found themselves in the same position. Of the most notable seventeenth-century poets, only George Herbert had the will as well as the desire to confine himself solely to sacred verse. Thus a seventeenth-century reader might be less likely to question the sincerity of *"His Confession"* and

"His Prayer for Absolution" and be more likely to empathize with Herrick's dilemma as a man and as a poet.

Herrick's being a priest as well as a poet has also been seen as a dilemma by some who question the Christian sincerity of the author of so many love poems, so many gross epigrams, and so many poems on pagan rituals and themes. At least John Donne, they note, was sufficiently embarrassed by some of his profane poems to try to remove them from circulation when he became Dean of London's St. Paul's Cathedral. Herrick, however, was vicar of Dean Prior until just before the publication of *Hesperides,* and it is likely that many of his works of "wanton Wit" were written well after he took holy orders. This is more likely to puzzle modern readers than it did Herrick's contemporaries, who did not widely share the post-Puritan notion that pastors' lives as well as their preaching and ministering must be wholly sacramental. That priests could appreciate their own sensuality and also exercise their creative imaginations seems to have been understood in the seventeenth century, as well as the distinction between art and life: "*Jocond his Muse was; but his Life was chast.*" It may have been that, like other impecunious university graduates of his time, Herrick went into holy orders because other opportunities were closed to him. Moreover, in his long ecclesiastical career he may never have been a model of traditional piety. But to doubt the sincerity of a priest who was expelled from the vicarage he occupied for 17 years because his principles prevented him from submitting to the Puritan regime, and who served in that same vicarage for 14 years after the Restoration, is to put the burden of proof on the doubter. In any case, sincerity never wrote a memorable line of poetry, much less a memorable poem, and it is Herrick's memorable poetry, sacred as well as profane, that concerns us here.

The Uses and Abuses of Religion

"In Robert Herrick," according to one scholar, "there was no split [between his being, his art, and his religion]: the man was one, and he practiced his art as an act of worship."[1] From this extreme statement of the case it logically follows that all of Herrick's poetry, "humane" as well as "divine," is "religious." But one need not go so far to be able to recognize that while there are few poems in *Hesperides* that are as plainly and orthodoxly Christian as those in *Noble Numbers,* Herrick's secular collection does contain a number of works that are religious in a broad sense of the term. It is with some of these that this and the next section will deal.

Although Robert Herrick was born, bred, and ordained in the Church of

England and lived in a period of explosive religious controversy, his devotional poetry does not have a markedly sectarian cast. Even his secular verse, like the prose of Sir Thomas Browne, is surprisingly free from the kind of malice toward all other sects that is commonly found in the literature of the period. There are, however, a few exceptions, one of which is a curious poem of definition entitled *"The Christian Militant"* (H-323). Here the tendency of Herrick to blend Christian and pagan elements—a tendency that has been the despair of some of his Victorian critics—manifests itself in satire.

From a historical point of view, the title of this poem is more reminiscent of the spirit of seventeenth-century English Puritanism than of Anglicanism. It recalls, for example, Puritan tracts like John Downame's *The Christian Warfare* (1604) and such phrases as "the true warfaring Christian" from the *Areopagitica* of Puritan England's spokesman, John Milton.[2] For Milton such a Christian is one who tests his faith, his reason, and his virtue by confronting evil in all of its guises and not submitting to it—an active as opposed to a passive Christian. That Herrick is developing a similar definition in *"The Christian Militant"* seems indicated by its opening: the true militant Christian, he asserts, is "A Man prepar'd against all ills to come, / That dares to dead the fires of martirdome" (ll. 1–2). The couplet is deceptive. To be prepared for possible misfortune is not only good Stoicism but common sense; but to try to prepare oneself for *all* possible misfortunes smacks of unhealthy pessimism if not paranoia. It also suggests a lack of faith in Divine Providence.

Moreover, one so thoroughly prepared runs small risk of having his faith tempered in "the fires of martirdome." Such a man would enjoy the security of one "That sleeps at home; and sayling there at ease, / Feares not the fierce sedition of the Seas" (ll. 3–4). The juxtaposition of this image of domestic safety and that of martyrdom's fires is ironic. Sleeping at home is a luxury zealous Christians (like John Bunyan, for example) enjoyed but rarely; and vicariously sailing the ocean (by perusing maps) is hardly the mark of the active man. On the contrary, such activities are, as chapter 3 pointed out, the kind enjoyed by the contemplative man who values quietude, retirement, and safety and seeks these in country living. Such a life could have a strong appeal for a moderate Anglican like Robert Herrick but would be despicable to a crusading Puritan. So far, then, Herrick has defined a contradiction—an unmilitant militant—and therefore a ridiculous figure. Ridicule is also conveyed through wordplay: "sedition," the act of rebelling against lawful authority, is an unusual metaphor for the sea's action unless "seas" is a pun on *sees,* the offices or powers of bishops. In the seventeenth century one of the chief sources of controversy between radical Protestants and the Church of England was its ecclesiastical hierarchy, which endowed bishops with considerable power and influence. To a zealous Puritan, the Anglican bishops, like their Catholic counterparts, were usurping Christ's own office as mediator between God and man and thus were "seditious."

Rather than take on the church hierarchy, however, this unmilitant militant stays safely in his rural retreat (Puritanism had a strong following among the English squirearchy), content to be one:

> That's counter-proofe against the Farms mis-haps,
> Undreadfull too of courtly thunderclaps:
> That weares one face (like heaven) and never showes
> A change, when Fortune either comes, or goes:
> That keeps his own strong guard, in the despight
> Of what can hurt by day, or harme by night:
> That takes and re-delivers every stroake
> Of Chance, (as made up all of rock, and oake:)
>
> (ll. 5–12)

Taken out of context, this could be an admiring portrait of one who confronts the tribulations of life with Stoic fortitude; indeed, it squares well with the Jonsonian notion of the good man that Herrick shares. But the description subtly subverts itself: for the true Puritan, there is no such thing as fortune or chance, only Divine Providence, and one's personal election makes itself manifest in activism, not Stoic acceptance. Moreover, the concluding lines of Herrick's definition are so preposterous—crucifixion was not a fate awaiting seventeenth-century Christians—and hyperbolic in tone that they render the portrait previously established grotesque:

> That sighs at others death; smiles at his own
> Most dire and horrid crucifixion.
> Who for true glory suffers thus; we grant
> Him to be here our *Christian militant.*

Finally, there is such a gap between the poem's early image of the hearthside hero and its concluding image of the crucified masochist that one's credulity is strained.

The careful reader of *"The Christian Militant,"* then, is left with one of two impressions: either that the poem's incongruities are unintentional and thus it is a more badly flawed work than Herrick typically turns out, or that its incongruities are deliberate, aimed at creating a covert caricature of the

kind of Puritan satirized by Ben Jonson as "Zeal-of-the-Land Busy" in
Bartholomew Fair. Moreover, it is improbable that a political being like
Herrick would never once give in to the impulse to expose the hypocrisy of
those who opposed everything he stood for—Royalism, Anglicanism, the
priesthood, sometimes even poetry itself. Whether or not "much of *Hesperides* should be seen as a subtle attack on what Herrick believed were the tendencies and values of Puritanism in seventeenth-century England," as
Achsah Guibbory has argued,[3] that description certainly fits "*The Christian
Militant.*" Finally, the latter is not *Hesperides'* only satire on religion; another is an ambitious work dedicated to counselor-at-law John Merrifield,
"*The Fairie Temple:* or, Oberons *Chappell*" (H-223). Here, however, the object of Herrick's mockery is Roman Catholicism rather than Puritanism.

So familiar and fully developed in the British Isles was the folklore of
the fairies and their realm that Spenser in *The Faerie Queene* (1591),
Shakespeare (in *A Midsummer Night's Dream,* c. 1595), Ben Jonson (in
his masque, *Oberon the Faery Prince,* 1611), Michael Drayton (in *Nimphi-
dia, the Court of Faery,* 1627), and other writers were accustomed to draw
heavily upon it. The popularity of fairy literature and the challenges to a
poet's imagination it posed clearly struck a responsive chord in Herrick,
for he wrote a total of five fairy poems, and they are among his longer
works. "*The Fairie Temple*" contains two formal divisions, the first being a
six-line dedication that asks which is finer, real temples made of "Lime, or
Wood, or Stone" (l. 4) or this one, whose architect is a poet. This amusingly self-serving affirmation of art introduces the poem's next division,
"*The Temple.*" Here Herrick describes the miniature church's decor, fixtures, and services in detail, and in addition catalogs its ecclesiastical staff.
Some passages are mainly descriptive, with Herrick, "the goldsmith's ap-
prentice, the master of filigree,"[4] carving out his reduced-scale images
with delicate craftsmanship—for example, in his lines (54–63) on the
fairy temple's altar:

> The Altar is not here foure-square,
> Nor in a forme Triangular;
> Nor made of glasse, or wood, or stone,
> But of a little Transverce bone;
> Which boyes, and Bruckel'd* children call
> (Playing for Points and Pins) *Cockall.***
> Whose Linnen-Drapery is a thin
> Subtile and ductile Codlin's† skin

> Which o're the board is smoothly spred
> With little Seale-work Damasked.
>
> **grimy*
> ***knuckle bone*
> *†apple's*

Made out of a bone used in children's games (which helps to reduce it in
importance as well as in size), the fairy altar is covered, not with the traditional finely figured linen cloth, but with an appleskin. For all its ingenious-
ness, whether poetry like this continues to amuse very much depends on the
taste of the modern reader. The observant and partisan seventeenth-century
reader, however, would have been able to enjoy passages such as this for the
political satire they entail: as L. C. Martin has pointed out (*PW,* 520),
Herrick's reference to the shape and composition of the altar slyly alludes to
a contemporary controversy about the proper shape, composition, and location of the church altar—one of those seemingly minor theological arguments that added fuel to what would become the firestorm of the Civil War.
Herrick's wit reduces such arcane matters to absurdity.

   "The Temple" is full of such satire, most of it directed at Roman Catholicism, although it is not entirely irrelevant to the Church of England in its
more Anglo-Catholic aspects: for example, the fairies' faith, like Anglicanism, is "a mixt Religion . . . Part Pagan, Part Papisticall" (ll. 23, 25), and "if
their Legend doe not lye, / They much affect the *Papacie*" (ll. 109–10).
The very juxtaposition of ancient polytheism and Romanism is in itself an
implied criticism, but Herrick goes further by combining the externals of
both religions in his description of the chapel. That description's opening
lines, for example, reveal a *"Temple of Idolatry"* (l. 6) where the Fairy King
Oberon "of *God-heads* has such store, / As *Rome's Pantheon* had not more"
(ll. 7–8). Herrick at once makes Catholicism guilty by association with paganism and mocks pagan animal-gods by reducing them in lines 14–18 to
mere insects: "Idol-Cricket," "*Idol-Beetle-flie,*" "*Idol-Canker*" (a worm), and
the "golden god, *Cantharides*" (a beetle). This catalog and Herrick's listing
of fairy saints' names notable for their silliness—"Saint *Tit,* Saint *Nit,* Saint
Is, Saint *Itis*" (l. 28), and several more—reduce Roman Catholic veneration
of the saints to absurdity. Herrick also ridicules the ornateness of Baroque
church decor: "where ye look, ye see, / No *Capitoll,* no [cornice] free, / Or
Freeze, from this fine Fripperie" (ll. 19–21). Line 21's alliteration alone
makes a joke of some of Christendom's architectural masterworks, includ-

ing many Anglican churches built before the Reformation. (Herrick's own church is architecturally relatively austere.)

Fairyland's holy men are treated no more gently. Like the clerics who even today guard the entrances to St. Peter's, "A little-Puppet-Priest" "squeaks" out his exhortations (l. 40) to arriving worshippers; another "pules" or whines his (l. 43). Meanwhile the chief priest stands at the altar "off'ring up the Holy-Grist" (grain, but perhaps with a pun on "ghost"), "Ducking in Mood, and perfect Tense, / With (much-good-do't him) reverence" (ll. 52–54)—in other words, suiting his bowings and noddings to the grammar of the liturgy, as if (sniggers the speaker in an aside) such ritual flourishes have anything to do with true spirituality.

Herrick also scores Roman Catholicism on other counts. The fairies' faith, he implies, is highly doctrinaire: they worship by the book—by "their Book of Canons," "their Book of Articles," and "their Book of Homilies" (ll. 78–82): "They have their Text for what they doe" (l. 77). Their services are depicted as being excessively elaborate, with ceremonial fixtures and robes ("Of cleanest Cobweb"), all of which are supposed to lend "sanctity" (l. 97) to the occasion. Also coming in for ridicule is the ecclesiastical hierarchy, with its "*mumbling Masse-priests*," "many a dapper *Chorister*," "*Canons*," and "*Cloyster-Monks*" (ll. 103–7); the Catholic practice of selling "*Pardons* and *Indulgences;*" and the Catholic emphasis on rosaries, relics, and incense (ll. 114–16).

"*The Fairie Temple*" continues for almost 30 more lines but does not so much end as stop, as Oberon finishes his devotions and moves off to dine—described in a sequel located further on in *Hesperides,* "Oberons *Feast*" (*H-*293). Neither the latter work nor any of Herrick's other fairy poems is satiric in mode. The charm of such works resides in their combination of two elements: the amusement provided by the analogies between the "little people's" world and the human world, and the appeal of simple miniaturism, the reduction of familiar things to the smallest imaginable size. Whatever fascination such poetry might have had in the seventeenth century, to a modern sensibility it may come across as at best ingenious, at worst as merely cute. Its satiric thrust gives "*The Fairie Temple*" a certain edge, even though as satire it is basically Horatian—good-humored, almost evenhanded, in that it could be taken as twitting Anglicanism as well as Catholicism and polytheism.

In an intolerant age, when Catholics often were regarded as subversives and were persecuted by deed and word, "*The Fairie Temple*" makes Herrick look relatively tolerant. In fact, he even appears to employ Roman Catholic elements to lend sanctity and significance to a more serious poem, "*The*

Funerall Rites of the Rose" (*H-686*). The criticism of F. R. Leavis—that this
work is a trifle, an extended and merely witty (but not metaphysical) conceit based on the resemblances between flowers and girls (36, 39–41)—has
been countered by Thomas R. Whitaker's observation that the poem's
main concern is the essentially religious one of "transcending the flux of life"
(19). Indeed, life's transiency is implicit in the bittersweet simplicity of the
poem's opening line: "THe Rose was sick, and smiling di'd." The sickness
of the rose and the ironic fact that she smiles as she dies (a cropped rose is
dead, but still lovely) personify her and thus remind readers of their own
relative fragility. The parallel is reinforced by the services that commemorate her passing:

> And (being to be sanctif'd)
> About the Bed, there sighing stood
> The sweet, and flowrie Sisterhood.
> Some hung the head while some did bring
> (To wash her) water from the Spring.
>
> (ll. 2–6)

Whether Herrick intended "Sisterhood" to evoke an image of roses as nuns
(roses like nuns "dress" alike) or more generally of flowers as maidens is uncertain, but the religious connotation of "Sisterhood" is strengthened by the
flowers' ritual actions: their sighs audibly mourn their sister's death; the
drooping blossoms of some make them appear to be bowing their heads;
others seem to bathe the rose with the dewdrops they have collected. Here
Herrick has created what William Oram calls

a sort of double exposure in which maidens are superimposed on blossoms: now
[the reader] imagines the figures as women . . . now . . . as flowers. The alternation
is pleasing: one of the pleasures of the poem lies in its fleeting animism, its capacity
to give the reader a glimpse of a sentient, sympathetic natural world.[5]

Neither the natural nor the human world, however, can achieve transcendence through ceremony; ceremony can only sanctify life's events. Although the "flowrie Sisterhood" keep "a solemne Fast," sing funeral songs,
"The sacred *Dirge* and *Trentall*" (another term with Catholic connotations),
and expend their natural "perfumes" like incense, the rose must be returned
to the earth from whence it came—ashes to ashes, dust to dust:

At last, when prayers for the dead,
And Rites were all accomplished;
They, weeping, spread a Lawnie Loom,*
And closed her up, as in a Tombe.
                                        (ll. 13–16)

*linen cloth

Although these last rites have more of a Christian than a pagan aura, almost
to the point where nature is in effect "Christianized," the poem conspicu-
ously fails to generate any Christian optimism. Moreover, there is something
to William Oram's comment that, despite its seemingly serious mood,
Herrick's vignette "never loses its whimsy" (rather like "The Faerie Temple").
Yet, as Oram acknowledges, the poem does confront the fact of death, however that fact may be mediated, rendered more manageable, by embodying
it in images of anthropomorphized flowers (214, 215).

Like so many of the "religious" poems in Hesperides, the actual religious
character of "The Funerall Rites of the Rose" remains elusive. Does it imply
an Anglican, a Catholic, or as Robert Deming has suggested, a Roman ceremony (114)? Such questions arise because, more than any other important
poet of his age, more even than Jonson, Herrick is one in whose imagination
and art the Christian and the pagan achieve a level of synthesis that must
have its source not merely in his learning and his literary talent but in his
fundamental personality.

Christian and Pagan

Readers who return to Herrick's complete works for the second time
may well perceive foreshadowings of His Noble Numbers throughout the
"Sacred Grove" of his secular poems. The difficulty is that such foreshadowings are liable to be overshadowed by Herrick's more apparent paganism. For example, two paired poems, "Mattens, or Morning Prayer"
(H-320) and "Evensong" (H-321), take their titles from Church of England services but are less than orthodox in content. In "Mattens," for example, the speaker-priest instructs the faithful to perform a Christian
ritual—make the sign of the cross—when they arise, but then proceed "to
sacrifice," which is not normally thought of as a feature of morning
prayers. (Only later in the poem is it implied that the sacrifice is
metaphorical—of the soul.) The worshippers are then told, "First wash
thy heart in innocence, then bring / Pure hands, pure habits, pure every-

thing" (ll. 3–4). Ritual purification as a prerequisite for participation is also not a universal feature of Christian worship. Such purification, however, is considered an essential preliminary to the kind of Roman ceremonies set forth in Tibullus (2.1.13–14) and in Jonson's Roman play, *Sejanus* (5.174–5), both of which Herrick's lines echo.[6] Yet the poem's final passage, with its allusion to Revelation 5.8 ("golden vials full of odours"), and its affirmation of the interdependence of one's soul, one's deeds, and one's aims, seems to reflect a Christian perspective:

> Next to the Altar humbly kneele, and thence,
> Give up thy soule in clouds of frankinsence.
> Thy golden Censors fil'd with odours sweet,
> Shall make thy actions with their ends to meet.
>
>   (ll. 5–8)

"*Evensong*" also echoes a passage from Revelation (*CP,* 174)—"I am Alpha and Omega, the beginning and the end, the first and the last" (22.13)—but the priest speaks of Jove rather than Jehovah: "BEginne with *Jove;* then is the work halfe done" (l. 1). Such a piety would be suitable to any religion, but to claim that "*Jove's* is the first and last" is more appropriate in a monotheistic Christian context than in a polytheistic one. "Jove" is, of course, a stock epithet for God in humanist literature, but Herrick's employment of it in a poem that appears from its title to treat a familiar ritual of the Church of England seems designed to shock. Both of these paired poems, then, exhibit Herrick's Christian-pagan synthesis, though that synthesis is more artfully achieved in "*Mattens*" than in "*Evensong.*"

A more ambitious example of Herrick's creative humanism is one of his wartime occasional pieces, "*A Dirge upon the Death of the Right Valiant Lord,* Bernard Stuart" (*H*-219), who was killed in battle in 1645. A proper funeral song, "*A Dirge*" is intended to be sung—according to Herrick's own directions—by a chorus and three soloists. It opens with the first soloist intoning a banishment of any who would profane the solemnity of the moment with noise (according to Robert Deming, a Roman ritual), and then an introduction to "this *Trentall*," a Christian dirge (120). The second soloist then sings a panegyric to the fallen lord that hints of Stuart's resemblance to the risen Lord:

> 2. Had Wolves or Tigers seen, but thee,
>   They wo'd have shew'd civility;
>   And in compassion of thy yeeres,

> Washt those thy purple wounds with tears.
> But since th'art slain; and in thy fall,
> The drooping Kingdome suffers all.

Like Adam and the second Adam, Stuart possessed the kind of perfect innocence that could make wild beasts tame. Stuart was also like Christ in that
he is associated with being washed with tears and with bleeding (the adjective "purple," suggesting both deep red and royalty, was frequently employed to describe Christ's wounds). Finally, like both the first and second
Adams, Stuart underwent a "fall" that affected a whole kingdom.

Even in an age accustomed to hyperbole, Herrick is sailing dangerously
close to blasphemy. Still, the chorus maintains this rhetorical pitch, vowing
to mourn Stuart's death themselves, "And if that will not suffice, / Thou
shalt have soules for sacrifice" (ll. 11–12)—as if Stuart were a man-god like
Caesar or a god-man like Christ. They will preserve his body, as Christ's
was, with spices and oils. At this point, however, Herrick reduces the poem's
intensity: he shifts from metaphor to metaphysics by having the third soloist
offer a ringing affirmation of the incorruptibility of Stuart's soul and its
immortality:

> 3. Live, live thou dost, and shalt; for why?
>   *Soules doe not with their bodies die:*
>   Ignoble off-springs, they may fall
>   Into the flames of Funerall:
>   When as the chosen seed shall spring
>   Fresh, and for ever flourishing.

These lines seem to sound a distinctively Christian note, but as L. C. Martin
has pointed out, both Ovid and Tacitus make similar claims.[7] The idea that
the flesh is the inferior embodiment of the spirit has its roots in Platonism as
well as in Christianity, as does the image of souls as the "chosen seed," the
seminal and eternal elements of humanity's being. The implication of rebirth into life eternal conveyed by "for ever flourishing" is, of course, pat-
ently Christian and serves as a counterweight to the earlier image of the
funeral pyre, a fixture of pagan ceremonies.

The dirge concludes in a similarly mixed vein as the chorus proclaims,
"And times to come shall, weeping, read thy glory, / Lesse in these Marble
stones, then in thy story" (ll. 21–22). The idea that marble and gilded
monuments are inadequate to the task of memorializing is conventional,
but there is ambiguity in the couplet's pivotal word, "glory." Glory as

earthly fame or reputation is sought by pagan heroes, but the aim of the Christian is heavenly glory alone. It is a commonplace of Christian thought that the pagan dies out of his glory, the Christian into his, but Herrick's commemoration of Bernard Stuart, with its extraordinary synthesis of the pagan and the Christian, has it both ways, elevating this fallen Royalist officer to saint as well as to hero.

When it comes to Hesperidean self-portraits in a religious vein, however, Herrick is modesty itself. For example, in *"On himselfe"* (*H*-306) this Anglican priest assumes a role associated with Catholicism, that of humble pilgrim:

> Here down my wearyed limbs Ile lay;
> My Pilgrims staffe; my weed* of gray:
> My Palmers hat; my Scallops shell;
> My Crosse; my Cord; and all farewell.
> (ll. 1–4)

*robe

The image is not that of Bunyan's pilgrim: his costume suggests a Catholic wayfarer, wearing a cross, a shell-shaped badge signifying that he had visited the shrine of St. James of Campostella (*CP*, 168), and a hat which may indicate that he had made a pilgrimage to the Holy Land. In his plain grey robe gathered by a simple cord he resembles a member of the order of Grey Friars. But this pilgrimage, of course, is the poet's life:

> For having now my journey done,
> (Just at the setting of the Sun)
> Here I have found a Chamber fit,
> (God and good friends be thankt for it)
> Where if I can a lodger be
> A little while from Tramplers* free;
> At my up-rising next, I shall,
> If not requite, yet thank ye all.
> (ll. 5–12)

*journeyings

Although Herrick could at most have been in his early fifties when he penned these lines, they depict a man approaching the end of life's journey, one who has finally found a home, a room in an "inn" where he can lodge comfortably until his long day ends—the parsonage at Dean Prior. (John Milton utilizes an almost identical conceit in his 1631 mock clegy, "Upon the University Carrier.") The poet's indebtedness to God, as needy mortal, and to his friends, as sociable Cavalier, too great to be repaid in this life, will be acknowledged in the next one. For the moment, as poet he can offer only the recompense of his words:

> Meane while, the *Holy-Rood** hence fright
> The fouler Fiend, and evil Spright,
> From scaring you or yours this night.
>
> (ll. 13–15)

crucifix

This triplet is a charm or versified spell to ward off evil and thus the kind of gift a poor parson or a poet could bestow on those to whom he is grateful— including, surprisingly (and touchingly) the reader and his loved ones ("you or yours"). The subgenre of the charm-poem is one at which Herrick tried his hand several times;[8] it accords with his notion (discussed further in chapter 6) that poems are forms of magic. As "charms" or "incantations" they possess extraordinary power.

Herrick's concluding charm in a way returns the poem to the vaguely Catholic mode of its beginning: charms, after all, smack somewhat of superstition, and one of the radical Protestants' criticisms of Catholicism was that it retailed superstitions more than it preached the Gospel. The poet's "Catholicizing" of himself, then, in *"On himselfe,"* might be an implicit rebuke of religious intolerance, particularly since the portrait that emerges is, more than anything else, that of Robert Herrick as Everyman.

Foreshadowings of the poet's *Noble Numbers* are also to be found in *Hesperides'* religious epigrams. Close to the spirit of *"On himselfe"* is *"Sufferance"* (*H*-1027): "IN the hope of ease to come, / Let's endure one Martyrdome." Whether life in this vale of tears is seen as pilgrimage or martyrdom, the hope of eternal rest is, of course, orthodox. Another religious epigram from Herrick's secular volume, *"Comforts in Crosses"* (*H*-1007), is similarly orthodox, but complexly so. It compresses into two lines (1) a seriously witty pun on "cross" as Christian symbol and as synonym for "misfortune," a pun that lends a double meaning to its title as well as its first line; (2) the Christian paradox that one must be defeated to become victorious, be humbled to be exalted; and (3) an allusion to the Fortunate Fall: "BE not dismaide, though crosses cast thee downe; / Thy fall is but the rising to a

Crowne." This is consolation at its most compact, an illustration of why both Jonson and Herrick regarded the epigram form so highly.

Another *consolatio* whose thought and spirit anticipate Herrick's *Pious Pieces* is "*Comfort to a youth that had lost his Love*" (*H*-1024). What might from its title be expected to be an avuncular response to a standard love complaint turns out to be something more serious, for the mistress in question is not coy but dead:

> WHat needs complaints,
> When she a place
> Has with the race
>   Of Saints?
>   (ll. 1–4)

Also peculiar here is the seeming curtness of the tone, which comes from Herrick's almost exclusive employment of monosyllabic words and his odd prosody: although not divided into regular stanzas, "*Comfort*" consists of six quatrains, each with three lines of iambic dimeter and one of iambic monometer, rhyming *abba*. (Herrick uses more short lines than any other important English poet, the extreme example being the self-epitaph, "*Upon his departure hence*," *H*-475, written exclusively in iambic monometer.) One reason for Herrick's employment of the poetics of terseness in "*Comfort*" may be the place of consolation in Christian doctrine. Since death for the faithful is the way to eternal life and the experience of God's superior love, excessive grief, even for a lost love, constitutes a kind of blasphemy. Doctrinally and possibly psychologically a firm tone may be what is needed in such cases.

The thrust of this poem is clear from its first quatrain: the lady is with the "Saints" and one does not mourn the blessed. What this means is made plain in the next two quatrains:

> In endlesse mirth,
> She thinks not on
> What's said or done
>   In earth:
> She sees no teares,
> Or any tone
> Of thy deep grone
>   She heares.
>   (ll. 5–12)

The essence as well as the being of the youth's lost love has been transfigured. Because eternal bliss, to be bliss, seemingly cannot be compromised
by awareness of sublunary suffering, heaven's "endlesse mirth" blocks his
pain out of his beloved's consciousness. Such a conclusion, brutal though it
may seem, follows logically from Christian doctrine. That doctrine, which
holds that heaven is a state of perfect happiness, gives Milton considerable
trouble in *Paradise Lost* and Herrick again in "*The white Island*" (see the
section on "Holy Living and Holy Dying" below). As a vision of heaven it is
the opposite of sentimental; and indeed, in heaven mere sentiment is
transcended:

> Nor do's she minde,
> Or think on't now,
> That ever thou
> Wast kind.
> But chang'd above,
> She likes not there,
> As she did here,
> Thy love.
> (ll. 13–20)

All that idealism associated with romantic love becomes irrelevant in
heaven: along with the negative aspects of eros, such love is subsumed
within a higher love. It would be difficult to imagine a more pointed or
more poignant illustration of the doctrine that death results in transfiguration. An operative principle of eternal life then would seem to be not so
much *contemptus mundi* as *annhilatio mundi*. The result is a vision of
heaven that, unlike more sentimental conceptions, bluntly emphasizes heav-
en's distance—and its detachment—from earthly existence.

The speaker's consolation has actually assumed the form of an argument
based upon taking Christian orthodoxy to its logical—if seemingly
extreme—conclusions. Once that orthodoxy and its interpretation are accepted by the youth, he can obtain peace of mind:

> Forebeare therefore,
> And Lull asleepe
> Thy woes and weep
> *No more.*
> (ll. 21–24)

Here the prosody remains terse and the tone logical, but the softer consonants and long vowels of these lines give them a gentler quality and convey some sense of compassion. In this "sacred" poem from Herrick's "profane" collection, then, dogma is ultimately mediated by humanity, a process that, as indicated below, is generally operative in the poet's *Noble Numbers* as well.

Religious Variety and Unity

The variety of those "humane" works classified in this chapter as religious is a reflection of the variety of Herrick's collection itself: varied in form, in prosody, in subject, in tone and mood, even in religious character—Christian-pagan, Protestant-Catholic—his poems nevertheless bear the impress of his unifying personality and his synthesizing poetic imagination. That this imagination is highly disciplined—the apparent eclecticism and randomness of *Hesperides* to the contrary—is clearly demonstrated in *His Noble Numbers,* where the poet's determination to create a more traditional body of devotional verse is manifest from the beginning. (This is not, of course, to imply that Herrick wrote all of his sacred poems after he composed his secular ones or even that he wrote them all in the same period of time: rather, the point is that the poems of *His Noble Numbers* have been collected and deliberately arranged with certain religious purposes in mind.) Herrick is still Herrick in *His Noble Numbers,* but his persona—in contrast to the array of lovers, wits, lyrists, philosophers, courtiers, patriots, social critics, etc., on display in *Hesperides*—seems very much to be that of the vicar of Dean Prior (although, somewhat surprisingly, he never explicitly identifies himself as a priest in *Noble Numbers*). Indeed, the congregation in his small country church might well have been a fair representation of the audience for his poetry in the seventeenth century. Some of that poetry would be readily accessible even to the unschooled, who could appreciate it when it was recited or sung; and some would be enjoyed mainly by university wits (like Herrick himself) and their sophisticated circle. The main body of his verse, however, would have been readable on some level by almost any literate individual of average intelligence. Some of his prayers, for example, are simplicity itself (although it can be a simplicity that is beyond many poets). Various lyrics and meditations blend the kind of piety and experience of everyday life that anyone who has led such a life can readily understand. A few epigrammatic poems, on the other hand, are theological in nature and too abstract to be easily comprehended.

As the beginning of this chapter indicated, the Herrick of *His Noble*

Numbers establishes his persona and that persona's situation in the three poems that introduce that volume. *"His Confession"* (N-1), conventions and autobiographical quibbles aside, is the ritual expression of a divided soul, Robert Herrick as true Christian as well as true poet. The next stage in the ceremony of redemption is penitence: accordingly, in *"His Prayer for Absolution"* (N-2) Herrick implies that his "wild unhallowed Times" and "unbaptized Rhimes" are things of the past. Readers will find this to be true in the sense that the poems that lie ahead in *Noble Numbers,* in the "reading future", so to speak, are literally "inlaid" with God, for his name, often in capital letters, appears in a majority of them.

Having settled these autobiographical issues to his own satisfaction, Herrick then addresses what may be the central issue of *His Noble Numbers,* perhaps of any believer's life, in a theological poem, *"To finde God"* (N-3). Its mode is that of a verse argument, the purpose of which is to demonstrate, through the *reductio ad absurdum* of a catalog of impossibilities, that God is beyond man's primitive apprehension:

> WEigh me the Fire; or, canst thou find
> A way to measure out the Wind;
> Distinguish all those floods that are
> Mixt in the watrie Theater.*
>
> (ll. 1–4)

*the ocean

Herrick has employed this technique before in *Hesperides,* in two love complaints in the manner of John Donne's lyric "Goe, and catch a falling starre"—*"His Protestation to Perilla"* (H-154) and *"Impossibilities to his friend"* (H-198)—and in a philosophical poem on oblivion as humankind's destiny, *"Proof to no purpose"* (H-720). (Herrick is something of a self-plagiarist, with a tendency to reuse what works.) *"To finde God"* continues in five more couplets to challenge the reader to perform impossible feats and then triumphantly concludes, "This if thou canst; then shew me Him / That rides the glorious *Cherubim"* (ll. 15–16). This is Herrick as Christian metaphysician. His argument's conclusion—that God is beyond human ken—follows logically from its premise, that even nature is in the main beyond humankind's grasp. The argument's organization is also logical, for each challenge is associated with one of the four known elements—fire, water, air, and earth.

The next *Pious Piece* appears to contradict the conclusion of *"To finde*

God," for its title is *"What God is"* (N-4). However, as it turns out this epigram simply takes its predecessor's conclusion a step further: "GOD is above the sphere of our esteem, / And is best known, not defining him." In other words, God is beyond not only our circumscription but our valorization, for only that whose limits can be fixed can be accurately valued. Note that for Herrick God *is* knowable: as succeeding sacred epigrams make plain, he predictably accepts what the Bible reveals about God. In fact, Ann Coiro has pointed out that a number of Herrick's two-line epigrams are "almost exact transcriptions" from John Gregory's 1646 prose work, *Notes and Observations upon some Passages of Scripture* (1988, 184–85).

Other sacred epigrams suggest that for Herrick certain kinds of human experience also can be valid sources for inferences about the deity. In *"Upon God"* (N-87), for example, we learn that the deity is present even amid life's familiar trials and tribulations:

> GOD when He takes my goods and chattels hence,
> Gives me a portion, giving patience;
> What is in God is God; if so it be
> He patience gives; He gives himselfe to me.

The epigram is a compound of simple faith, of Christian Stoicism, and of a rather subtle theological conception about the relationships among divine essence, divine existence, and divine extension.

Given Herrick's predeliction for the pastoral vision, what is surprising about *His Noble Numbers* is its lack of evidence that he put much store in that other source of insights about God so widely valued in the seventeenth century, "The Book of the Creatures," God's own creative work, the natural world. In *Paradise Lost* Milton laments that his blindness prevents him from perusing "the Book of knowledge fair . . . of Natures works" (3.47, 49), but Herrick reserves such explorations for *Hesperides*. Indeed, in *Noble Numbers* he can show more faith in human authority as a source of revelation, as the fifth poem of "His Pious Pieces," *"Upon God"* (N-5), suggests: "GOD is not onely said to be / An *Ens,* but *Supraentitie.*" The authority doing the "saying" may be Aristotle, for *ens* is the Aristotelian term for *being* (*supraentitie,* then, is "the being beyond being"). As to the meaning and significance of this theological opinion, however, the poet, uncharacteristically, offers no help.

The Herrickean persona of metaphysician and theologian looms large in *Noble Numbers,* partly through sheer numbers: many of this collection's poems are theological epigrams that, like *"What God is"* and *"Upon God,"* offer terse ex cathedra pronouncements on a variety of religious subjects. Although these short poems are rarely anthologized and have received little attention from Herrick scholars, taken together they give a distinctively intellectual, learned, and didactic cast to *His Noble Numbers,* evoking the impression of a persona who is by turns donnish and parsonish. In fact, after the collection's two opening autobiographical poems, the next 14 could be classified as theological epigrams—on the whole somewhat abstract and cerebral but still capable of evoking brief but intense bursts of feeling from the reader who is passionately involved in religious thought. If Donne had written holy epigrams instead of holy sonnets, they might not have been entirely unlike Herrick's.

Miriam Starkman has described *His Noble Numbers* as "a large, metrical prayer book [containing] creeds and graces, confessions and thanksgivings, litanies and dirges, nativity and circumcision songs, anthems and carols, plus a large body of near catechical wisdom" (the holy epigrams).[9] But "prayer book" is misleading: while Herrick's collection contains prayers and allusions to prayer aplenty, it is, like George Herbert's *The Temple,* first and foremost a gathering of devotional *poems* carefully arranged for artistic effect.

This wide variety of sacred modes and moods is unified by not only the Herrickean persona but by its quintessential Protestantism, a Protestanism unqualified by the occasional Anglo-Catholicism and ubiquitous paganism of *Hesperides.* For example, a poem straightforwardly entitled *"His Creed"* (*N-78*) sets forth what can be viewed as the doctrinal base of *His Noble Numbers.* Like a number of Herrick's "profane" meditations, it begins with the speaker contemplating his own death. Unlike most of those in *Hesperides,* however, this speaker's confrontation with death concludes not with oblivion but with a vision of an afterlife:

> I Do believe, that die I must,
> And be return'd from out my dust:
> I do believe, that when I rise,
> Christ I shall see, with these same eyes:
> I doe believe, that I must come,
> With others, to the dreadfull Doome:
> I doe believe, the bad must goe
> From thence, to everlasting woe:
> I doe believe, the good and I,
> Shall live with Him eternally.
>
> (ll. 1–10)

It is poems such as these that have sometimes led Herrick's religion and his religious verse (in spite of the evidence of the theological epigrams) to be characterized as simple and even simplistic or childlike. *"His Creed,"* however, like all credos, is intended to be a brief and summary statement of faith, not a theological discourse. Like a catechism it simply affirms the Christian promise of resurrection (the controversy regarding when resurrection takes place is glossed over), judgment, and the disposition of the "good" (with whom the speaker unself-consciously and confidently includes himself) and the "bad." What those moral terms mean is left unstated, as if they are self-evident. Even what heaven and hell entail is left open.

The specifically Protestant cast of Herrick's credo emerges toward the poem's conclusion:

> I do believe, I shall inherit
> Heaven, by Christs mercies, not my merit:
> I do believe, the One in Three,
> And Three in perfect Unitie:
> Lastly, that JESUS is a Deed
> Of Gift from God: *And here's my Creed.*
> (ll. 11–16)

Herrick indicates his Protestantism by affirming salvation through faith alone rather than through faith and works (anything that earns one "merit"), a doctrine associated with Catholicism. On the whole, however, *"His Creed"* is less sectarian than it is quintessential Christianity, Christianity stripped down to a few basic though hardly simple doctrines. Therefore, it is the kind of poem a child or an unlettered adult could hear and memorize with relative ease, a versified catechism of the kind that a country preacher might make good use of. Moreover, located about a third of the way through *His Noble Numbers,* some of which are at best abstruse, *"His Creed"* reminds us that the speaker is not a scholar of divinity but a humble poet whose verses can have a pastoral (i.e., ministerial) function. There is nothing quite like it in the notable devotional poetry of the seventeenth century, as there is nothing quite like *His Noble Numbers.*

Herrick has been criticized for not being Donne or Crashaw or Milton or Herbert (Press, 31), yet a careful reading of his *"Pious Pieces"* will reveal an occasional "passionate apprehension of Christian dogma," a touch or two of "mysticism," frequent exaltations of "God's majesty," and expressions of a desire to "attune himself to God's will." The real question, of course, is not whom Herrick is like as a devotional poet but what he is like.

God and the Individual

Contributing importantly to the Protestant character of *His Noble Numbers* is the poetry's deinstitutionalized quality. Recent criticism has properly emphasized the importance of ceremony in Herrick's poetry, but the rituals of his religious collection are more often private than public; that is, they are formal communications between a speaker and his God rather than between an assembled congregation and the Almighty. The church as an institution—its history, dogma, traditions, and culture—do not figure in Herrick's devotions as they do in the sacred verse of the Anglican George Herbert or the Catholic Richard Crashaw. Even the clergy and the ecclesiastical hierarchy are conspicuous by their absence, as is any continuing emphasis on the Bible. *His Noble Numbers* begins with a self-confessed poet-sinner in search of a God whom he can hardly find or understand: "'Tis hard to finde Gode, but to comprehend / Him, as He is, is labour without end." This epigram, "*God not to be comprehended*" (N-8), is only the eighth poem in the collection, but it is already the third to pose the problem faced by the Protestant believer who is obliged to develop a unique relationship with God. Thus a kind of pattern is established that helps give shape to this devotional miscellany: it is as if Herrick were combining the roles of poet-theologian and Everyman. Sometimes he is the former, presenting "*An Ode on the Birth of our Saviour*" (N-33) or explaining the nature of "*Sin*" (N-100) or "*Evil*" (N-101); sometimes he is the latter, simply expressing "*His wish to God*" (N-115) to end his days piously and quietly or trying to find hope in a colloquy "*To God, on his sicknesse*" (N-84). Sometimes, as in "*To God*" (N-232), he is both—humble sinner as well as religious thinker.

Herrick begins the latter poem with a negative invocation that portrays God as the Old Testament's Yaweh, the God of wrath:

> COme to me God; but do not come
> To me, as to the gen'rall Doome,
> In power; or come Thou in that state,
> When Thou Thy Lawes didst promulgate,
> When as the Mountaine quak'd for dread,
> And sullen clouds bound up his head.
>
> (ll. 1–6)

The God of Judgment Day and the giver of the Ten Commandments to Moses is too awful for an ordinary mortal to bear. The speaker seeks a colloquy, not a confrontation; he is an Everyman, not a hero of religion. Accordingly, he requests a less "Miltonic" God, one less majestic and intimidating:

> No, lay thy stately terrours by,
> To talke with me familiarly;
> For if Thy thunder-claps I heare,
> I shall lesse swoone, then die for feare.
>
> (ll. 7–10)

The effect of the poem's rhetoric and imagery is to make the situation "Biblical": it is as if Herrick has stepped into the pages of the Old Testament and into an era when one might actually receive a visitation from the Almighty. So vividly is the scene envisioned that the reader may forget that the poem is an extended metaphor for a state of mind—one individual's intensely emotional effort to imagine his deity. It becomes easy too to empathize with him when, quite humanly, he hopes to evoke the New Testament God of love rather than the angry Old Testament God:

> Speake thou of love and I'le reply
> By way of *Epithalamie,*
> Or sing of *mercy,* and I'le suit
> To it my Violl and my Lute:
> Thus let Thy lips but love distill,
> Then come my God, and hap what will.
>
> (ll. 11–16)

With these lines Herrick's Everyman assumes the additional role of poet-musician: if God arrives bearing a message of love for all humankind, the speaker will respond with a song celebrating his soul's marriage to Christ; if the deity appears as poet, singing of his compassion for humanity, Herrick will accompany the divine lyric. Such harmony between the individual soul and the Almighty constitutes the universal religious ideal. Note, however, that Herrick will have it on his own terms: the mode of the final couplet is conditional. That couplet will appear less presumptuous, however, when it is recalled that the poem is not so much a colloquy with God as an expression of desire for such a colloquy; it is also a kind of indirect spiritual self-portrait.

The Christian assurance that humankind is the continual recipient of such divine love and mercy is reiterated throughout *Noble Numbers* and helps to set that volume's tone. This is not to say that the converse—that humanity is also continually judged and punished by God—is absent: Herrick's seventh "Pious Piece," for example, is *"Gods Anger without Affection"* (N-7). It is followed within the space of a few pages by epigrams such as *"Affliction"* (N-10); *"Calling, and correcting"* (N-19)—"GOD is not onely mercifull, to call / Men to repent, but when He strikes withall"; *"No escaping the scourging"* (N-20); *"God has a twofold part"* (N-22), which involves making "His Children smart"; *"Persecutions profitable"* (N-24); and *"Whips"* (N-26)—"GOD has his whips here to a twofold end, / The bad to punish, and the good t'amend [make better]." Modern readers, accustomed to less rigorous versions of Christianity, may find a strain of religious masochism in such works, but as *"Whips"* implies, it follows from Original Sin that even "the good" require correction. Indeed, as one of the most extraordinary epigrams of *His Noble Numbers* puts it, *"Good men* [are] *afflicted most"* (N-108):

> GOD makes not good men wantons,* but doth bring
> Them to the field, and there to skirmishing;
> With trialls those, with terrors these He proves,
> And hazards those most, whom the most He loves:
> For *Sceva,* darts; for *Cocles,* dangers; thus
> He finds a fire for mighty *Mutius;*
> Death for stout *Cato;* and besides all these,
> A poyson too He has for *Socrates.*
>
> (ll. 1–8)

*layabouts

J. Max Patrick notes that all of the men Herrick lists are heroes of antiquity—Scaeva, a brave Roman centurion; Cocles, a defender of Rome; Mutius, who defied pain and death; Cato, a noble suicide; and, of course, the unjustly doomed philosopher Socrates (*CP,* 489n). All were brought to the test by God—and met it. All proved worthy combatants in life's warfare. "But bastard-slips [the unworthy]," the poem concludes, "and such as He dislikes, / He never brings them once to th'push of Pikes" (ll. 11–12); they remain spiritual "noncombatants." Like John Milton, Robert Herrick "cannot praise a fugitive and cloistered virtue . . . that never sallies out and sees her adversary" (*JM,* 728). Virtue must be active; it must be tested.

What is extraordinary and yet ultimately so Herrickean about these lines is, of course, that the "good men" given as examples are not Christian heroes but "virtuous pagans." None of this would be surprising if *"Good men af-flicted most"* were to be found in *Hesperides;* in *His Noble Numbers* the poem stands out as a reminder of Herrick's deep-seated Christian humanism. It also implicitly rebukes the intolerant Christian for whom nonbelievers can-not be "good men."

Although it is an illustration of Herrick's Christian realism to recognize that the good do suffer and for reasons, poems like *"To his ever-loving God"* (*N*-51) are more characteristic of Herrick's vision of the relationship be-tween God and humans. L. C. Martin has pointed out that this poem ech-oes several of Herrick's own works,[10] but the one that it most calls to mind is the poem from *Hesperides* discussed earlier in this chapter, *"On himselfe"* (*H*-306). The central metaphor of both is the quest or journey of life. In *"On himselfe"* this metaphor is couched in terms of a pilgrimage, but in *"To his ever-loving God"* it becomes simply that most familar means of travel in the seventeenth century, a journey on foot. In that time, as in life, such a form of travel was not easy:

> CAn I not come to Thee, My God, for* these
> So very-many-meeting hindrances,
> That slack my pace; but yet not make me stay?
> Who slowly goes, rids** (in the end) his way.
>
> **because of*
> ***expedites*

The question raised in lines 1–3 is answered by the homily of line 4: the ob-stacles that life puts between the individual and God may retard one's jour-ney to Him, but in matters of the spirit as of travel, "slow but sure" is the watchword. Only God, however, can insure progress, so his aid is invoked:

> Cleere Thou my paths, or shorten Thou my miles,
> Remove the barrs, or lift me o're the stiles:
> Since rough the way is, help me when I call,
> And take me up; or els prevent the fall.
>
> (ll. 5–8)

The assumption behind this prayer is of a personal god, one whose eye is on individual wayfarers and who, in mercy and love, will come to their aid. Concrete images of bars (to entrances) and stiles (steps over fences) lend a

rural English character and thus a kind of homely familiarity to the extended metaphor, as does the image of the traveler's final destination:

> I kenn my home; and it affords some ease,
> To see far off the smoaking Villages.
> Fain would I rest; yet covet not to die,
> For feare of future-biting penurie.
>
> (ll. 9–12)

The archaic verb "kenn," meaning "to catch sight of," reinforces the very
ordinariness and thus the universality toward which the poem builds. There
can scarcely be a more welcome feeling than at the first sight of home after a
long journey. The relief that is felt is enhanced by Herrick's image of humanity's celestial home, not as the Heavenly City but as a cluster of villages
whose smoking chimneys promise shelter, warmth, and light. For the reader
familiar with *Hesperides,* Herrick's image invokes the world of English pastoral to generate a fresh, indeed a unique, image of the Christian heaven.

The weary traveler, however, cannot yet rest—cannot die—because he
feels inadequate and impoverished: he believes that he has not been able to
lay up for himself sufficient treasures in heaven. Should he die in this condition, his spiritual future might be jeopardized. It is this, which translates
into his love of God rather than some un-Christian love of life, that impels
him to continue his journey: "No, no (my God) Thou knowst my wishes
be / to leave this life, not loving it, but Thee" (ll. 13–14). The intense apostrophe, "No, no (my God)," echoing as it does the negation of the opening
line, brings the poem full circle and reminds the reader that, although it
takes the form of an allegory, *"To his ever-loving God"* is also a colloquy between Everyman and his God. This poem's expression of the almost easy familiarity between Herrick and the Almighty when that relationship is at its
happiest is even more pronounced in one of the few relatively well-known
poems of *His Noble Numbers,* "A Thanksgiving to God, for his House"
(*N*-47).

Technically, *"A Thanksgiving"* is a kind of hymn, a celebration of God's
gifts; however, it lacks the stanzaic division of the typical hymn, being a catalog of blessings rather than a series of linked thoughts, and its metrical
pattern—couplets with one iambic tetrameter and one iambic dimeter
line—may make it almost unsingable. Nevertheless, out of these somewhat
unpromising materials Herrick creates a memorable vision of a distinctively
English, distinctively Christian, yet almost "Hesperidean" way of life:

> LOrd, Thou hast given me a cell
>   Wherein to dwell;
> And little house, whose humble Roof
>   Is weather-proof;
> Under the sparres of which I lie
>   Both soft, and drie;
> Where Thou my chamber for to ward
>   Hast set a Guard
> Of harmlesse thoughts, to watch and keep
>   Me, while I sleep.
>   (ll. 1–10)

Here the emphasis is threefold: on the humbleness of the speaker's situation, on the security and contentment it brings him, and on his indebtedness to God for it all. Beginning to emerge as well, in the allusion to the speaker's innocence, is another of Herrick's idealized self-portraits. In himself, he informs us, Christian humility is joined with a Roman sense of hospitality:

> Low is my porch, as is my Fate,
>   Both void of state;
> And yet the threshold of my doore
>   Is worn by'th poore,
> Who thither come, and freely get
>   Good words, or meat.
>   (ll. 11–16)

While poor people are rare in traditional pastoral, they are very much present in the Christian view of the human condition and in the poet's Hesperidean pastoral of rural England. As he redelineates this world in *"His Thanksgiving,"* Herrick also characterizes himself as one of its citizens: since he has already indicated that he is not gentry, it follows that he must be one who is obliged by his religion to succor the physically and spiritually needy. He does so despite the modesty of his circumstances: his parlor, hall, and kitchen are all "small"; his buttery or pantry, his bin for storing food, and even his loaves of bread are all "little." Only a few sticks make an adequate fire, "Close by whose living coale I sit, / And glow like it" (ll. 25–26). The image is one of the most appealing in Herrick's poetry: the warmth of the fire matched by the inner glow of a man at peace with himself and his God.

The final movement of *"A Thanksgiving"* reaffirms that all blessings come from God. Although the vegetables on Herrick's table are ordinary English produce—"Pulse" (peas and beans), "Worts" and "Purslain" (herbs), "Water-cresse," and "my beloved Beet"—their very variety suggests God's bounty. Moreover, they are "seasoned" by the poet's contented state of mind. Also leavening the loaf of this spiritualized Good Life is good cheer, and it too is God-sent:

> 'Tis thou that crown'st my glittering Hearth
> With guiltlesse mirth;
> And giv'st me Wassaile Bowles to drink,
> Spic'd to the brink.
> (ll. 37–40)

The passage is an implicit rebuke of Puritans and other abstemious Christians for whom pleasure seemingly can never be "guiltlesse," who fail to understand that strong drink is as much a gift of God as fertile land, "teeming" hens, "healthfull Ewes," and cows whose "conduits . . . Run Creame, (for Wine)" (l. 50). "All these, and better," Herrick concludes, God sends him, "to this end":

> That I should render, for my part,
> A thankfull heart;
> Which, fir'd with incense, I resigne,
> As wholly Thine;
> But the acceptance, that must be,
> My Christ, by Thee.
> (ll. 53–58)

The poem itself is, of course, a demonstration of the poet's "thankfull heart" as his inventory of God's blessings has been a demonstration of divine love. Such love is repaid by love, the gift of the only thing the worshiper has to give, his heart. The poem thus moves from receiving to giving, from the speaker's acceptance of what he needs to Christ's acceptance of what He desires.

Besides being a lesson in Christian gratitude, "*A Thanksgiving to God, for his House*" becomes an implied portrait of Herrick as rural resident and of marginal English country life in the seventeenth century—poetically enhanced, of course, but probably not by much: as mentioned above, "His House," the modest old parsonage at Dean Prior, still stands, and the Devonshire countryside that surrounds it is likely as pleasant—and almost as primitive—as it was in Herrick's day.

Holy Living and Holy Dying

Committed as Herrick is to a conception of a God of love and mercy, it is understandable that Christ, the traditional exemplar of these qualities, should figure importantly in *His Noble Numbers*. However, it is worth noting that of the 37 "Pious Pieces" that to some extent treat Christ, a majority of them deal with only two events in his life—the Nativity (eight poems, appearing mainly toward the beginning of the collection) and the Crucifixion (16 poems, appearing mainly toward its end). The remaining 13 tend to present Christ in abstract rather than in dramatic and poetic terms. What all this indicates about Herrick as Christian and as poet can only be conjectured.

For Christians both events certainly are highly dramatic demonstrations of God's love for and mercy toward humankind. And while other events in Christ's life are apt for poetic rendering, the Nativity and the Crucifixion are among the most visual and sensual—that is, capable of being imagined through the senses. Moreover, because the Nativity and the Crucifixion not only involve ceremony but have become incorporated into Christian ceremony they had to have been of special interest to a poet as fascinated with ritual as Robert Herrick. In fact, ceremonial elements figure significantly in a number of these poems—for example, "*A Christmas* Caroll, *sung to the King in the Presence at* White-Hall" (*N*-96).

This carol is evidence that Herrick did have an audience for his sacred verse and a distinguished one at that. (Four other devotional poems—*N*-17, *N*-97, *N*-102, and probably *N*-98—were also performed before the court.) Additional evidence that Herrick was not an unknown versifier is supplied by a footnote appended to the carol: "*The Musicall Part was composed by Master* Henry Lawes." Lawes, who wrote the music for Milton's *Comus* and was also a principal performer in that mask, was one of the most distinguished of the period's musicians, as Herrick himself confirms in "*To* M. Henry Lawes, *the excellent Composer of his Lyricks*" (*H*-851). And music does receive the emphasis in "*A Christmas* Caroll": it is a fairly elaborate production featuring four solo voices and a chorus and including a "*Flourish*" or brass fanfare. The chorus opens with a seven-line stanza proclaiming the purpose of the ritual and setting the celebratory mood:

> *Chor.* WHat sweeter musick can we bring,
> Then a Caroll, for to sing
> The Birth of this our heavenly King?
> Awake the Voice! Awake the String!

> Heart, Eare, and Eye, and every thing
> Awake! the while the active Finger
> Runs division with the Singer.

The great event itself is presented in mythic time, as if it has just occurred, collapsing the distant past into the lyrical present. The theme is that of awakening from the long sleep of the Old Dispensation and paganism into a new world of light and life. The unique but unobtrusive prosody of the stanza bears witness to Herrick's craftsmanship: its first five lines, mainly in iambic tetrameter, constitute a quintet, all featuring the same masculine rhyme, whereas the two final lines comprise a distich with feminine rhymes. Moreover, "Finger" and "Singer" happen to possess initial morphemes that rhyme with the masculine rhyme of the quintet. Although the remainder of the carol is less metrically complex, it does feature couplets, tercets, and a quatrain in varying arrangements.

The choral introduction is followed by the flourish and three solos, the first two of which are tercets on a theme also developed in Milton's "Nativity Ode"—that the sacred birth brought not only peace on earth and good will to men but a transformation of the order of nature: night becomes day, winter becomes spring:

> 1. Dark and dull night, flie hence away,
>   And give the Honour to this Day
>   That sees *December* turn'd to *May*.

By transforming the month that marks the death of the year and the dead of winter into May, the month of the rebirth of the natural world and human vitality, the Nativity actually accomplishes what the myth of pastoral has always promised—to create a springtime world. The second soloist, not understanding this, asks why "all things here / Seem like the Spring-time of the yeere?" (ll. 12–13). This question is reiterated by the third soloist, in lines in which Judea and the English countryside meet in the fragrance of a pastoral image, and its answer is finally supplied by the fourth soloist:

> 3. Why do's the chilling Winters morne
>   Smile, like a field beset with corne?
>   Or smell, like to a Meade new-shorne,
>   Thus, on the sudden? 4. Come and see
>   The cause, why things thus fragrant be:
>   'Tis he is borne, whose quickning Birth

> Gives life and luster, publike mirth,
> To Heaven, and the under-Earth.

The fallen world is transfigured because the birth of Christ is "quickning," giving life and light and joy to the dying year and an "under-Earth" that has been in decline since the Fall of Man.

The reaction of humankind, represented by the singers, to this cosmic event constitutes the carol's closing movement:

> *Chor.* We see Him come, and know him ours,
> Who, with his Sun-shine, and His showers,
> Turnes all the patient ground to flowers.
>
> 1. The Darling of the world is come,
>   And fit it is, we finde a roome
>   To welcome Him. 2. The nobler part
>   Of all the house here, is the heart,
>
> *Chor.* Which we will give Him; and bequeath
> This Hollie, and this Ivie Wreath,
> To do Him honour; who's our King,
> And Lord of all this Revelling.

Christ is the God of nature whose sun/son-shine and showers, love and mercy, transform earth into a new Eden, a Christianized "*Sacred Grove.*" But the Son has come primarily to renew humankind, not all nature. The irony that the world affords no room for its "Darling" is resolved in terms of the familiar metaphor of the human body as the temple of the holy spirit, whose most fitting chamber for Christ's dwelling place is the heart. The metaphor also reinforces the ambiance of mythic time, conveying the sense of a Christ who is alive now as he was then because he lives in the *sancta sanctorum* of the human heart. Therefore the singers enthrone him in their surrendered hearts and mark his new reign by tendering him the traditional Christmas plants, the holly and the ivy. That Christ is king over all human-kind is also traditional; that he is the Master of the Revels of his own birth-day is distinctively Herrickean, the poet's affirmation of not only the proper joy of Christmas but of the joy of Christianity in an age in which Christmas itself would be banned, and joy and religion could be deemed antithetical.

In sharp contrast to the lyrical mood and tone of "*A Christmas* Caroll" is the dramatic ode, "*Good Friday:* Rex Tragicus, *or Christ going to His Crosse*" (N-263). The latter is the first of a series of nine poems with which Herrick

brings *His Noble Numbers* to a dramatic conclusion. These poems make up
what Robert Deming has called "Herrick's Passion play," possibly based on
the poet's "own observations of Christmas pageants in rural dramatic pres-
entations" (76). In "*Good Friday*" the king of comedy, master of the Christmas festivities of "*A Christmas* Caroll," becomes a tragic king—chief actor
in the drama of his own fall. It is doubtless no coincidence that this is one of
Herrick's rare "*Pious Pieces*" written in iambic pentameter, the standard
meter for serious English verse drama.

"*Good Friday*" is complexly theatrical: its subject, Christ's passion, is inherently dramatic; it is perceived and presented by the poem's speaker in
theatrical terms (e.g., Christ as tragic hero); and the speaker himself, with
whose mental state the reader is to identify, is both actor and audience, an
unwilling party to and observer of the tragic action. The poem as a whole
consists of an internal apostrophe addressed to Christ by one who is pre-
sumed to be a faithful follower and present at the event. Because he perceives the situation in terms of drama, the speaker in a sense becomes the
tragedy's imagined director or stage manager:

> PUt off Thy Robe of *Purple,* then go on
> To the sad place of execution:
> Thine houre is come; and the Tormentor stands
> Ready, to pierce Thy tender Feet, and Hands.
>
> (ll. 1–4)

Because it is intended to mock the King of Kings as King of the Jews, the
robe of majesty is to be removed so that the drama's final act can be played
out. The audience, the brutish masses, and the bit players have grown bored
or surly by the delaying of their "entertainment":

> Long before this, the base, the dull, the rude,
> Th'inconstant, and unpurg'd Multitude
> Yawne for Thy coming; some e're this time crie,
> How He deferres, how loath He is to die!
> Amongst this scumme, the Souldier, with his speare,
> And that sowre Fellow, with his vinegar,
> His *spunge,* and *stick,* do ask why Thou dost stay?
>
> (ll. 5–11)

The mood here is complicated. On the one hand, Herrick makes use of dramatic irony to intensify the emotional atmosphere: the reader knows what

the Roman with the spear will do, for example, although the soldier himself as yet does not. At the same time, like a Breughel painting, the scene is highly realistic, not only in its employment of historical details but in its satirically accurate evocation of the members of the crowd, with their brief attention spans and their flair for cruel banter. Even the speaker himself is not above punning on the character of the sadist who will give Christ vinegar for water. Such dark humor clashes with and thus intensifies the horror of the action and calls attention to its ultimate absurdity.

The speaker–stage manager then returns his focus to the "guiltlesse man" whose arrival, not as a common thief but "like a Person of some high account," will mollify the restless audience:

> The *Crosse* shall be Thy *Stage;* and Thou shalt there
> The spacious field have for Thy *Theater.*
> Thou art that *Roscius,* and that markt-out man,
> That must this day act the Tragedian.
>
> (ll. 17–20)

Like the pity and fear Aristotle theorized were the fundamental responses to tragedy, the effects of this enactment will be, we are told, "wonder and affrightment" (l. 21). Herrick's blunt metaphors set the stark scene. The "star" of this play-within-a-poem—its Roscius (a tragic actor)—will be Christ, "Whom all the flux of Nations comes to see" (l. 23). The two condemned thieves are mere supernumeraries; its protagonist is at the heart of this drama: "this Scene from Thee takes life and sense, / And soule and spirit[,] plot, and excellence" (ll. 26–27).

These "stage directions" to the most notable of all tragedies conclude with the speaker's ironic exhortation to raise the curtain: "Why then begin, great King! ascend Thy Throne / And thence proceed, to act Thy Passion" (ll. 28–29). Christ is urged to give such a performance as will stun "Hell, and Earth, and Heav'n" and cause even "those, who see Thee nail'd unto the tree," the scornful mob, to "praise and pitie Thee" (ll. 34–35). In response to the operations of the "Lawes of Action"—on one level the principles of tragic acting, on another the divine providence that ordained this tragedy—Christ's followers will undergo catharsis, will "both sigh, and weep." They will then act out the ritual of the tragic denouement by seeing to it that its protagonist has been embalmed and then "sweetly buried" (ll. 38–39). No mention, of course, is made of the Resurrection, which will transform this tragedy into a divine comedy of cosmic proportions.

Ode, apostrophe, soliloquy—"*Good Friday*" manages, for all of its theatrics and its theatrical subject, to open Herrick's "Passion Play" series on a powerful, somber note. Since the persona can hardly be construed as actually speaking aloud to Christ at this point in the historical action, the poem may be most appropriately read as an interior monologue. Its long-range purpose is, like "*A Christmas* Caroll," to draw readers into mythic time, where, through Herrick's persona they become witnesses to the Passion and thus learn about its implications for themselves through vicarious experience. Claude J. Summers has suggested yet another purpose, as "a prophetic warning of the fate that threatens the 'player-King,' as Milton would later characterize Charles I." Summers argues that the poem's "surface text" in fact "ill-conceals" an anticipation of Charles's demise that translates the latter's execution into a martyrdom.[11] What Herrick's point would be in writing a poem predicting the martyring of a sitting monarch, to whom several celebratory poems are addressed and to whose successor the entire collection had been dedicated, is not clear. Such a poem could be viewed as at best insensitive, at worst seditious, neither of which Robert Herrick was. Certainly internal evidence that would warrant such a reading is slender, and the poem could well have been written long before the possibility of executing Charles I began to be publicly bruited about.

The success of "*Good Friday*" is due in large measure to the vividness and originality with which Herrick re-creates a familiar event from the life of Christ. The effect of making the poem's speaker a part of the scene he contemplates is to bring readers, as they share the speaker's thoughts, into that scene as well. Seventeenth-century readers, in fact, would be accustomed to such a process because it was integral to a popular religious exercise of the time, the formal meditation. To perform this exercise meditators attempt to visualize some event of religious import to the extent that they seem actually to be experiencing it; they then try to understand the spiritual significance of this "experience"; and, finally, they initiate a conversation with God on the basis of what they have come to understand. First formulated by St. Ignatius Loyola, the formal meditation had, according to Louis L. Martz, gained such currency in England by the end of the sixteenth century that it would significantly influence the devotional poetry of John Donne and his disciples.[12]

Although Herrick obviously is much more a Son of Ben than a metaphysical poet, at least one poem in addition to "*Good Friday*" stands as evidence that he seems to have been aware of the meditative tradition, its practices, and its uses for poetry—"*His Meditation upon Death*" (N-230). Despite its title and its opening lines, however, "*His Meditation*" is more a poem *about* meditation than it is an actual meditation itself.[13] It opens with

Herrick imagining himself on his own death bed or at least in the last stage
of his life: "BE those few hours, which I have yet to spend, / Blest with the
Meditation of my end." Concentrating on one's future death as an aid to
holy living as well as to holy dying was common meditative practice. What
should follow this announcement of the meditator's subject is the first formal stage of the exercise, "the composition of place." Here the event to be
focused on is so envisioned—"composed" in one's imagination—that it is as
if it were actually taking place (like Christ's Passion in *"Good Friday"*).
Herrick, however, begins to philosophize about the correlation between a
long life and the good life:

> Though they be few in number, I'm content;
> If otherwise, I stand indifferent:
> Nor makes it matter, *Nestors* yeers to tell,*
> A multitude of dayes still heaped on,
> Seldome brings order, but confusion.
> Might I make choice, long life sho'd be with-stood;
> Nor wo'd I care how short it were, if good:
> Which to effect, let ev'ry passing Bell
> Possesse my thoughts, next comes my dolefull knell.
>
> (ll. 10–12)

*metaphorically, to grow old

This, of course, is a Herrick we have encountered before. The serious neo-
Epicurean who faces the brevity of human existence with equanimity, who
cares more for the quality of his life than its length, is a familiar figure from
Hesperides. But here there is an important difference: instead of responding
to death by affirming life, this Herrick vows to meditate upon his own
death each time he hears the melancholy tolling of the funeral bell, a bell
that he, like John Donne in his familiar seventeenth meditation, imagines is
tolling for himself. And if that is not enough, Herrick will also meditate
upon his death when he retires to bed each night:

> And when the night perswades me to my bed,
> I'le thinke I'm going to be buried:
> So shall the Blankets which come over me,
> Present those Turfs, which must cover me:
> And with as firme behaviour I will meet
> The sheet I sleep in, as my Winding-sheet.
>
> (ll. 13–18)

Here Herrick contemplates how he will effect a "composition of place." Typically, he employs whatever props are available as aids to the imagination: thus his blankets become the earth that will cover his grave and his bedsheet the cloth that customarily was wound about the corpse. To the modern reader, systematically envisioning one's bed as a grave may appear less pious than morbid, but in the seventeenth century such exercises were regarded as being conducive to "firme behaviour"—to confronting the fact of death with Christian-Stoic poise.

Herrick envisions the crisis of his dramatic "composition of place" as his falling asleep (dying) and its climax as his awakening (resurrection) and appearance at "that *Gen'rall Doome*, / To which the Pesant, so the Prince must come" (ll. 23–24), the Last Judgment. Then mere remorse will be futile: "Teares, at that day, shall make but weake defence; / When Hell and Horrour fright the Conscience" (ll. 27–28). Such images are less powerful than those of "*Good Friday*" because Herrick has in effect subverted the process of "the composition of place": by describing rather than dramatically re-creating his "composition" he puts himself (and the reader) at two removes from the religious experience. Moreover, in this much modified meditation, as Robert Deming has pointed out (105–6), there is no formal second stage, in which the meditator attempts to come to grips with the vicarious experience previously created. Rather, he moves immediately to the third stage, the colloquy, where he vows to reform himself: "Let me, though late, yet at the last begin / To shun the least Temptation to a sin" (ll. 29–30). The colloquy is usually an imagined conversation with God, but it can, as here, take the form of a dialogue with the self (Martz, 37). His holy living, Herrick trusts, will ensure his being "safe in death": he will undergo transfiguration, "rise triumphant in [his] Funerall" (l. 36).

Although, as we have seen, Herrick writes a great deal about death— death in the abstract, the deaths of others, even his own death—it is ironic that when he endeavors imaginatively to "experience" his own end, he backs away from it. In psychological terms he erects a defense against his mortality by distancing it, projecting it "outside" himself.

This sort of pattern is, with variations, repeated in another well-known poem from *His Noble Numbers*, "*His Letanie, to the Holy Spirit*" (N-41). But whereas "*His Meditation*" describes a projected "composition of place," initially at least "*His Letanie*" dramatically envisions the deathbed scene:

> 1. IN the houre of my distresse,
>   When temptations me oppresse,

And when I my sins confesse,
> Sweet Spirit comfort me!

2. When I lie within my bed,
> Sick in heart, and sick in head,
> And with doubts discomforted,
>> Sweet Spirit comfort me!

The adverb "When," which begins all but the first stanza, to some extent undercuts the poem's immediacy by projecting the event into the future. Despite this rhetorical distancing, however, Herrick's images, like this one of the dying man afraid to close his eyes in sleep, can still be affecting:

3. When the house doth sigh and weep,
> And the world is drown'd in sleep,
> Yet mine eyes the watch do keep;
>> Sweet Spirit comfort me!

Herrick also transforms his serious poem into black comedy with deathbed humor, pointed satire on "artlesse" (unskillful) physicians who think only of their fees and whose "cures' only kill (stanzas 4–5), as well as on insincere "comforters":

7. When the tapers now burne blew,
> And the comforters are few,
> And that number more then true;
>> Sweet Spirit comfort me!

At the same time the illusion of physical realism is maintained through such details as the blue flame of the dwindling candle and the dying man being forced to nod in response to the last rites, "'Cause my speech is now decaid" (stanza 8). There is also the psychological realism of the speaker being mentally "tost about; Either with despaire, or doubt" (stanza 9), and in his terrifying visions of Satan and of hell, "When the flames and hellish cries / Fright mine eares, and fright mine eyes," and of Judgment Day (stanzas 10–12). Even projected into some dim future, Herrick's images possess a cumulative power, taking the speaker (and the reader) from the dying man's ritual confession of sin to the terror and uncertainty of his final moments. As in *"His Meditation,"* no analytical stage interrupts the speaker's outpourings. There is no formal colloquy either, only the prayerful refrain that concludes each stanza, "Sweet Spirit comfort me!"

There is little reason to doubt that a poet of Herrick's skill was capable of composing a conventional meditative poem if he chose. Perhaps "*His Meditation*" and "*His Letanie*" are experiments in a devotional form that turned out to be too constraining to his talents. On the other hand, even the verse meditations of John Donne and George Herbert are seldom as strictly patterned as Donne's own prose meditations, *Devotions upon Emergent Occasions* (1624). Donne, of course, composed the latter after he had actually undergone a near fatal illness. But Robert Herrick was healthy enough to live a quarter century or more after he had written his modified meditations upon death: that he may have attempted them then more as exercises than as re-creations of personal experience may help explain their elusiveness. The elusive quality of Herrick's vision of the afterlife in "*The white Island: or place of the Blest*" (N-128), however, is even more difficult to explain.

The image of heaven as a white island appears to be original with Herrick, so readers come to it devoid of associations. The pleasant landscape of "smoking Villages" in "*To his ever-loving God*" (N-51) bears at least a distant relationship to the heavenly city of Christian tradition, but what does the image of a white island convey? Purity and innocence, of course, but little warmth; security, perhaps, but also isolation. Fortunately, the poem's first stanza clarifies Herrick's controlling metaphor—worlds are islands:

> IN this world (the *Isle of Dreames*)
> While we sit by sorrowes streames,
> Teares and terrors are our theames
>   Reciting.
>   (ll. 1–4)

The seventeenth-century reader, accustomed to thinking of "this world" as a vale of tears, might have been less likely than modern readers to be disconcerted by the idea that reality is unreal, a dream world that, as in the legend of Plato's cave, is merely a shadow of another reality—in this case, Hades, or even hell. Nevertheless, Herrick's vision is surprisingly grim for the poet of *Hesperides,* which he himself associates with the green and pleasant British Isles. It is grim too for the composer of that poem of spiritual contentment, the previously discussed "*A Thanksgiving to God for his house.*"

What Herrick's image of this world as nightmare does accomplish is to make death seem a welcome release:

> But when once from hence we flie,
> More and more approaching nigh
> Unto young Eternitie
>   Uniting:
>
> In that *whiter Island,* where
> Things are evermore sincere;
> Candor here, and lustre there
>   Delighting.
>   (ll. 5–12)

An exhilarating sense of flight, of soaring upward, transforms the mood and makes it positive, as does the whimsy of "young Eternitie" ("young," because eternity transcends the force that ages, time). What we are flying to, however, remains somewhat abstract: on the white island "things" are true, pure; there we find pleasure in "candor"—"brilliant whiteness"? "purity"? "justice"? "kindliness"? (*OED*) all of the above?—and "lustre"—"refulgence"? "luminosity"? "glory"? (*OED*). It is all very positive but vague, lacking shape and substance, and somehow not especially real (like Milton's heaven in Book 3 of *Paradise Lost*). Still, the contrast with this world, one that seems to be the fearful product of our fallen imaginations, is marked:

> There no monstrous fancies shall
> Out of hell an horrour call,
> To create (or cause at all)
>   Affrighting.
>   (ll. 13–16)

Sin, like Macbeth, murders sleep, making nightmares. The "Blest," having transcended sin and labor, have no need of sleep. Eternal vigilance seems to be the price of heaven, but it is vigilance over immortal pleasures:

> There in calm and cooling sleep
> We our eyes shall never steep;
> But eternal watch shall keep,
>   Attending
>
> Pleasures, such as shall pursue
> Me immortaliz'd, and you;

And fresh joyes, as never too
Have ending.
(ll. 17–24)

Herrick's fifth stanza self-destructs: sleep is "calm and cooling," but the blessed sleep no more. Logically it is possible to accept eternal insomnia in heaven—where there is no labor, no fatigue, rest is superfluous—but emotionally the idea of perpetual wakefulness, even to enjoy perpetual bliss, is problematical. (Milton recognized the problem: in the heaven of *Paradise Lost* there is night and angels do rest.) Compounding such difficulties are the abstractions of the last stanza: what are heaven's "Pleasures" and "fresh joyes," one wonders, and in what sense might they "pursue" the blessed?

"*The white Island*" does not so much conclude as stop, as if Herrick's heart is not in it. What is missing are the vivacity and concreteness with which he recounts the pleasures of the pastoral world in *Hesperides* and the quiet joys of his country life elsewhere in *Noble Numbers*. Indeed, because of the way in which he has developed this poem he is forced to renounce the concrete for the abstract, the sensuous for the spiritual, the "*Sacred Grove*" for the "*white Island*." It could be argued that such is the logic of Christian doctrine, which has always been more vague on the subject of heaven than on that of hell, that "*The white Island*" is the result of the same kinds of artistic choices Milton made in book 3 of *Paradise Lost*. Or it might be conjectured that a poet like Herrick, whose inclination is to affirm life, may have felt considerable anxiety about death and life after death, devout Christian though he was. Some of that anxiety, then, may find unconscious expression in the peculiarities of "*The white Island*." Unconscious avoidance of the question of the afterlife may also be why so much of *His Noble Numbers* is devoted to the celebration of holy days, to the pleasures and the hardships of the Christian life, to understanding God and the relationship between God and humans, and to establishing a positive and personal relationship with God in the here and now rather than in the sweet by-and-by. Herrick's mind, his imagination, and his art are finally and essentially oriented to this world, to this life.

This is not to suggest that, as has been charged, Herrick as a devotional poet merely glosses over his fundamental paganism with a thin veneer of ritual (Press, 30–35). As this chapter has indicated, and as the studies of DeNeef and Deming have demonstrated, for Herrick ritual is feeling as well as form, meaning and purpose, a fundamental way of expressing secular as well as spiritual experience. Because ritual seems to shape his imagination and his art as much as personal experience, it does not follow that his poetry or his Christianity will seem less authentic or will be less affecting for readers than the art and the religion of Donne, say, or Herbert. Nor does it follow that because Herrick's sensibility found pagan art and thought congenial, and because he (as much as any poet of his age) was able to synthesize an ancient Mediterranean world-view and a seventeenth-century English one, the result must be a dilution and a diminution of his Christianity and his Christian verse. That the Christian humanism which is so much admired in poets like Milton is cause for reservations about a poet like Herrick may well say more about the biases of his critics than it says about Herrick's poetry.

Finally, it is worth reiterating that, regardless of the problematical arrangement of his book of poems, Herrick is one poet, not two—not a secular poet and a devotional poet, not a genius and a hack. The conspicuous presence of effective and essentially religious poems in *Hesperides* and of the Stoic and Epicurean motifs and classical elements in *His Noble Numbers* lend unity, continuity, coherence, and intellectual and emotional richness to his magnum opus. There is no reason to doubt that Herrick took his religion as seriously as he took his art—if less reason to care. This chapter has attempted to show that he is capable of making art—affecting, meaningful, and memorable art—of his religion; as he announces toward the end of *Noble Numbers:*

> THe work is done; now let my *Lawrell* be
> Given by none, but by Thy selfe, to me:
> That done, with Honour Thou dost me create
> Thy *Poet,* and thy *Prophet Lawreat.*
> (*To God* [N-262])

George Herbert could have not hoped for more, although he would not have been so presumptuous as to express it. Herrick, typically, is straightforward: throughout his book he has been searching for someone to dub him "Poet"—and make it stick. He has found Him, and, as Milton came to understand, as God is a poet, to be God's poet is to be a prophet, to give expression to God's word.

Chapter Six

"The Pillar of Fame" and "This Sacred Grove": Themes of Poetry, Poets, and Immortality

The year 1648 was not the best of times for Robert Herrick to publish a book of poems, much less a book consisting chiefly of pastoral, amatory, epigrammatic, and devotional pieces. He had been expelled from his vicarage for his Royalist sympathies a year earlier and the Royalist cause was all but lost. Charles I, whom *Hesperides* celebrates, would be executed in January of 1649. Herrick's timing, along with some careless readings of his book, led to an earlier critical view that he was a poet so absorbed by his world of art that he was unaware of the real world around him turned upside down by the Civil War. This view, in which Herrick becomes a kind of unworldly late Elizabethan, and *Hesperides* a literary anachronism, has now, fortunately, been discredited.

Far from regressing to a mythic "merrie Englande," Herrick's poetry mediates between "the drooping West" (the war-torn West Country)—the world as it is—and the "*Sacred Grove*"—the world as it can be. The involvement of *Hesperides* in history has been amply demonstrated by such scholarship as Leah Marcus's study of anti-Puritanism in Herrick's pastorals, Ann Coiro's analyses of his poems occasioned by the Civil War, and Claude J. Summers's examination of reflections in *Hesperides* of the political tensions of the time.[1] Specifically, the careful reader will find, interspersed among love poems and serious or scurrilous epigrams and bucolics, occasional verses on the political and martial fortunes of King Charles, on specific wartime events, and on heroes fallen in the Royalist cause.[2]

Herrick's awareness of and concerns about the turbulent times are also demonstrated in apparently less topical poems. "*The bad season makes the Poet sad*" (*H*-612), for example, is a complex hybrid—half occasional and specific, half general and ambiguous. The ambiguity begins with the title: in what sense is the season "bad," the reader wonders, and for that matter what is mean by "season"? Clarification does not come with the first couplet, which admits to at least three levels of interpretation: I am, says Herrick, "DUll to my selfe, and almost dead to these / My many fresh and fragrant Mistresses." Triggered by the alliterating "DUll" and "dead," the tone seems to be that of a love complaint. Read in the specific context of *Hesperides,* however, the "Mistresses" may not be flesh-and-blood women but the possibly fictional Julias and Corinnas of the love poems, or they may even be those poems themselves. In either event *"The bad season"* would appear to be about poetry, not passion. The next two couplets seem to confirm as much:

> Lost to all Musick now; since every thing
> Puts on the semblance here of sorrowing.
> Sick is the Land to'th'heart; and doth endure
> More dangerous faintings by her desp'rate cure.
>
> (ll. 3–6)

Here England has become Herrick's foremost mistress. Her heartsickness is the political and religious conflicts of the time and her swooning is a consequence of the insult to her body politic brought on by the battles between the Royalists and the Parliamentarians. The Civil War is the "bad season," and it has not only depressed Herrick but ruined him for poetry itself (his "Musick").

The situation thus set, the poem's second movement expresses a desperate hope for the future through an invocation of the past, a cry for a return to the idyll of the prewar era:

> But if that golden Age wo'd come again,
> And *Charles* here Rule, as he before did Raign;
> If smooth and unperplext the Seasons were,
> As when the *Sweet Maria* lived here:
> I sho'd delight to have my Curles halfe drown'd
> In *Tyrian Dewes,* and Head with Roses crown'd.
> And once more yet (ere I am laid out dead)
> *Knock at a Starre with my exalted Head.*
>
> (ll. 7–14)

Here historical reality is framed in terms of art. Herrick hopes for the stabilization of the monarchy, with the King's authority no longer challenged and once again appropriately exercised. With such a change in the political weather the world of the "*Sacred Grove,*" over which Charles and his queen used to preside, would become repastoralized; moreover, the poet, no longer "sad," would be able to recapture his former Anacreontic spirit and once more enjoy the kind of life in which his poetry flowed, and in which his apotheosis, his achievement of literary fame, seemed more assured. Herrick's political bias, of course, is evident in these verses' nostalgia for the prewar years (although that nostalgia is not, it should be noted, expressed at the Puritans' expense). Located midway through *Hesperides*, "*The bad season*" reminds us that Herrick is merely human, a political being whose songs have been performed for royalty, whose spirits are, like ours, affected by current events, and whose creativity depends on more than his muse.

In "*Farwell Frost, or welcome the Spring*" (H-642), another partial allegory, Herrick's pastoralism again mediates between art and life and demonstrates their symbiotic relationship. In this poem, also located near *Hesperides'* midpoint but several pages after "*The bad season*," the latter's fond hopes are brought into focus: winter is over and, given the cyclical nature of things, the winter of England's political discontent must likewise come to an end. Herrick's political intent, however, is not apparent at the start of this poem: it appears to be a conventional spring song, couched in the luxuriantly artificial rhetoric of traditional bucolics:

> FLed are the Frosts, and now the Fields appeare
> Re-cloth'd in fresh and verdant Diaper.*
> Thaw'd are the snowes, and now the lusty Spring
> Gives to each Mead a neat enamelling.
> The Palmes put forth their Gemmes, and every Tree
> Now swaggers in her Leavy gallantry.**
> The while the *Daulian Minstrell*† sings
> With warbling Notes, her *Tyrrean* sufferings.
>
> (ll. 5–8)

> *damask
> **finery
> †nightingale

Palm trees and classical nightingales seem to locate the poem at a far remove from the realities of English country life. All that we appear to have here is a fanciful personification of a seasonal change: acting as landscape painter, spring transforms the brown meadows into bright green, and trees, like young maids, deck themselves in leafy finery.

With the second stage of the allegory, however, a gradual unpacking of its political meaning begins to take place:

> What gentle Winds perspire? As if here
> Never had been the *Northern Plunderer*
> To strip the Trees, and Fields, to their distresse,
> Leaving them to a pittied nakednesse.
> And look how when a frantick Storme doth tear
> A stubborn Oake, or Holme* (long growing there)
> But lul'd to calmnesse, then succeeds a breeze
> That scarcely stirs the nodding leaves of Trees.
>
> (ll. 9–16)

*type of oak

The "*Northern Plunderer*" is literally the north wind, which in winter commits rape upon green and growing nature, but figuratively it is the Parliamentary forces that have been devastating England. (Some of the monarchy's strongest opposition came from the north, particularly Scotland.) The oak is possibly a symbol of Charles I himself, around whom the storm of civil war has raged.

With the next line it becomes clear that the structure of the poem has been that of an extended simile:

> So when this War (which tempest-like doth spoil
> Our salt, our Corn, our Honie, Wine, and Oil)
> Falls to a temper, and doth mildly cast
> His inconsistent Frenzie off (at last)
> The gentle Dove may, when these turmoils cease,
> Bring in her Bill, once more, *the Branch of Peace*.
>
> (ll. 17–22)

The state of the nation has been Herrick's true subject all along. Wine and oil are not English products; their presence here is the poet's way of suggesting that before war came his country was a kind of Arcadia, a tropical paradise. Civil war itself is characterized as an aberration, a sickness in the body politic that, in the natural course of things, must give way to health again. The effect of the figure is to take some of the onus (earlier established) off the Roundheads, for a sickness is not necessarily someone's fault. Thus a poem that appears to be developing into political propaganda concludes on a note that is, if not conciliatory, at least somewhat tolerant and optimistic: peace is possible, in our time. According to Achsah Guibbory, Herrick's concept of history is cyclical. Thus "*Farwell Frost*" expresses his sense that

History is essentially an extension of nature in the realm of human affairs, exemplifying the same cyclical pattern as the seasons. Consequently, the Civil War is not for Herrick an example of chaotic disorder, but rather part of the natural order. (143)

It is a conception natural to a classicist and pastoral poet, an attempt to dally with surmise, false or true, by imposing an artistic vision upon the facts of life.

Art as Response

That Herrick's Hesperidean vision did not blind him to English reality is further demonstrated in two poems about rural Devonshire, where he spent 33 years as poet and priest. As noted in chapter 3, the autobiographical "*Discontents in Devon*" (*H*-51) bitterly proclaims the frustrations of living in the West Country in its first quatrain; then, in its second, Herrick ruefully acknowledges that his bucolically induced unhappiness and boredom paradoxically enough seem to stimulate his creativity, enabling him to compose "Ennobled numbers for the Presse" (l. 7). "Ennobled numbers," a phrase Herrick may have recalled when he came to give a title to his devotional collection, here simply means "good poetry." After he has proclaimed himself a pastoral poet in the series of verses that introduces *Hesperides,* this bemused antipastoral, placed early in the collection and before any of his celebrated bucolics, comes as something of a surprise. It serves notice that Herrick can be a realist as well as a romantic pastoralist, capable of looking critically and analytically at his world, his art, and himself.

Much later in *Hesperides,* a poem entitled "*His Lachrimae, or Mirth, turn'd to mourning*" (*H*-371) has Herrick taking a different tack. Here he complains that he has lost his "mirth," his vivacity, since he has been sent to Devonshire; moreover,

2.   Before I went
         To banishment
     Into the loathed West;
         I co'd rehearse
         A Lyrick verse
     And speak it with the best.

"Banishment" was a Roman punishment, and Herrick's Rome was London, his birthplace. He and others have reported that Ben Jonson used to hold dinner parties in London taverns where, amid hearty eating and drinking, he and his "sons" would recite their poetry to each other. In the West Country, Herrick grumbles, he is far removed from such sources of inspiration. Those who have been dutifully reading their way through *Hesperides* may recognize that this poem appears to contradict "*Discontents in Devon.*" Such a contradiction may, however, remind us that poets can be as baffled as anyone by the mystery of their own creativity and by the question of the relationship between that creativity and their life situations. The kind of self-consciousness about himself as artist and about the tension between his art and his life Herrick exhibits here and elsewhere, commonplace in modern poets, is unusual for the seventeenth century; it further distinguishes the "unifying personality" of *Hesperides* and helps to ground its world of art in the realm of psychological as well as physical reality.

As has been suggested earlier, Herrick's pastoralism is a principal way in which he mediates between "the loathed West" and the "*Sacred Grove,*" between a sometimes unsatisfactory existence and one ameliorated by art. But mediation is a two-way street: if art can improve on reality, reality can also modify art, as Herrick illustrates in two paired poems, "*The meddow verse or Aniversary to Mistris* Bridget Lowman" (*H*-354A) and "*The parting verse, the feast there ended*" (*H*-355). Bridget Lowman's uncle and aunt, Sir Edward and Lady Giles, are buried in Herrick's church, and on their tomb is engraved an epitaph almost certainly written by the poet (*H*-354B). There is no reason to doubt that the Mayday festival which both poems ritually frame actually took place. "*The meddow verse*" constitutes a ceremony of welcome, extended to Bridget as May Queen. Its opening is reminiscent of a better known Herrickean May Day poem, "Corinna's *going a-Maying*":

> COme with the Spring-time, forth Fair Maid, and be
> This year again, the *medows Deity.*
> Yet ere ye enter, give us leave to set
> Upon your Head this flowry Coronet.
>
> (ll. 1–4)

"*The meddow verse*" is also an anniversary poem because Bridget has been the "Princesse of the Feast" before ("This year again"). The sign of her office is the crown of flowers Herrick places on her head or perhaps the "flowery Coronet" of the poem itself. Her presence and the holiday transform the Devonshire countryside, he says, into a "Fairie land," by folk tradition (and literary tradition) a higher reality. The poem ends with a priestly blessing and the hint of an admonition: "Full mirth wait on you; and such mirth as shall / Cherrish the cheek, but make none blush at all" (ll. 11–12). Herrick has a knack for making one word, judiciously chosen and placed, do multiple duty. The good humor in the pun of "Cherrish," for example, makes the finger-wagging that follows less magisterial than avuncular: "Have the kind of fun that will caress your cheeks by making them cherry-red, but not the kind that would cause embarrassment." Even in "Fairie land" proprieties are to be observed.

The mood is altered from allegro to penseroso in "*The parting verse.*" The May Day revels now are ended:

> LOth to depart, but yet at last, each one
> Back must now go to's habitation:
> Not knowing thus much, when we once do sever,
> Whether or no, that we shall meet here ever.
>
> (ll. 1–4)

The lines are prosaic, but they capture the inevitable note of melancholy implicit in "The party's over—time to go home—how about next year?" "Fairie land" does not last forever, and poets age:

> As for my self, since time a thousand cares
> And griefs hath fil'de upon my silver hairs;
> 'Tis to be doubted whether I next yeer,
> Or no, shall give ye a re-meeting here.
> If die I must then my last vow shall be,
> You'l with a tear or two, remember me,
> Your sometime Poet. . . .
>
> (ll. 5–11)

Holidays are paradoxical: their pleasures are reminders of the pains of everyday existence; their recurrence is a reminder of life's transiency. But the plea to Mistress Lowman to remember him whose poetry commemorated her nudges Herrick out of his mood of self-pity before his address can become merely maudlin:

> but if fates do give
> Me longer date, and more fresh springs to live:
> Oft as your field, shall her old age renew,
> *Herrick* shall make the meddow-verse for you.
>
> (ll. 11–14)

Bridget's "sometime Poet" has recovered his wonted Stoicism and the tentative optimism that comes from his sense of the cyclical nature of things. Nature is renewed, so there may be hope for aging poets. In any case, the paired poems imply a kind of transcendence for those involved: Bridget Lowman and Robert Herrick are both named in them.

Herrick refers to himself by name in his verse more than any other important poet. The practice might seem merely narcissistic, except that this self-naming is seldom as self-glorifying as Jonson's, for example. Nor is it merely autobiographical, for such references are seldom very revealing. The most appropriate term for Herrick's practice is "self-reflexivity," and it grounds his collection in space and time, in the sense of the material reality of a person's life, even though neither that space, that time, nor that life may be very specifically set forth. Of course, self-naming is also Herrick's way of establishing the provenance of a work—there can be no doubt who wrote *"The parting verse"*—thus doubly ensuring that his name will be eternized.

Art as Nature Improved

The *"Sacred Grove"* represents a pastoral vision of the ideal, but that vision is rarely merely fanciful; rather, it is an ideal that accommodates the real. Nothing less is possible for one who sees art as part of, not separate from, human nature, as Herrick's epigram *"Upon Man"* (H-394) indicates:

> MAn is compos'd here of a two-fold part;
> The first of Nature, and the next of Art:
> Art presupposes Nature; Nature shee
> Prepares the way to mans docility.

The *OED*'s definition of *art*—"Human skill as agent, human workmanship. Opposed to *nature"*—is relevant here, but Herrick seems to intend something more. If by "Nature" he means man's physicality, his existence as a creature or living thing, then "Art" would be that which endows that physical being with human agency, with mind and passion, spirit and will. (The adverb "here" permits the inference that elsewhere, as in heaven, humankind may be differently constituted.) This, of course, would be a broad, almost anthropological, definition of art, one that includes but is not limited to the process of making cultural artifacts like poems. For Herrick, then, art in any sense is not so much opposed to nature (in the sense of life) as complementary to it: human corporeality "presupposes"—is the necessary condition of—noncorporeal being, our "higher humanity." In this way human corporeality undergirds our socialization, our becoming less creaturely and more civilized, more "docile." Art "improves" us, makes us more human, just as it improves nature, perfecting what is fallen. The implication is that, in the words of Herrick's contemporary, Sir Thomas Browne, "Nature is not at variance with Art, nor Art with Nature. . . . Art is the perfection of Nature" (*RM,* 23). Or, as Herrick's mentor, Ben Jonson, puts it, "without Art, Nature can ne're be perfect; &, without Nature, Art can clayme no being" (*BJ,* 586). What poets do, then, is to draw upon those resources that humanize them and employ those resources to impose a higher reality on the human order and the order of nature. Nature is where the art of poetry begins, and nature transformed is where the art of poetry ends.

"*Upon man*" sets forth basic principles of Herrick's esthetic with the seriousness and abstraction of a philosophical discourse, but his interest in esthetic issues also manifests itself in less solemn contexts, such as his poems about women's clothes. Trivial as these "meditations on the psychology of dress" may appear to be, they are, as John Press notes, "a mark of [Herrick's] interest in aesthetic theory and a pointer to the nature of his poetic endowment" (10).

One such "meditation" is the much-anthologized "*Delight in Disorder*" (*H*-83), a poem probably inspired by the second stanza of Ben Jonson's lyric, "Still to be neat, still to be drest," where the natural look in fashion is endorsed; Jonson writes:

> Give me a looke, give me a face,
> That makes simplicity a grace;
> Robes loosely flowing, haire as free:
> Such sweet neglect more taketh me
> Than all the adulteries of art;
> They strike mine eyes, but not my heart.

Here not only do art and nature seem to be antithetical, but artifice is perceived by Jonson as corrupting, "adulterating," the natural. Herrick, however, since he views art and nature as complementary, calls for a compromise between an "artless art" that comes as close as possible to the completely natural and sheer artifice;[3] that compromise is hinted at in the apparent paradox of his title and his apparently paradoxical opening couplet:

> A Sweet disorder in the dresse
> Kindles in cloathes a wantonnesse:

A Lawne* about the shoulders thrown
Into a fine distraction:
An erring Lace, which here and there
Enthralls the Crimson Stomacher.**
A Cuffe neglectfull, and thereby
Ribbands to flow confusedly:
A winning wave (deserving Note)
In the tempestuous petticote:
A carelesse shooe-string, in whose tye
I see a wilde civility:
Doe more bewitch me, then when Art
Is too precise in every part.

*linen stole
**decoration worn beneath bodice lacings

Like a psychologist of esthetics, Herrick works back from effect to stimulus. "Wantonnesse" like beauty is, of course, in the mind of the beholder and can range in intensity from feelings of raging lust to a sense of mild titillation. That Herrick has the latter more than the former state in mind may be implied by his word choice: the "disorder" he admires—a kind of studied carelessness—"Kindles" an erotic response rather than inflames one.

Herrick's tactic here initially is to anthropomorphize women's clothes, endowing them with the reactions of male admirers. The resultant covert metaphor evokes the male fantasy of being as close to a lady as her very clothes—draped about her shoulders like a "Lawne" or embracing her torso like "erring" ("wandering" but also "forward") lace. Herrick then turns to natural imagery to underscore his compromise esthetic: ribbons should "flow confusedly" like streams, while the greater bulk of a petticoat should exhibit the surging movement of the sea itself. Art and nature can even meet in the tying of a shoelace. The phrase "a wilde civility" is another of Herrick's memorable oxymorons (like Jonson's "sweet neglect" and Herrick's own "cleanly-*Wantonnesse*") that encapsulates a complex idea: the function of art is to control, give "civility" to, "wilde" nature, and thus improve it. However, a look that is too "precisely" contrived, like art whose artifice is too obvious, will lack magic, will never "bewitch" beholders. It may be no coincidence that on the page opposite *"Delight in Disorder"* in *Hesperides'* first edition is a poem discussed in chapter 3, *"To* Dean-bourn" (*H*-86), in which Herrick complains about the "warty incivility" that Devonians share with their landscape. Neither the arts of living nor the fine

arts have redressed their "wildness," made them "civil." They are nature in
the raw and thus living examples of an extreme.

The paradoxical principle of "wilde civility" also figures importantly in a
poem whose title and theme might seem to contradict *Delight in Disorder,*
another of Herrick's meditations on esthetics, *"Art above Nature, to* Julia"
(*H*-560). As L. C. Martin has noted (*PW,* 541), in this poem—as in numerous others—Herrick is indebted to Robert Burton, a passage of whose
Anatomy of Melancholy reads as follows:

It is a question much controverted . . . whether natural or artificial objects be more
powerfull? . . . for my part, I am of opinion, that though Beauty itself be a great
motive . . . artificial is of more force, and much to be preferred. (3.2.2.3)

Herrick, however, slightly qualifies Burton's opinion in a series of conditional statements about Julia's fashion sense that makes up most of this
single-sentence, 16-line poem:

> WHen I behold a Forrest spread
> With silken trees upon thy head;
> And when I see that other Dresse
> Of flowers set in comeliness. . . .
>   (ll. 1–4)

In spite of his title, Herrick's rhetoric implies the complementary relationship of art and nature: Julia's hat may look like a wild "Forrest," but its trees
are of silk, and the flowers that make her appear so comely are artificial
ones, embroidered upon or woven into her dress.

Awkwardly, the art-nature metaphor is abandoned in the next four
lines—where the arrangement of Julia's lace is compared to the sails of a
ship—but then resumed in an image of the geometry of her hairdo: "Then,
when I see thy Tresses bound / Into an Ovall, square or round" (ll. 9–10);
her hair is natural, but arranged with almost mathematical artifice.

The poem's series of dependent clauses is completed in a grammatical
and thematic conclusion that clearly echoes *"Delight in Disorder"* (Herrick
imitates himself almost as frequently as he imitates other writers):

> Next, when those Lawnie Filmes I see
> Play with a wild civility:
> And all those airie silks to flow,
> Alluring me, and tempting so:

> I must confesse, mine eye and heart
> Dotes less on Nature, then on Art.
>
> (ll. 13–18)

When Julia walks, her linen and silk clothes billow about and stream like nature's own winds and waves, their "wild civility" imitating that "orderly disorder" that the seventeenth century found in nature. The effect for him, Herrick self-mockingly admits, is erotic, but his attribution of its cause to art more than nature has been partly undercut by his own language: it is actually the combination of art and nature that has reduced him to doting. Despite the poem's title, then, its esthetic is in essence consistent with that of "*Delight in Disorder,*" and its borrowings from the earlier poem (earlier, at least, in *Hesperides*) suggest as much. In one sense, as Achsah Guibbory has observed, the true subject of both poems is "the sexuality of aesthetics"—what it is about someone's look that attracts us to them.[4] More generally, as A. J. Murphy has argued, the poems enunciate a principle that underlies a fundamental artistic tension of *Hesperides* and is reflected in that collection's structure, "which is controlled yet seems so uncontrolled."[5]

A direct application to poetry itself of the principle implied by "a wild civility" is made by Herrick in "*A Request to the Graces*" (*H-914*). In this poem the Graces, who traditionally are associated with the Muses and with other powers capable of enhancing life, are invited to become the poet's editors:

> POnder my words, if so that any be
> Known guilty here of incivility:
> Let what is graceless, discompos'd, and rude,
> With sweetness, smoothness, softness, be endu'd.
>
> (ll. 1–4)

If the Muses are the direct sources of poetic inspiration, the Graces apparently preside over revision. Thus they are asked to bring their art to bear to improve any of the poet's verses smacking of "incivility," raw naturalness in any form. That Herrick's poems could be "guilty" of anything anthropomorphizes them: the feminine Graces, then, become governesses as well as editors, lending grace to any "graceless" poems, transforming rough-sounding girls into perfect ladies. Indeed this poetic finishing school is to make coquettes of them so that they will attract readers:

> Teach it* to blush, to curtsie, lisp, and shew
> Demure, but yet, full of temptation too.
> *Numbers** ne'r tickle, or but lightly please*
> *Unless they have some wanton carriages.*[†]
>
> **each "uncivil" poem*
> ****verses*
> [†]*implications*

The metaphor is sexual, its meaning, esthetic: unless a poem is capable of somehow attracting readers, it will go unread—a seemingly self-evident point, yet one often overlooked in discussions of poetry that emphasize intellectual content and "high seriousness." Here again Herrick shows himself to be a highly self-conscious poet who is very aware of his audience and its psychology. While the conceit he employs may seem to trivialize his subject, it is often a mistake to assume that when Herrick is not being solemn he is not being serious. Like any poet, he had to recognize that some of his poems were more popular than others, and like any poet he thought about it. Unlike most poets, however, he wrote about his conclusions in "esthetic meditations" like *"A Request to the Graces,"* poems that, taken together, reveal a sophisticated philosophy of art.

Poetic Art as Craft

Herrick has been more praised for his craftsmanship than for any of his other qualities as a poet. Ironically enough, although such praise has led to his work being widely read and well loved—few anthologies of verse in English printed in the last hundred years have failed to contain some of his poems—it has not always resulted in his being much respected. Being regarded as a superlative craftsman has sometimes contributed to a distorted sense of him as a poet—the image of Herrick as a wordsmith with little to say, lacking in "tough-mindedness" and "strong feeling." This misperception is a result of glossing over too much of his poetry, including those poems where he is thoughtful and passionate about the craft of poetry itself.

In his *Discoveries* Herrick's acknowledged mentor, Ben Jonson, announces, "For a man to write well, there are required three necessaries: to read the best authors, observe the best speakers, and much exercise of his own style" (*BJ,* 566). As to the second bit of advice, it is likely that, as a young man about Cambridge and London, Herrick heard some first-rate speakers, including the literati of Jonson's own circle. The more than fourteen hundred poems of his *Hesperides* and the evidence of his revisions of a number of them demonstrate that Herrick "exercised" his "style." And with regard to Jonson's first precept, Herrick's extensive familiarity with those whom his age regarded as "the best authors"—classical poets like Anacreon, Catullus, Martial, and Horace—has been thoroughly documented by studies of his sources and influences going back more than a century. Herrick's reading was not, however, confined to the "Ancients": as his editors have shown, he was also well acquainted with some of the "best authors" among the "Moderns," and, in particular, with Ben Jonson himself. If the poems that Herrick directed to Jonson are taken at even an approximation of their face value, it was chiefly from "Father Ben" that his preeminent literary "son" learned his craft.

"*Upon Master* Ben. Johnson. *Epigram*" (*H*-382) is one of the few of Herrick's many epigrams classified as such, perhaps as way of reminding the reader that Jonson is here being honored in a poetic mode of which he himself was a master. It begins with an epithet for Jonson that combines the inscription on his tomb in Westminster Abbey ("O rare Ben Jonson") with Robert Burton's characterization of Jonson as the spiritual head of English versifiers, "our arch Poet" (*CP*, 203n):

> After the rare Arch-Poet JOHNSON dy'd,
> The Sock grew loathsome, and the Buskins pride,
> Together with the Stages glory stood
> Each like a poore and pitied widowhood.
> The Cirque* prophan'd was; and all postures rackt:
> For men did strut and stride, and stare, not act.
>
> (ll. 1–6)

*theatre

Jonson's death has almost killed off theater itself: comedy and tragedy, symbolized respectively by the classical "Sock" and "Buskin," and the stage itself has in Jonson lost its lord and master. Associating Jonson with terms from the lexicon of Roman theater implies that he is not merely a humanist but a "Modern Ancient." At this point Herrick shifts to the indirect tribute of satire: he commends Jonson's own acting with a biting condemnation of the post-Jonsonian generation of thespians who posture rather than act, who "squeake" rather than "speake," who lack inspiration, "Holy-Rage," and who therefore receive "No clap of hands, or shout" (ll. 6–10)—in contrast to Jonson, whose applause "Did crack the Play-house sides, or cleave her roofe" (l. 12).

Next, Jonson the master playwright is by inference praised for his artistry and learning through mockery of weaker writers: "*Artlesse the Sceane was:* and that monstrous sin / Of deep and *arrant ignorance* came in" (ll. 13–14). In a poem Herrick may be recalling here, the famous elegy "To the Memory of My Beloved, the Author Mr. William Shakespeare," Jonson himself had praised Shakespeare's art (here, his literary talent) and nature (his knowledge of life):

> Yet must I not give Nature all: Thy *Art*
>   My gentle *Shakespeare,* must enjoy a part.
> For though the *Poets* matter, Nature be,
>   His Art doth give the fashion.

Herrick then is celebrating Jonson for the same qualities Jonson praised in Shakespeare. Jonson has been criticized for committing an indiscretion by mentioning Shakespeare's "small *Latine,* and lesse *Greeke,*" and Herrick likewise touches on a sore point, the audience's hissing of what Herrick extolls as Jonson's "Unequal'd Play, the *Alchymist*" (l. 16). After condemning such perversity, Herrick envisions the death of "all witt" or genius (another of Jonson's requisites of a poet) for all time: wit will appear again only with Jonson's own resurrection, on the Final Day. Herrick's apotheosizing of Jonson, which parallels Jonson's famous apotheosis of Shakespeare at the conclusion of "To . . . Shakespeare," is the final element that transforms Herrick's epigram into a kind of miniature elegy. Along with its conventional expressions of mourning for and admiration of the deceased, it is an angry poem, as elegies often are, exhibiting considerable hostility toward the survivors, of whom the poet, obviously is one: it is as if Herrick is displacing his own guilt at surviving his "father." Of additional interest, and complicating the psychology of this epigram, is the fact that although it initially characterizes Jonson as a poet, it actually celebrates him as an actor and playwright—neither of which Robert Herrick was.

On the other hand, Herrick amply praises Jonson's achievement as a poet elsewhere, such as in the epitaph, "*Upon* Ben. Johnson" (*H*-910). A conventional poem of its kind, it adopts the fiction that it is to be engraved on Jonson's tombstone in Westminster Abbey's "Poets' Corner," where he, "the Best," lies "with the rest / Of the Poets." Equally conventionally, the reader of the epitaph is invited to investigate Jonson's "Story," his life and works, for only they can adequately convey "his glory." More original and interesting is the poem to Jonson that follows this epitaph, *"An Ode for him"* (*H*-911). As stanza 1 indicates, it is to be a highly personal kind of ode:

> AH *Ben*!
> Say how, or when
> Shall we thy Guests
> Meet at those *Lyrick* Feasts,
> Made at the *Sun,*
> The *Dog,* the triple *Tunne?*
> Where we such clusters had,
> As made us nobly wild, not mad;
> And yet each Verse of thine
> Out-did the meate, out-did the frolick wine.
>   (ll. 1–10)

The informality of Herrick's address is only qualified by the formality of his prosody—five couplets of widely varying line lengths, 1/2, 2/3, 2/3, 3/3, 3/5. Although Jonson himself is hailed in familiar fashion, Herrick's Anacreontic characterization of the now-ended revels of "the Sons of Ben" endows them with an almost Roman dignity. They were held in ordinary London taverns, but to Herrick they were festivals of poetry. Even though a good deal of wine ("clusters") was consumed, the consequences were not drunkeness, he claims, but "noble wildness," literary ecstasy, evoked chiefly by Jonson's recitations of his own poems.

After this remembrance of good things past, Herrick invokes the dead Jonson's aid for the immediate future:

> My *Ben*
> Or come agen:
> Or send to us,
> Thy wits great over-plus;
> But teach us yet
> Wisely to husband it;
> Lest we that Tallent spend:
> And having once brought to an end
> That precious stock; the store
> Of such a wit the world sho'd have no more.
>   (ll. 11–20)

Here the Anacreontic–urban London context of the first stanza is replaced by a Biblical-georgic one. Jonson, possessively addressed as "My Ben" (as

Jonson referred to "My . . . Shakespeare"), is asked to return from the dead,
Christlike, or at least to intercede, like a saint of poetry, on behalf of his
"sons." He is begged to bestow on them merely the excess of his genius,
which they, like good husbandmen, will use judiciously. By alluding to the
parable of the talents in John 25, Herrick dignifies himself and Ben's other
"sons" by associating them with those dutiful servants who wisely employed
what their master had entrusted to them, and he honors Jonson by
obliquely comparing him to a beneficent deity. (The fact that each stanza
approximates the shape of a pyramid, traditionally monuments to god-
kings, is not coincidental.) The ode's graceful yoking of classical and Christian metaphors, its unique combination of nostalgia and compliment, and
its plain language and intricate prosody all demonstrate that, despite the
protestations of the second stanza, Herrick has already received his portion
of Jonson's "wits great over-plus."

Although Herrick loved Jonson as Jonson claimed to have loved
Shakespeare—"this side Idolatry"—he must have appreciated the wisdom
of Ben's dictum that, while true poets should hold the great masters up as
models, they must regard them as "guides, not commanders" (*BJ*, 525).
Poets, in short, must be open to whatever their great predecessors can teach
them but finally must be themselves. Whatever poets absorb from their
models (and both Jonson and Herrick absorbed a great deal), they must re-
create so that something new is made out of something old. As Jonson
phrased it, the poet must "be able to convert the substance or riches of an
other poet to his own use. . . . Not, to imitate servilely (as Horace saith),
and catch at vices for virtue, but to draw forth out of the best and choisest
flowers, with the bee, and turn all into honey" (*BJ*, 585–86). This dictum
indeed is the theme of Herrick's witty epigram, "*Upon his Verses*" (*H*-681):

> WHat off-spring other men have got,
> The how, where, when, I question not.
> These are the Children I have left
> Adopted some; none got by theft.
> But all are toucht (like lawfull plate)
> And no Verse illegitimate.

The controlling metaphor of poems as the poet's "children," his flesh and
blood, suggests something of Herrick's pride in his craft. His way of conveying this serious viewpoint, however, is unsolemn: his sly remark that he does
not inquire too closely into the circumstances in which children (and poems)
have been acquired by other men (and poets) leaves open the possibility that

some of them have even been kidnapped (plagiarized). His own poetic off-spring, however, Herrick claims, are either originals or honest imitations—not a bastard among them. All are like silver or gold tableware, whose genuineness can be tested by rubbing, that is, by careful reading. Moreover, as Achsah Guibbory has observed, "By publicly recognizing these poems as his own, [Herrick] ensures that, like other men's sons, they will carry on his name. His poems are thus the progeny who provide him with immortality" (1978, 80).

The covert joke of the epigram is the male's fear of being cuckolded, of always wondering whether his children are his own. Its serious implication involves Herrick's sense of his integrity as a poet. As self-presentation *"Upon his Verses"* is accurate: in accordance with the age's practice and Jonson's precepts, Herrick frequently imitates, occasionally translates, and in some cases borrows directly. But because, as Jonson recommends, he brings his own vision and style to his synthesis of a poem's elements, Herrick remains a highly original poet.[6]

One advantage of following what Dylan Thomas called his "craft or sullen art"[7] is that it can bring the poet fame. This, along with the fact that so many seventeenth-century gentlemen and ladies were "scribblers," may help explain the cynicism of the epigram, *"Fame makes us forward"* (H-448): "TO print our Poems, the propulsive cause / Is fame, (the breath of popular applause)." Although "forward" can mean merely "eager," in the context of the epigram it more likely signifies "presumptuous" or "immodest." In *Lycidas* Milton describes fame paradoxically as "That last infirmity of noble mind." There is little that is noble or even particularly cerebral in Herrick's description of fame: his technical-sounding phrase "propulsive cause" comes close to making poets machines driven by their egos. Moreover, the adjective "popular" almost always has a pejorative connotation in the seventeenth century, so the irony of Herrick's description is twofold: fame is mere breath, hot air, and it is the breath of the undiscriminating populace, the great unwashed. Of course, this satiric observation comes in the middle of a book of poems that was apparently published at its author's own initiative and under his supervision. Although here again Jonson established the precedent, the age had by no means abandoned the notion that real gentlemen and ladies did not publish their verses. Since Herrick takes pains not to exempt himself—he refers to "our Poems"—*"Fame makes us forward"* may do more than counterbalance *"Upon his verses"* and similar self-serving poems: it also acts as a defense, preempting criticism by offering self-criticism, and possibly as a kind of catharsis, assuaging the poet's guilt for being "forward."

Herrick is even cynical about legitimate fame, the subject of the epigram *"Glorie"* (*H*-623): "I Make no haste to have my Numbers read. / *Seldome comes Glorie til a man be dead.*" Again, the self-presentation can be supported: Herrick did not rush into print but waited until he was 57 years old. As to his recognition as a poet while he was alive, there is only one extant reference to him before the publication of *Hesperides* in 1648 and few after that (Patrick, 1978). It would be well after his death—a century and a half, at least—before "glorie" was finally to be his. This historical fact for the reader compounds the irony already present in Herrick's satirical epigram about unfavorable critics, *"Upon the same* [the Detracter]" (*H*-174):

> I Ask't thee oft, what Poets thou hast read,
> And lik'st the best? Still thou reply'st, The dead.
> I shall, ere long, with green turfs cover'd be;
> Then sure thou't like, or thou wilt envy me.

Every poet is condemned to be a "modern poet" and fated to encounter the elitist position that only the "Ancients" or at least the safely dead are worth reading. Such inevitabilities lend more of a rueful than a bitter tone to the epigram, although there can be no doubt that its final clause conceals a sting: it implies that a reader who does not like Herrick's poetry has to be a contemptible wretch.

Even in the best of times for poetry—and the seventeenth century was one of the best—publishing one's poems is an act of faith: therefore, the cynicism Herrick sometimes displays toward the world of letters must have been relatively weak or occasional. In fact, the stronger impression that a reader of *Hesperides* is likely to receive will be that Herrick exhibits considerable faith in poetry, a judicious estimation of his own talents, and a determination to utilize those talents to their fullest, even though (as he acknowledges) he is not always able to do so: sometimes "the holy fier / Either slakes or doth retire" (*"Not every day fit for Verse"* [*H*-714]).

"Holy fier"—inspiration—is what the true artist brings to his art; reworking, laboriously improving what that fire yields, is where the craftsman living within the true artist surfaces. It is Herrick the craftsman who appears in *"His request to* Julia" (*H*-59):

> JUlia, if I chance to die
> Ere I print my Poetry;
> I most humbly thee desire
> To commit it to the fire:

> Better 'twere my Book were dead,
> Then to live not perfected.

This is a trebly deceptive work. From its title it should be a love poem, even if this early in the book a reader were not aware that Julia is first among mistresses. But the love it chiefly displays is the poet's implied love of himself and of his poetry, which is also a form of self-love. Taken at face value the poem is an anachronism because it appears in the book, *Hesperides;* therefore, an important purpose for including it has to be the image of its maker it presents. Finally, the poem is a fantasy because Herrick knows very well his book is imperfect and in fact will joke about its "Aberrations" very shortly in *"To the generous Reader"* (*H*-95). What is left is the poem's conventionality or, as some of Herrick's readers would have it, its ceremonial nature and functions. Since writing poetry was in the seventeenth century still supposed to be an activity primarily for gifted amateurs, a plea that one's verses be destroyed if they were not suitable for publication seemingly disavows any commercial motivation or itch for praise. Herrick expects his reader to recognize that the poem is a ritual proclamation of his dedication to his craft. But even that commendable purpose will to some extent be subverted if the reader notes that the epigram immediately preceeding *"His request to* Julia" is entitled *"Ambition"* (*H*-58): "IN man, Ambition is the common'st thing; / Each one, by nature, loves to be a King," and the poem that follows is the cynical epigram whose title is its theme, *"Money gets the masterie"* (*H*-60). If evidence were needed that Herrick can sometimes feel ambivalent about writing poetry, this deployed triptych is it. On the other hand, the fact that he deliberately devises an implicit confessional of this sort suggests the extent of his self-awareness and his candor.

Both of these qualities are also present in an epigram on the poet's motivation, *"Parcell-gil't* [partly gilded] *Poetry"* (*H*-1000): "LEt's strive to be the best; the Gods, we know it, / Pillars and men, hate an indifferent Poet." This translation of lines 372–73 of Horace's *Ars Poetica* is unacknowledged, which gives the illusion of spontaneity and immediacy to Herrick's plea to his fellow poets to try harder. Mediocrity, he warns, is rejected by the supernatural order, the order of nature ("men"), and even by the order of the inanimate, the pillars around whose bases booksellers displayed their merchandise (*CP*, 408n.)—or possibly even the pillars that, in Herrick's symbolism, represent fame.

As self-conscious as he is about his contemporary audience, it comes as no surprise that Herrick also thinks a good deal about his future audiences. A poem that comes relatively early in *Hesperides, "Lyrick for Legacies"* (*H*-

218), establishes his sense of his place in the history of poetry but, more poignantly, displays a childless and impecunious man's sense of how he may figure in the lives of generations yet unborn:

> GOld I've none, for use or show,
> Neither Silver to bestow
> At my death; but thus much know,
> That each Lyrick here shall be
> Of my Love a Legacie,
> Left to all posterity.
> Gentle friends, then doe but please,
> To accept such coynes as these
> As my last Remembrances.

J. Max Patrick notes that the poem echoes Acts 3.6: "Silver and gold have I none; but such as I have give I thee" (*CP*, 56n.). In each case the "coynes" bestowed are more valuable than precious metals because they are expressions of *agape*—all-embracing love for humanity. Like coins, poems are artifacts as well as symbols: both are produced by craftsmen and embody value. But a legacy of mere coins is always insufficient because they can be distributed only to a limited number of people, whereas poems can be willed "to all posterity." We normally think of a coin as legal tender rather than as a memento, but poems are "remembrances" in two senses: as things to be passed along to posterity, they force poets to remember their human audiences, future as well as present, and as means by which posterity will remember the poet, they constitute a living memorial.

Poets have as much need of memorials as their fellow human beings, being like them, mutable. We live, as "*A Lyrick to Mirth*" (*H*-111) puts it, only "WHile the milder Fates consent." In that interim, the lyricist urges,

> Let's enjoy our merryment:
> Drink, and dance, and pipe, and play;
> Kiss our *Dollies* night and day:
> Crown'd with clusters of the Vine
> Let us sit, and quaffe our wine.
> Call on *Bacchus;* chaunt his praise;
> Shake the *Thyrse,* and bite the *Bayes*.
> (ll. 2–8)

No English poem could seem more Roman. Its speaker is a sensuous philosopher, whose world view could not be more opposite to that of a Christian:

life is wholly contingent, not part of a grand design; its extent entirely depends on the capricious fates. To watch and pray, then, is senseless: living through the senses is the answer. No pale "L'Allegro" he, Herrick's speaker sees excess as success, not merely drinking wine but gulping it down, even invoking the god of wine and drunkenly commandeering his symbolic javelin and chewing on his leafy crown.

Grown godlike with wine, this uninhibited pagan will resurrect the legendary poet Anacreon, not to affirm the spirit but the senses: "Rouze *Anacreon* from the dead; / And return him drunk to bed" (ll. 9–10). Mention of a dead Greek poet calls to mind a dead Roman one—"Sing o're *Horace*"—and, soberingly, universal mortality—"for ere long / Death will come and mar the song" (ll. 11–12), not to mention the singer and maker of "*A Lyrick to Mirth.*"

At this point the poem should be over. But Herrick adds two more surprising lines: "Then shall *Wilson* and *Gotiere* / Never sing, or play more here" (ll. 13–14). And the reader wonders, how did these two moderns get into this imitation of an ancient poem? According to J. Max Patrick, Dr. John Wilson was professor of music at Oxford and James Gouter or Gaultier was a French lutenist (*CP,* 56n). By naming actual living artists, men apparently acquainted with him or of whom he knew, Herrick dramatically underscores the point that they are as doomed as long-dead Horace and Anacreon. And so is he—and so are we. Herrick had to have realized that few of his readers then (and fewer still in posterity) were likely to know who Wilson and Gaultier were. (He could not have anticipated an annotated edition of *Hesperides.*) And this compounds the irony: these notable musicians are doomed to oblivion except as they are immortalized by being named in Herrick's lyric. It is not much of a joke, but then there is little that is mirthful in "*A Lyrick to Mirth,*" nor is mirth either its addressee or its real subject. Rather, its implied subject, and one that becomes increasingly important in *Hesperides,* is the eternizing power of poetry: Anacreon and Horace are remembered through their verses and even John Wilson and James Gaultier will enjoy the glimmer of immortality this poem provides. This is the consolation of the "religion of poetry" and one of the sources of the poet's power.

Poetry as Religion

Although the religion of poetry has no bible, no volumes of history and dogma, no organized priesthood, no congregations of worshipers, and no temples, it is an ancient faith. Its origins are unknown, but its creed can be

traced back at least to the first century B.C., and more specifically to the
poets of Rome's Silver Age—Horace, Ovid, Catullus, Tibullus, and Martial. The first article of that creed—that poetry alone is immortal—makes
up the conclusion of one of Herrick's best-known pieces, "*To live merrily
and to trust to Good Verses*" (*H*-201). The exuberant themes of this poem
are announced in its title and are given vivid expression in its main body—
the first in stanzas 1–10 and the second in the final three stanzas. Herrick's
craftsmanship is also very much in evidence here. The work's structure is
ceremonial, based on the ritual of the alcoholic toast as it would be performed at the kind of "*Lyrick Feasts*" to which Herrick refers in his ode to
Ben Jonson; that structure, however, is also argumentative, advocating the
classical precepts of the poem's title.

    The first three stanzas (ll. 1–12) of "*To live merrily*" set its scene and
mood and characterize its speaker:

> NOw is the time for mirth,
>   Nor cheek, or tongue be dumbe:
> For with the flowrie earth,
>   The golden pomp is come.
>
> The golden Pomp is come;
>   For now each tree do's weare
> (Made of her Pap and Gum)
>   Rich beads of *Amber* here.
>
> Now raignes the *Rose,* and now
>   Th'*Arabian* Dew* besmears
> My uncontrolled** brow,
>   And my retorted† haires.
>
> **scented oil*
> ***uninhibited look*
> †*slicked back*

Clearly, the setting is the "*Sacred Grove,*" the springtime world of pastoral,
with its landscape of flowers and trees decked out like bejeweled ladies. The
speaker borrows the sensuous conventions of Anacreon to convey his exuberant, Dionysian mood. What that mood will lead to, however, is not the
"mirth" of wine, women, and song, but a kind of literary orgy. With considerable ceremony the speaker proposes a series of toasts, each of which cele-

brates a classical poet and the virtues of the wine in which the toasts are drunk.

The Bacchanalian spirit of the occasion is conveyed by the humor of each toast, some of which borders on the crude. For example, according to the toastmaster, the Spanish wine is so potent that it would have restored the sight of the blind bard himself:

> *Homer*, this Health to thee,
>   In Sack of such a kind,
> That it would make thee see,
>   Though thou wert ne'r so blind.
>   (ll. 13–16)

More subtle humor distinguishes the next toast. By playing upon the similarity between "Virgil" and "Virginia," the toastmaster suggests that the sack being imbibed is as rich as the fabled American colony:

> Next, *Virgil,* Ile call forth,
>   To pledge this second Health
> In Wine, whose each cup's worth
>   An Indian Common-wealth.
>   (ll. 17–20)

The choice of Virgil is an appropriate one here, for his *Aeneid* is the account of the founding of another commonwealth. No such dignity, however, is accorded to Ovid, in spite of the fact that he is the favorite Roman poet of Herrick's age, if not of Herrick himself. In fact he becomes the victim of the toastmaster's witty play on his name, Publius Ovidius Naso ("nose"):

> A Goblet next Ile drink
>   To *Ovid;* and suppose,
> Made he the pledge,* he'd think
>   The world had all *one Nose*.
>   (ll. 21–24)

*toast

In J. Max Patrick's paraphrase, Ovid "would find the [wine's] aroma so rich that he would think the world had one nose, and that he was smelling with it" (*CP,* 115n.). Although the joke is on Ovid, it is an appropriate one for so sensuous a poet. There is no joking, however, when it comes to one of Robert Herrick's favorite poets, the Roman lyricist, Catullus:

> Then this immensive cup
>   Of *Aromatike* wine,
> *Catullus,* I quaffe up
>   To that Terce Muse of thine.
>   (ll. 25–28)

This toast continues the previous one's theme of the wine's fragrance but is most notable for its explicit compliment to the poet being honored. Catullus's inspiration is said to yield verses that are "Terce"—burnished, trim—high praise from one who labors after such qualities in his own poetry.

At this point, after having drunk four generous toasts, the toastmaster, clearly feeling the effects of his bibulousness, interrupts his own ritual by crying out to the god of wine:

> Wild am I now with heat;
>   O *Bacchus*! coole thy Raies!
> Or frantick I shall eate
>   Thy *Thyrse* and bite the *Bayes.*
>   (ll. 29–32)

Flushed with sack and losing control, the toastmaster comically threatens to play the life of the party by acting out the Roman equivalent of wearing a lampshade on one's head—attempting to devour the pine cone atop Bacchus's symbolic thyrsus or staff as well as the god's crown of laurel. But in spite of being in an alcoholic whirl, the speaker manages to resume his ceremonial toasts:

> Round, round, the roof do's run;
>   And being ravisht thus,
> Come, I will drink a Tun
>   To my *Propertius.*
>   (ll. 33–36)

Of interest is the possessiveness of the toastmaster toward this little-known elegiac poet: he is "his" Propertius, suggesting that he is especially valued. Another lesser known Roman poet is the recipient of the next "pledge": "Now, to *Tibullus,* next, / This flood I drinke to thee" (ll. 37–38). The hy-

perbole of imbibing a veritable "flood" of wine to this rather obscure versifier calls attention to the witty paradox that has been the structuring principle of the vinous ritual—the poets have been toasted in a generally
descending order of literary importance, from Homer to Tibullus, but the
pledges drunk to each are quantitatively in inverse proportion to that order:
Homer and Virgil, of epic fame, rate only a cup of wine each, while Ovid
merits a goblet, Catullus an "immensive cup," Propertius a "Tun" or huge
cask, and Tibullus a "flood." What can compound the humor here is the
reader's recognition, after reading some two hundred of *Hesperides'* poems,
that Herrick is more a kindred spirit of the lesser known poets than he is of
Homer and Virgil—a comic irony certainly not lost on Herrick himself. Yet
another irony is that this work's catalog of worthies does not mention
Horace, the Roman poet Herrick is by modern consensus most like.
Gordon Braden has pointed out that the opening clause of "*To live merrily*"
echoes Horace, as does its penultimate stanza; these, along with other observations, lead Braden to conclude ingeniously that "Horace is not mentioned
[in this poem] because, in some sense, Horace is speaking" (1978, 139).

If Horace goes unmentioned, Tibullus is accorded the dubious dignity of
being mentioned twice. His name recalls something to the toastmaster's
wine-soaked brain, and with the ponderous wisdom and weighty seriousness of the very drunk, he sees an opportunity to turn priest: "But stay," he
interposes, "I see a Text, / That this presents to me" (ll. 39–40). That
"Text" or passage from holy writ is proclaimed in the next stanza, and it is
taken, not from the Bible, but from Ovid's *Amores* (3.9, 39–40):

> Behold, *Tibullus* lies
>   Here burnt, whose smal return
> Of ashes, scarce suffice
>   To fill a little Urne.
>   (ll. 41–44)

The irony that even a productive poet must end up as a handful of ashes is
given more immediacy by Herrick's poetic fiction that his toastmaster actually has the funerary urn of Tibullus before him. This irony, however, is
moderated by the fact that, minor poet though he is, Tibullus's name is remembered and his verses continue to be read. Thus, the logic of the toastmaster's brief "sermon":

> Trust to good Verses then;
>   They onely will aspire,

> When Pyramids, as men,
>   Are lost i'th'funerall fire.
>
> And when all Bodies meet
>   In *Lethe** to be drown'd;
> Then onely Numbers sweet,
>   With endless life are crown'd.
>   (ll. 45–52)

river in Hades

Ars longa, vita brevis. Life is short and even monuments crumble into oblivion, but art endures. To preserve a name or a life, trust poetry. The waters of Lethe ensure that everyone is eventually forgotten, except those whom "Numbers sweet"—good poetry—have immortalized. "*To live merrily and to trust to Good Verses,*" then, is self-validating: besides being a high-spirited affirmation of good times and good poetry and an amusing characterization of literati in their cups, it has wittily memorialized a gallery of poets as well as its author for close to three and a half centuries.

Immortality, then, is the promise of the "religion of poetry," a promise Herrick refers to often enough to make it appear that he believed in it or at least very much wanted to. It is on his mind in "*An Hymne to the Muses*" (*H*-778), where he presents himself as a priest of the religion of poetry. Here he honors the nine muses as his inspiration and his instructors, who teach him how to make his "measures ravishing." His tribute concludes with a request that they confer on him the laurel wreath that symbolizes his status as a poet and that will ensure that his memory shall be ever green:

> Then while I sing your praise,
> My *Priest-hood* crown with bayes
> Green, to the end of dayes.
>   (ll. 9–11)

It is serendipity that this "*Hymne*" is immediately followed in *Hesperides* by the poem that, as much as any other, has led Herrick to be recognized as a poet, "*Upon* Julia's *Clothes*" (*H*-779).

It is also as a member of poetry's priesthood that Herrick offers "*His Prayer to* Ben. Johnson" (*H*-604). In the epigram that precedes this small ritual of poetry's religion, "*To his Booke*" (*H*-603), Herrick once again exhibits a degree of nervousness about *Hesperides'* reception: "all here is good" (l. 3), he protests, but will it be liked or even understood? Aware that even

Ben Jonson, a poet laureate, had his critics, Jonson's "son" seeks all the help
he can get:

> 1. WHen I a Verse shall make,
>   Know I have praid thee,
>   For old *Religions* sake,
>   Saint *Ben* to aide me.

Herrick chose the verb of his opening line advisedly, because to Jonson a
poet was first and foremost a "maker," one who takes the raw material of
"nature" or life and fashions it into art (*BJ,* 582). In the general Christian
usage of the time, Jonson could properly be called a saint in the sense of his
soul now being in heaven. Praying for his intercession, of course, is the religion of poetry borrowing from Roman Catholic practice: Jonson's "canoni-
zation" as a preeminent man of letters has endowed him, it is implied, with
special mediatory powers. J. Max Patrick suggests that the phrase "old religion" may refer to the bonds of Jonson's and Herrick's friendship or more
generally to ancient notions about duty and loyalty (*CP,* 283n.); however,
the poem's controlling metaphor, identifying concepts of poetic influence
and inspiration with Christian practice, makes it more likely that it is the religion of poetry Herrick has in mind. He goes on to promise that in the
"temple" of poetry's religion he will perform all of the requisite rituals to ensure Jonson's blessing—dedicate poems to him, maintain his reputation,
and include more poems mentioning Jonson's name in his "*Psalter,*"
Hesperides itself:

> 2. Make the way smooth for me,
>   When I, thy *Herrick,*
>   Honouring thee, on my knee
>   Offer my *Lyrick.*
>
> 3. Candles Ile give to thee,
>   And a new Altar;
>   And thou Saint *Ben,* shalt be
>   Writ in my *Psalter.*

Since he is Jonson's "son"—"thy" Robert Herrick—any of his lyrics could
be said to honor his literary father. There is fortuitousness as well as craft in
the rhyming of "*Herrick*" and "*Lyrick,*" but such self-naming has more profound purposes: it grounds what is otherwise a charming tour de force in

cultural history, immutably linking the younger to the older poet and thereby giving little-known Robert Herrick a historical reality approximating that of famed Ben Jonson. Moreover, by naming his own name, Herrick is eternizing himself along with Jonson. Thus he as well as "Saint *Ben*" is guaranteed an appearance in his "psalter," the book containing this poem. The synecdoche of candles and altars transforms Herrick's book into a temple of the religion of poetry, "the Church of Saint Ben."

The wit of "*His Prayer*" need not subvert the essential seriousness of its theme—that poetry is for poets at least akin to a religious phenomenon, with dogma and ceremonies of its own and with its own kind of spirituality. It also has its own articles of faith, such as "trust to good verses," an idea sufficiently important to bear repeating, as Herrick does, for example, in an epigram coming just before "*His Prayer*," "*On himselfe*" (*H*-592):

> LIve by thy Muse thou shalt; when others die
> Leaving no Fame to long Posterity:
> When Monarchies trans-shifted are, and gone;
> Here shall endure thy vast Dominion.

This is one of 16 poems bearing the same innocuous title, a significant phenomenon in itself: no other important poet formally addresses himself so frequently or inserts himself so insistently into the reader's consciousness. Each reading of his book "resurrects" him, or at least his self-image. *H*-592 is distinctive, though, on several counts. It affirms the doctrine of "trust to good verses" in a considerably more magisterial tone than does "*To live merrily.*" For all of Herrick's ardent Royalism, it reminds us that monarchies too succumb to "*Times trans-shifting*," as that of the Tudors did and that of the Stuarts soon would. And, by way of contrast, it crowns poets the kings of their own eternal kingdoms. *Hesperides* is even a "vast Dominion"—"vast," perhaps, compared to the small island that makes up Stuart England. Although earlier poems had variously honored Prince Charles, the king, and the queen as the rulers of Herrick's "*Sacred Grove*," increasingly they appear to be titular monarchs only: *H*-592 makes explicit what has become more and more evident—that Robert Herrick is the creator of the poetic world that is *Hesperides* and its rightful ruler and that by his decree the religion of poetry is that dominion's official faith.

The transcendence of the natural world's transiency that the poet achieves when he creates his deathless verse–world is given metaphysical dimensions in a unique and ambitious poem, "*The Apparition of his Mistresse calling him to* Elizium" (*H*-575). At first glance "*The Apparition*" looks like

Hesperides' "pagan" version of *His Noble Numbers'* "*The white Island*" (N-128): it too is a vision of the afterlife, but an afterlife for poets and lovers rather than for the pious, one set in a technicolor pastoral rather than a pale paradise. In form the piece is a hybrid, a combination of and variations on the dream vision and the invitation poem. While it is never made explicit that the lady has come to Herrick in a dream, at the conclusion it is disclosed that her apparition has appeared to him in the dead of night. Moreover, "*The Apparition*" is in a sense an invitation to death rather than to love—or at least to love in the hereafter—and in the end has much more to do with poetry than with romance. Finally, "*The Apparition*" is for *Hesperides* a relative rarity, a poem whose persona is female—although there is little except its title and an allusion to the speaker's amorous relationship to the poet to mark out this "dialogue of one" as "feminine."

Three main movements constitute "*The Apparition*": a description of Elizium as Herrick's "*Sacred Grove*" translated to the next world; an account of its happy inhabitants and their pleasures; and the lady's hurried conclusion of her speech brought on by the advent of day. To evoke the vision of Elizium, which, according to classical mythology, was that paradisaical region of Hades reserved for those favored by the gods, Herrick calls upon his memory of Tibullus (*CP,* 275n.) and his pastoral muse:

> COme then, and like two Doves with silv'rie wings,
> Let our soules flie to'th'shades, where ever springs
> Sit smiling in the Meads; where Balm and Oile,
> Roses and Cassia crown the untill'd soyle.
>
> (ll. 1–4)

Never is death, which looms so large in *Hesperides,* more delicately and romantically glossed over than here, in the image of two turtle doves, the birds of love, gliding into the bucolic landscape of Elizium. Here death has no sting; this is the poetry of transfiguration.

The pastoral world the lady's language evokes resembles the one depicted in Michael Drayton's "The Description of Elizium" that serves as his prelude to *The Muses Elizium* (1630). Herrick's is also a land of milk and honey, of oils and spices, of naturally sensuous beauty,

> Where no disease raignes, or infection comes
> To blast the Aire, but *Amber-greece* and *Gums.*
> This, that, and ev'ry Thicket doth transpire*
> More sweet, then *Storax*** from the hallowed fire:

Where ev'ry tree a wealthy issue beares
Of fragrant Apples, blushing Plums, or Peares
And all the shrubs, with sparkling spangles, shew
Like Morning-Sun-Shine tinsilling the dew.

(ll. 5–12)

*exhale
**sweet gum

This is Herrick in his more classically pastoral mode: other than a possible echo of Jonson's "To Penshurst" in the catalog of fruits, there is no hint of English rural life present. Incense imagery and exotic terms like "*Storax*" lend an air of the foreign to the scene, as do the painterly images of the greenery.

True to the tradition of pastoral, this is the world of eternal spring:

Here in green Meddowes sits eternall May,
Purfling the Margents, while perpetuall Day
So double gilds the Aire, as that no night
Can ever rust th'Enamel of the light.

(ll. 13–16)

It is personified May and Daytime who "paint" this picturesque scene. May, the most pleasant month, is Elizium's only season, and through her act of "Purfling the Margents"—"richly embroidering the meadows' edges" (*CP*, 275n.) with her flowers—she "frames" the landscape. Bright daytime forever tinges the very air with gold. The poet calls attention to the artifice of his vision by his use of painterly language: this is an "enameled" world, a world of art rather than of nature, and thus one that never rusts or decays. However, here, as in "*The white Island*," a certain uneasiness about night can be detected: Elizium too is depicted as a world of "perpetuall Day," as if such an unfamiliar condition would spell perfection to all readers.

To complete his scene, one which a seventeenth-century artist of the Picturesque like Poussin might have painted, Herrick adds idealized human figures:

Here, naked Younglings, handsome Striplings run
Their Goales for Virgins kisses; which when done,
Then unto Dancing forth the learned Round
Commixt they meet, with endlesse Roses crown'd.

(ll. 17–20)

Elizium is a paradise of "cleanly-*Wantonnesse*": like naked Greek athletes, the young men run races, but here they win kisses, not laurel wreaths; those kisses, however, lead not to coupling but to stately formal dance, "the learned Round." This can be regarded as yet another example of unconsummated eroticism that bothers those critics of Herrick who pant after the explicit, discount the artistic advantages of decorum, and underestimate the healthy sexual imaginations of readers. Herrick's, however, are not lovers on a Grecian urn, denied sexual intercourse forever; that their happiness is complete is implied by the symbols of love which crown them.

The seductive promise his mistress holds out is that she and Herrick are to become participants in this romantic scene:

> And here we'l sit on Primrose-banks, and see
> Love's *Chorus* led by *Cupid;* and we'l be
> Two loving followers too unto the Grove,
> Where Poets sing the stories of our love.
>
> (ll. 21–24)

These lines effect the transition between the poem's first and second movements, for this is a paradise not only of lovers but of poets, and Herrick is here presented as both. It is appropriate that the procession of lovers has as its destination the "Poets' Corner" of the "*Sacred Grove*," for it is the poets who elevate life to art, love to legend, to "stories."

The second movement of "*The Apparition*" makes concrete a corollary of the religion of poetry, that poets are favored by the gods. To the appeals of Elizium's beautiful landscape and of a romantic reunion with his love is added the promise that Herrick will eternally consort with the famed poets of history, and as a peer. These poets, mainly Ancients, but joined by a few favored Moderns, are cataloged in approximately chronological order. That catalog begins with the "*Divine Musaeus*," chronicler of the legendary love of Hero and Leander who, like Herrick and his mistress, were separated by death. The list continues with "honour'd *Homer*," enthroned as a monarch, whose readings from his epics draw a "crowd of Poets" simply "To heare the incantation of his tongue" (l. 30). This illustrates what is for Herrick another corollary of the religion of poetry—that verses have magical or hypnotic power which can induce altered states in their audience.

Among the poets who follow in the lady's catalog, special attention is focused on Anacreon, to whose bacchanalian verses Herrick, as we have seen, more than once pays the sincerest form of tribute. Speaking through the persona of the apparition, he returns the compliment to himself with a vision of Anacreon in Elizium reciting from *Hesperides:*

> Ile bring thee *Herrick* to *Anacreon,*
> Quaffing his full-crown'd bowles of burning Wine,
> And in his Raptures speaking Lines of Thine.
>
> (ll. 32–34)

The legendary Greek poet will welcome his young successor, and both will "rage"—be elevated to poetic ecstasy—and "drink and dance together." By this time the resemblances between "*The Apparition*" and "*To live merrily and to trust to Good Verses*" have become more and more apparent, as do the contrasts between this vibrantly warm, colorful, and lively vision and the sterile luminosity of "*The white Island.*" That, as man, Herrick was able to reconcile Elizium and the "*place of the Blest*" remains uncertain; that, as poet, his heart is in Elizium is self-evident. Where else could he enjoy seeing both "stately *Virgil,*" with whom he has little in common, and a poet with whom he shares much, "witty Ovid," by

> Whom faire *Corinna* sits, and doth comply*
> With Yvorie wrists, his Laureat head, and steeps
> His eye in dew of kisses while he sleeps.
>
> (ll. 40–43)

*embrace

This vignette too seems straight out of a seventeenth-century painting, but not because Herrick provides a great deal of detail. Indeed, its vividness is achieved, in a manner of speaking, with mirrors—with an abstract descriptive adjective here ("witty," "faire") and a synecdoche there ("Yvorie wrists," "his Laureat head"). The reader's imagination supplies the rest.

Other Roman poets, including "soft *Catullus,*" "sharp-fanged *Martial,*" the satirical poet, and "towering . . . *Horace,*" to whom Herrick has also been compared, are awarded places in Elizium's "spacious Theater" (doubtless a natural amphitheater) because they are regarded as being divinely inspired, capable of poetic "frenzies." Among the Moderns, only three are admitted to this select crew, all of whom are best known as playwrights. Two of the names may surprise the contemporary reader, for they are familiar today mainly to drama specialists:

> Among which glories (crown'd with sacred Bayes,
> And flatt'ring Ivie) Two recite their Plaies,
> *Beumont* and *Fletcher,* Swans, to whom all eares
> Listen, while they (like Syrens in their Spheres)
> Sing their *Evadne.*
>
> (ll. 49–53)

Collaborators in numerous tragedies (such as *The Maid's Tragedy,* in which
the title figure is named Evadne), tragicomedies, and comedies, Francis
Beaumont and John Fletcher were more esteemed in the seventeenth century than they are today. Indeed, they were viewed by some as Shakespeare's
successors. That Herrick subscribed to such a view is suggested not only by
the passage above, but by the fact that an earlier version of it honored "the
sweet swan of Avon" along with Beaumont in an allusion to: "*Shakespeare*
and *Beamond,* Swans, to whom all eares / Listen, while they call back the
former yeares / To teach the truth of Scenes" (*PW,* 489). As a drama critic
Herrick is conventional: he appears to praise Shakespeare and Beaumont
because their plays convey "truth" (not necessarily facts) as Renaissance his-
toriography decreed works based on history should do. The revised version
offers a typical compliment to the lyrical enchantment of Beaumont and
Fletcher's plays. What is of most interest, however, is the change itself. Did
Herrick revise the passage to align himself more closely with a popular
view? Had he seen or read plays by the collaborators and changed his mind?
Or had the death of John Fletcher in 1625 (nine years after the deaths of
Shakespeare and Beaumont) suggested a revision in an earlier version of the
poem? It is unlikely we shall ever know.

One reputation that is never qualified throughout *Hesperides* is, of
course, that of Ben Jonson, the third Modern Herrick identifies as a citizen
of Elizium. After explaining that Elizium holds more delights than Herrick
can imagine, the ghostly lady invites him to a "capacious roome"

> In which thy Father *Johnson* now is plac't,
> As in a Globe of Radiant fire, and grac't
> To be in that Orbe crown'd (that doth include
> Those Prophets of the former Magnitude)
> And he one chiefe.
>
> (ll. 57–61)

Although there were several "sons of Ben," the impression is given that
Herrick is an only child ("thy Father *Johnson*"). The complex and ambigu-

ous image developed here elevates the poet himself along with Jonson. The "capacious roome" seems to be the old Sun tavern where Jonson used to hold court, but the Sun has now become cosmic, transmogrified into "a Globe of Radiant fire." It then is equated with the celestial dwelling place of the prophets, among whom Jonson has become preeminent. This last characterization is of particular interest because it seems to show Herrick aligning himself with Milton's religious view of the poet as a type of prophet; Milton, however, is thinking primarily of the Christian poet, Herrick, of the poet as an adherent to the religion of poetry.

But neither the reader nor Herrick actually gets to see Jonson. Just as anticipation is at its height, the cock crows, "the prime of day" is seen to "break from the pregnant East," and the apparition abruptly exclaims, "'tis time / I vanish; more I had to say; But Night determines here, Away" (ll. 64–66). Here, that is, back on earth, night is in control (whereas, as we have seen, "perpetuall Day" rules in Elizium). Thus the lady has to obey the law of the supernatural that all spirits must return to their resting places before daybreak. With this unexpected development, the poem simply stops. The Latin tag *Desunt nonnulla* below the title of the poem had warned the reader that "some things are missing"—the phrase Christopher Marlowe uses for the same purpose at the close of his *Hero and Leander;* but like the poem's female persona this is another aspect of Herrick's fiction: "*The Apparition*" is successful just as it stands, a unique synthesis of dream vision, pastoral, invitation to love, and encomium that celebrates poetry and poets, including its own poet. This poem, then, is a special contribution to the *mythos* of the religion of poetry and an artistic realization of what may have been one of Robert Herrick's chief defenses, the denial of death, and one of his central fantasies, eternal life through eternal art.

Poetry as Salvation

That poetry perpetuates the poet is an article of faith so fundamental to Herrick that he displays Ovid's version of it on the very title page of *Hesperides* as that volume's motto, *Effugient avidos Carmina nostra Rogos:* "Our songs shall escape the eager funeral pyres." The thought is repeated so often in Herrick's collection that it becomes a kind of incantation, a charm against anxieties apparently persistent and profound, not so much about death as about oblivion, about being forgotten. For example, past the midpoint of *Hesperides,* the epigram, "*Verses*" (H-790), asks, "WHo will not honour Noble Numbers, when / Verses out-live the bravest deeds of men?" A Stoical two-line epigram on happiness and one on desire follow, and then

Herrick returns to the religion of poetry in an epigram whose title announces its theme, "*Poetry perpetuates the Poet*" (*H*-794):

> Here I my selfe might likewise die,
> And utterly forgotten lye,
> But that eternal Poetrie
> Repullulation gives me here
> Unto the thirtieth thousand yeere,
> When all now dead shall re-appeare.

Here the general principle about "Noble Numbers" (successful poetry) expressed in "*Verses*" is given specific and personal application. The strong
feeling implicit in the adverb "utterly" lends a poignancy to the initial couplet, expressive perhaps of the regretfulness of a childless man in an age in
which one's descendents were expected to perpetuate one's memory. This
state of mind, however, is contravened with a metaphor, one conveyed in a
single Latinate word. "Repullulation" means "regeneration," "the act of
budding and flourishing again." Herrick's buried metaphor, then, is of the
poet as a green plant: he will be reborn each time his poetry is read and will
thus attain a kind of immortality "Here," on earth, until he achieves the immortality of the faithful Christian on Judgment Day, "When all now dead
shall re-appeare." This is to take place in "that great Platonick yeere" ("*His
Winding Sheet*" [*H*-515]), at the end of a cycle of thirty thousand years "in
which the heavenly bodies were supposed to go through all their possible
movements and return to their original relative positions" (*OED*). Herrick's
association of this pagan belief with that of Doomsday suffuses his otherwise immodest claim for the power of his poetry with an aura, at least, of
sanctity.

The central metaphor of "*Poetry perpetuates the Poet*" in a sense resolves
the paradox of Herrick's pastoral vision: although death will eventually remove him from the order of nature and he, unlike its buds and blossoms,
cannot "repullulate," in his imitation of the order of nature, his "*Sacred
Grove*," he will live until the end of time. But poetry, in perpetuating the
poet, perpetuates his subjects as well. We have seen Herrick make assurance
double sure by occasionally taking himself as his own subject, even to enter-
ing his own name in his own text. But *Hesperides* also becomes an instru-
ment for immortalizing Herrick's relatives, friends, patrons, and heroes.
Their names, sometimes their social roles, and sometimes their deeds or key
moments in their lives are preserved in his poems, like (to borrow his own
image) lilies in crystal. Gone, they will not be forgotten. Nor is this merely

Herrick's fond hope. Like other poets of the time who shared his quasi-
religious faith in poetry (Shakespeare is but one example), he simply had to
look at the historical record. Oblivion had been the fate of the wealthiest,
the most powerful, and the most pious personages of Homer's age, but
Homer is remembered. Virgil is still loved, those he memorializes in his
poems are still admired, even though most of first century B.C. Rome is dust
and those who inhabited it, even the mightiest, have been forgotten. Poetry's religion, then, seems able to keep its promise. And keeps it still, for
Michael Oldisworth lives:

> NOr thinke that Thou in this my Booke art worst,
> Because not plac't here with the midst, or first.
> Since Fame that sides with these, or goes before
> Those, that must live with Thee for evermore.
> That Fame, and Fames rear'd Pillar, thou shalt see
> In the next sheet *Brave Man* to follow Thee.
> Fix on That Columne then, and never fall;
> Held up by Fames *eternall Pedestall*.

Ironically, Herrick did not get the name he sets out to preserve quite right:
his title for the poem is "*To the most accomplisht Gentleman Master* Michael
Oulsworth" (*H*-1092). Ann Coiro points out that Michael Oldisworth,
who had strong parliamentary sympathies and worked successfully against
the king's cause, "represents everything Robert Herrick might be assumed
to loath," but concludes that he is honored in this poem "because he is of the
new order," a representative of what could seem in the late 1640s to be a
historical inevitability" (1988, 142). This rationale requires that Herrick,
who chose to be expelled from his vicarage rather than submit to the new
order, would nevertheless dignify that order by praising Oldisworth. It is
more likely that the latter is here addressed as a prominent acquaintance,
possibly even a friend (in spite of his politics) because, as Coiro herself mentions, Herrick probably knew Oldisworth as Member of Parliament for his
region and as secretary to the Earl of Pembroke, who may have been a pa-
tron of the poet (1988, 142).

Certainly the tone of this epigram of praise is good-humored, even familiar, and central to its strategy is a comic if bookish conceit having to do with
the positioning of "*To* . . . Oulsworth" in the printed text. Herrick seems to
imply—his language here is atypically obscure—that the placement of this
poem almost at the end of *Hesperides* has to do with saving the best for last.
His book is a pantheon of worthies, all of whom, like Oldisworth, will re-

ceive eternal fame when *Hesperides* has been read through and been pronounced a success. Thus, fame precedes those honored early in the volume
and "sides" with those celebrated in midvolume in the sense that it takes
time for readers reading through *Hesperides* to recognize that Herrick's are
indeed "Good Verses," "Noble Numbers," truly capable of immortalizing
their subjects. But by the time they get to the poem to Oldisworth, these
readers (it is implied) will be certain that this poetry will live forever. The
symbol of this accomplishment is the hieroglyphic poem that concludes
Hesperides, "The pillar of Fame" (H-1129), which Herrick says Oldisworth
will be able to "see" from his niche in the pantheon because it is printed "In
the next sheet"—the sheet of paper adjacent to the one on which
Oldisworth's own epigram is printed. Oldisworth is instructed to gaze fix-
edly on "That Columne" (and the poem is patterned to look like a column)
and recognize that it "supports" him and all the rest in the Hesperidean
"Temple of [Herrick's] *Heroes"* (H-496).

This is an extraordinary example of the self-reflexivity of perhaps the
most self-reflexive collection of important poetry in English. Here, as
throughout *Hesperides,* Herrick shows himself to be unusually aware of
himself as a man and a poet *as both are represented in his poems,* and unusually aware as well of his poems' representation of his social relationships and
his personal situation. This heightened awareness also extends, of course, to
the human subjects and dedicatees of his poems and, significantly, to all of
his readers. Moreover, as we have already noted, Herrick is also very conscious of the juxtapositions and other typographical arrangements of those
poems in his book, in the printed and bound text. No other poet of consequence takes poetry's religion so far, from an artistically convenient piety to
a living faith that finds expression in the very conceptualization of his book,
as well as in his art itself.

Both the recipients of Herrick's eternizing and his readers are continually
reminded of poetry's metaphysical power. For example, one of those epigrams of praise in the "midst" of *Hesperides, "To his worthy Kinsman, Master* Stephen Soame" (H-545), combines Christianity and poetry's religion to
come up with a striking metaphor for *Hesperides'* honorees—as comprising
another chosen people. Herrick's second cousin has become, he is told, "one
of my righteous Tribe" (l. 2), all of whom speak the same language, are
similar kinds of persons, and share the same deportment and faith. They are
also "Saints," "canonized" by poetry, and recorded in the poet's "eternall
Calendar" or catalog of saints (l. 10), *Hesperides.*[8] In "*To his faithfull friend,
Master* John Crofts, *Cup-bearer to the King*" (H-804), *Hesperides* even becomes the heavens themselves, "my spacious Sphere," in which Crofts and

the poet's other select friends, his "few Immortals," become stars, "As Lamps for everlasting shining here" (ll. 7–8). Crofts's apotheosis is a quid pro quo: "FOr all thy many courtesies to me" (l. 1). The central conceit, however, of "*To Mistresse* Katherine Bradshaw, *the lovely, that crowned him with Laurel*" (*H*-224), is the more familiar one of the "*Sacred Grove.*" Although the poem appears little more than a tenth of the way through the collection, it assumes that the reader understands already that Herrick thinks of himself as a pastoral poet and that to be a pastoral poet can include being an epigrammatist, particularly one who specializes in epigrams of praise:

> MY Muse in Meads has spent her many houres,
> Sitting, and sorting severall sorts of flowers
> To make for others garlands; and to set
> On many a head here, many a Coronet.
>
> (ll. 1–4)

Words are flowers, and woven together by a true poet they become poetic garlands that confer immortality. In fact, by this juncture of *Hesperides,* Herrick has already garlanded 18 identifiably real people, including a sister-in-law, the royal family, two brothers, his father, a cousin, three lords, two bishops, a knight and his lady, a friend, a lawyer, and a lady. None of these, however, has returned the favor by giving Herrick's Muse "a day of Coronation"—by writing a poem to him. Ironically, Katherine Bradshaw, who has not thus far been immortalized, has not only written a poem to him but in that poem (which is not extant) has officially proclaimed him "poet": "Till you (sweet Mistresse) came and enterwove / A *Laurel* for her, ever young as love" (ll. 7–8). Nothing will do, then, but that Herrick reciprocate on his muse's behalf: "You first of all crown'd her; she must, of due, / Render for that, a crowne of life to you" (ll. 9–10). Herrick's requirements for admission to his pantheon, his tribe, his "*Sacred Grove,*" then, are various and include reciprocity for services rendered. Such a practice, looked askance at, perhaps, in our age, was de rigueur in the seventeenth century, when poetry's power to immortalize or simply to effect favorable "public relations" made it count for considerably more than it does today.

Herrick's confidence in poetry's religion and his artistic poise are demonstrated, paradoxically, by his capacity to subvert his own credo to give his collection comic relief. Thus, only one short poem separates the epigram "*To Mistresse* Katherine Bradshaw" (*H*-224) and an epigram in praise of liquor, "*To the most vertuous Mistresse* Pot, *who many times entertained him*" (*H*-

226). This amusing encomium even begins with echoes of the Bradshaw poem, with the poet looking back at his work: "When I through all my many Poems look, / And see your selfe to beautifie my Book," I think, he says, that because the liquor pot has inspired him, the "Region" that is *Hesperides* is filled with light. But this artistic triumph, he confesses, is not his, but Mistress Pot's, who is begged to "Guild [make bright] still with flames this Firmament [of the 'world' of his book], and be / A Lampe Eternall to my Poetrie" (ll. 5–6). It is fitting, he continues, that he eternize the liquor pot since she is the "mistress" who has enlightened him so that the poetry he writes will live forever.

On a more serious note, the promise of immortality that the religion of poetry makes to the poet often assuages Herrick's intimations of his mortality as a man, as another epigram *"Upon himself"* (*H*-507) suggests:

> TH'art hence removing, (like a Shepherds Tent)
> And walk thou must the way that others went:
> Fall thou must first, then rise to life with These,
> Markt in thy Book for faithfull Witnesses.

Yet another example of the self-reflexivity of Herrick's poetry, this poem is in essence a metaphor of his life and art. Its first line echoes Isaiah 38.12— "Mine age is departed, and is removed from me as a shepherd's tent" (*CP*, 251n.)—and this echo lends a note of Christian Stoicism to his observation that the days of his life are being "packed up" and carried off. The poem's sense of quiet acceptance is reinforced by the verb "must" in the next line, and in that line's Bunyanesque image of the wayfaring toward death that everyone undertakes. The verb "Fall" expresses the fatal link between Robert Herrick and Adam, whose own fall doomed Robert Herrick to fall into the grave. The epigram's first two and one-half lines have been traditional, even religiously orthodox, but its conclusion, grounded in the religion of poetry, skirts blasphemy, as Herrick becomes his own second Adam. His resurrection, his "ris[ing] to life," is not through Christ but is self-accomplished, the result of his becoming a living memory in the minds of those named in his poems—his "faithfull Witnesses."

One such witness is the Earl of Dorset, to whom the epigram immediately preceding *"Upon himself"* is dedicated. In that poem (*H*-506) Dorset is celebrated as a severe critic who has praised Herrick's poetry, and it is with plain gratitude that Herrick reciprocates: *"Few live the life immortall. He ensures / His Fame's long life, who strives to set up Yours"* (ll. 15–16). Dorset

thus becomes yet another entry in the register (the religion of poetry's coun-
terpart to Christianity's heavenly register) that is *Hesperides*.

Even "living Witnesses" like Robert Herrick's various worthies, however,
must die; the only witnesses that do not—whose memories are impervious
to *"Times trans-shifting"*—are his poems themselves. They constitute his
last line of defense against the dark, as the hieroglyphic *"His Poetrie his Pillar"* (*H*-211) affirms:

> 1. ONely a little more
>   I have to write,
>   Then Ile give o're,
>   And bid the world Good-night.
>
> 2. 'Tis but a flying minute,
>   That I must stay,
>   Or linger in it;
>   And then I must away.

The foreshortening of lines 1–2 (along with the abbreviated line lengths)
reinforce a sense of life's brevity, which even this early in *Hesperides* is recognizable as one of the volume's dominant themes. The comfortable ritual of
going to bed conveys a sense of death's naturalness and endows this confrontation of the poet's mortality with quiet Stoicism. Behind Herrick's
philosophical poise, however, he still feels a sense of urgency, expressed in
the extreme foreshortening of the image of "a flying minute," the irony of
"linger," and what sounds like the cry of one who has fallen behind
schedule—"I must away."

As it sometimes does, Herrick's contemplation of his own death leads
him to protest the near universality of oblivion, here in an apostrophe to
Time:

> 3. O time that cut'st down all!
>   And scarce leav'st here
>   Memoriall
>   Of any men that were.
>
> 4. How many lye forgot
>   In Vaults beneath?
>   And piece-meale rot
>   Without a fame in death?

Like death itself, time is a grim reaper, but what disturbs Herrick most is
not the inevitability of death but that so many die and leave no trace. There
is nothing to commemorate that we once lived except the horrible trash of
the charnel house. Being forgotten is the final obscenity. To his readers
Herrick has no consolation to offer, but he can console himself with the possibility of his own "Memoriall":

> 5. Behold this living stone,
>   I reare for me,
>   Ne'r to be thrown
>   Downe, envious Time by thee.

> 6. Pillars let some set up,
>   (If so they please)
>   Here is my hope,
>   And my *Pyramides.*

There is a touch of daring, perhaps even of the heroic here (a pose Herrick
adopts infrequently): he throws down the gauntlet of immortal poetry before time itself. Time will envy him, he claims, because Robert Herrick will
be self-immortalized: he is in the process of erecting a memorial that time
cannot vandalize, the living memorial of his poetry. Most mortals can only
rely on pillars of stone; seen whole on the page, "*His Poetrie his Pillar*"
assumes the shape of a pillar of words that will forever stand there. *Hesperides,* then, by extension is comprised not merely of three, but of many
"*Pyramides,*" of skyward-pointing word-tombs within which Robert
Herrick will be preserved. So bold a claim can be viewed as presumptuous,
except for the fact that Herrick realistically qualifies it: his immortality, he
says, is his "hope," not a certainty. Such a note is appropriate to the early
placement of "*His Poetrie his Pillar*" in the order of *Hesperides,* for its reinforces Herrick's fiction that he is composing the book as he goes along, in
the same order in which the reader is reading it.[9] By the end of *Hesperides,*
however, his most famous pattern poem, "*The pillar of Fame*" (H-1129),
will make its claim of immortality without qualification.

The fear of oblivion Herrick expresses in "*His Poetrie his Pillar*" turned
out to be well founded. Although today the visitor to Herrick's church at
Dean Prior can view a stone commemorating the poet prominently sited at
the foot of the church tower, it does not mark his "Vault." In fact it was only
recently placed there by the former owners of Herrick's old vicarage to represent the original tombstone, which did not survive the ravages of "envious

Time." Moreover, Herrick also turned out to be prophetic about his poetry. While the "*Sacred Grove*" of his *Hesperides* disappeared from the maps of English poetry for a time, Herrick's epigram "*To his Booke*" (*H*-240)— "THou art a plant sprung up to wither never, / But like a Laurell, to grow green for ever"—has proved reasonably accurate. Long after he died, the parishioners of Dean Prior recalled stories about him and had some of his poems by memory, even though his work fell out of favor among the literati. Today, when he is more esteemed by scholars and critics than ever and when more people than ever before have read at least a few of his poems in school and college anthologies, to millions who do not even know his name, "Gather ye rosebuds while ye may" has a familiar and somehow gratifying ring.

In a sense, Herrick's book itself is the overarching symbol of his poetry. Whether he represents *Hesperides* as a "*Sacred Grove,*" as a "Laurell ever green," as a calendar of "saints," as a "City . . . of *Heroes*" (*H*-365), or as a memorial pillar, his collection comes to serve as the ultimate affirmation and demonstration of his faith in poetry's religion—and in himself as poet. His book is the subject of its own opening poem, of poems scattered strategically throughout the 1648 volume, and of the climactic poem of his "Humane Works," "*The pillar of Fame*" (*H*-1129):

> FAmes pillar here, at last, we set
> Out-during *Marble, Brasse,* or *Jet.*
>   Charm'd and enchanted so,
>   As to withstand the blow
>   Of   overthrow:
>   Nor shall the seas
>   Or   OUTRAGES
>   Of storms orebear
>   What we up-rear,
>   Tho Kingdoms fal
>   This pillar never shall
>   Decline or waste at all;
> But stand for ever by his owne
> Firme and well fixt foundation.

Ann Coiro has observed that "Of the final eight poems in *Hesperides,* the first six epigrams are farewells to poetry," and that Herrick speaks as himself for the last time in the poem immediately preceding "*The pillar,*" "*On himselfe*" (*H*-1128) (1988, 214, 215). In the latter epigram the poet bluntly announces, "THe worke is done," and instructs "young men, and maidens" (who may always be his best audience) to crown him with the poet's "Mirtle Coronet" in recognition of his arduous artistic labors, his suffering "in the Muses *Martyrdome*" (l. 4). His tone is nothing if not self-assured: poetry itself will mourn when Robert Herrick is gone—"The Muses will weare blackes, when I am dead" (l. 6).

As John Kimmey has indicated, *"The pillar of Fame"* is recited by an anonymous "we," possibly the boys and girls (or the Muses) referred to in the preceding poem (1971, 263). Given the fiction of *Hesperides'* sequential composition it follows that the poet "dies" in the interval between "*On himselfe*" and "*The pillar of Fame.*" The "pillar," then, is at once a hieroglyphic poem, an emblem of *Hesperides,* the poet's grave marker, and a ritual pronouncement upon the setting up of that marker. That pronouncement's theme is, appropriately enough (given Herrick's affinity for Horace), a variation upon one of that Roman poet's more stately lines— *Exegi monumentum aere perennius* ("I have achieved a monument more enduring than brass"). Herrick's mourners, then, are to be understood as affirming what he had been hoping or asserting all along—that his fame as a poet guarantees that he will not be forgotten.

Although Herrick has been characterized as a mere maker of light verse, it is the substance or solidity of *Hesperides* upon which *"The pillar"* insists. At the same time Herrick's poetry is also said to be magic, for it represents the triumph of art over nature, of stasis over flux, of humanity over temporality. Thus, for one last time, *"The pillar of Fame"* implicitly poses the central problem of *Hesperides*—how is death to be confronted?—and triumphantly proclaims Herrick's final solution to that problem—the immortalizing power of poetry.

Chapter Seven

The "Criticks" and *"This Sacred Grove"*: Herrick's Reputation

Few important English poets have been more openly concerned about their fame and their ongoing reputations as writers than Robert Herrick—or have had fewer illusions about the circumstances upon which such fame can depend. Previous chapters have called attention to the poet's careful arrangement and printing of the collection upon which his reputation would depend and to his high degree of self-consciousness about those readers who could give him fame or deny it. Moreover, a number of his epigrams realistically and unhappily anticipate that *Hesperides* will meet assorted "criticks" (i.e., condemners), "detractors," and "soure" readers. In general, anticipating the reception of his book, he comes to expect that he will be misread by some, disliked by others, and ignored by many.

In all of these respects Herrick proved to be a prophet. It was his fate to be largely neglected for more than a century and a half after the publication of *Hesperides* and then for some time to be damned with the faint praise of the fastidious, distorted by enthusiasts, or bowdlerized by the censorious. It is a fascinating exercise in the history of literary taste and education and in the relativism of literary evaluation to read through Elizabeth Hageman's chronologically arranged bibliographical work *Robert Herrick: A Reference Guide* (see bibliography) and observe the wide variations in the appreciation and understanding of Herrick's poetry over time.

For the most part ignored in the age of Pope and Samuel Johnson, Herrick was throughout much of the nineteenth century regarded as being of mainly antiquarian, sentimental, or prurient interest. (The frequency and intensity with which his poetry is condemned for its so-called coarseness in this period suggests something amounting almost to an obsession.) Gradually consensus tagged him a "minor poet," an unhelpful classification that has inhibited the full understanding of his achievement to this day.

The late Victorian period, however, did see the beginning of substantive discussions of *Hesperides* that provided the foundation for modern Herrick scholarship and criticism. Edmund W. Gosse, for example, while acknowledging the poet's "wonderful art and skill," was put off by the erotic and scatalogical poems to the point that he disparaged Herrick's capacity for seriousness and strong emotions.[1] However, another of Herrick's editors, Alexander Grosart, saw in the poet "a deeper vein of thinking and feeling than is commonly suspected," revealed, for example, in poems on change and death. Such poems display "an unlifted shadow of melancholy that must have lain broad and black over Herrick, a melancholy which was neither transient nor a mere concession to the fashion of the age."[2] Yet another Victorian editor, F. T. Palgrave, supported Grosart by pointing out that "the light mask of classicism and bucolic allegory" that Herrick's poetry could sometimes wear concealed his essential seriousness of thought and feeling.[3] But Grosart and Palgrave did not pursue their speculations further, and the possibility that Herrick was capable of "high seriousness" was not taken very seriously for some time.

Despite their inevitable limitations as critics, Victorian scholars did help establish Herrick as one of those English poets with whom anyone with pretensions to culture must at least be acquainted. It will be recalled that Swinburne, for example, went so far as to claim that Herrick was England's greatest lyric poet (xi), and that high praise, coming from an accomplished poet, doubtless did much to sustain the "Herrick revival" of the late nineteenth century. Swinburne's authority also helped to establish the theory that the "tasteless" epigrams were probably intended to be functional, lending contrast and variety to *Hesperides* (xii).

The proliferation of scholarly and selected editions of Herrick in the last two decades of the nineteenth century culminated in the almost simultaneous publication of the first two full-length studies of the poet, F. W. Moorman's *Robert Herrick: A Biographical and Critical Study* (London: John Lane, the Bodley Head, 1910), and Floris Delattre's *Robert Herrick: Contribution a l'étude de la poesie lyrique en Angleterre au dix-septième siècle* (Paris: Felix Alcan, 1911). Both books reflect their era's penchant for biographical criticism, sometimes drawing dubious inferences about the poet from the poetry and about the poetry from the poet's life. Similarly, both works exhibit the age's interest in literary sources and influences and in esthetic evaluation, often at the expense of the analysis and interpretation of the poetry itself. While both now seem dated, these two books served the needs of their time, for there were to be no more full-length studies of the poet for over a half a century. Indeed, through the 1920s and 1930s, interest in Herrick slackened, until a new generation of critics undertook a cursory reexamination of his work.

F. R. Leavis, T. S. Eliot, Douglas Bush, Alan Gilbert, and Cleanth

Brooks[4] all endeavored to put biographical, philological, and other issues aside in the interest of addressing *Hesperides* itself, its individual poems and its nature and functions as a collection. Although still preoccupied to an extent with issues like major and minor poetry and esthetic value, these scholars raised criticism of Herrick to a new level of sophistication by keeping matters of qualitative judgment as well as pedantic nit picking to a minimum. Nevertheless, the first edition of this book (1966) was in part a reaction to issues raised two decades earlier by Leavis and Eliot in particular, in the process, however, falling into a critical trap—not only defending Herrick against the charge that he was merely a "minor poet" but arguing that he was in fact a "major" one. Such classifications have probably made little difference to dedicated readers of poetry; however, it is true that, perpetuated in scholarship and in anthologies and textbooks, they may skew the perceptions of scholars as well as students. The argument over Herrick's status did, however, lead to a conclusion that subsequent criticism has profitably tested—that *Hesperides* does exhibit Eliot's "unity of underlying pattern" and "continuous *conscious* purpose," and thus is a collection that needs to be read as a whole rather than merely sampled (43–45).

Despite some of its value judgments, the attempt of this book's first edition to place Herrick's achievement in relation to those of his contemporary and near-contemporary poets retains a certain utility, for it offered a quantitative as well as qualitative perspective on earlier seventeenth-century English poetry generally. It is still worth noting, for example, that Herrick's canon is not only more extensive than those of Carew, Suckling, and Lovelace put together, but that Herrick wrote in a greater variety of poetic modes—their output of devotional poetry, for example, is modest by comparison—and that he imitated a wider range of ancient and modern models than did his fellow Cavalier poets. Such facts need to be taken into account in any thoroughgoing consideration of "the Sons of Ben." It is also true that, of the metaphysical poets, only George Herbert wrote more devotional verse than Herrick—and Herbert wrote no secular poetry at all. With regard to secular poetry, Herrick's output is larger and more varied than either Donne's, with whom he has little in common even as a love poet, or Marvell's, with whom he shares an interest in, among other things, politics and the pastoral tradition. But it is "Father Ben," of course, whom he most resembles—except that Herrick is much more of a love poet and a pastoralist. A full consideration of his "Jonson connection," however, has yet to appear.

However unique Herrick's own genius was—and by consensus it was genius and it was unique—Ben Jonson was the source and fountain of his being as a poet, as the younger man readily and publicly acknowledged. The contribution of *Hesperides* to the stream of classical and neoclassical English poetry that issued from Jonson's pen initially is difficult to estimate. While there is no evidence that Herrick was read by Milton or Marvell, or by neoclassical poets like Dryden and Pope, his poems circulated in manuscript and his book must have confirmed the soundness of Jonson's theories of poetry and the poet for more than a few subsequent readers.

The number of scholarly readers of Herrick has increased measurably since the publication of this book's first edition in 1966, which itself was the first full-length study of the poet in more than a half-century. Almost all of their efforts are worth examining, but the few singled out below can be considered required reading.

Three articles by John L. Kimmey published in the 1970s invited a generation of New Critics, accustomed to close readings of individual poems of *Hesperides,* to take a more holistic approach, to pay more attention to the poet's arrangement of his poems and to his book's overall design.[5] To oversimplify Kimmey's general argument, the organizing principle of *Hesperides* is held to be a narrative one: like the typical sonnet sequence, it follows a loose story line. Thus, in "Robert Herrick's Persona" Kimmey suggests that the roles of poet, lover, exiled Londoner, and (in *Noble Numbers*) penitent are pivotal to the general "narrative" of Herrick's book—a "story" of yearning for literary immortality, of inconclusive love affairs, of aging, of unsettledness, and of humble faith. Additional Herrickean personae—"the preacher, the social critic [and] the shrewd observer of men and manners"— are analyzed in Kimmey's study of "Robert Herrick's Satirical Epigrams" (313). In the 151 poems of this type in *Hesperides,* Kimmey argues, Herrick as moralist focuses on man's "physical imperfections, his social and professional foibles, and his gross sins" (313), all of which compromise the vision of the good life to which *Hesperides* aspires.

Finally, Kimmey's "Order and Form in Herrick's *Hesperides*" offers an overview of Herrick's collection, proposing that a tonal shift complements the book's developing loose narrative, with the volume growing progressively more serious and culminating in the general sobriety and piety of *Noble Numbers.* While Kimmey's hypotheses have yet to receive a rigorous testing—no exhaustive study of the diverse patterns that make up the design of *Hesperides* has so far found its way into print—the validity of much of his general theory is self-evident. Moreover, his work has spurred such long overdue inquiries into Herrick's "poem clusters" as Ann Baynes Coiro's "Herrick's 'Julia' Poems," and has performed the immensely valuable service of reminding Herrick scholars that they must be wary of missing the "*Sacred Grove*" for the trees.

Hesperides has importance not only as Robert Herrick's only book but as a key document in the tradition of Cavalier poetry. Thus, while Earl Miner's *The Cavalier Mode from Jonson to Cotton* does not and cannot focus on Herrick exclusively, it was the first attempt to do for "the Sons of Ben" what a number of critical studies (including one of Miner's own) had earlier done for the metaphysical poets—attempt to make sense of the poetic output of several individuals with distinctive talents but linked by artistic, political, social, religious, and other allegiances. The Cavaliers, he argues, typically write in a "social mode" that distinguishes them from the introspection of the "School of Donne" and the public mode of Milton and the neoclassicals. There is much in Herrick's work, of course, to support such a view: his is a poetry of love and friendship, of people who are the blessings or the banes of everyday life, of familiar nature, of the pains and pleasures of ordinary existence; all of these, according to Miner, are typical Cavalier themes. While he can be introspective, Herrick is not preoccupied with subjective states; while he can occasionally adopt public stances, the circle within which he centers himself is on the whole a modest one, not much greater than that of Everyman. Not a gallant like Suckling, Lovelace, and Carew, Herrick is still very much the Cavalier poet and the Son of Ben.

In 1974, the tercentenary of the poet's death, one of those coincidences occurred which suggests that scholarship, like other phenomena, has rhythms of its own—the publication of two full-length critical studies of Herrick, both of them focusing on him as a ritualistic poet and as a poet of ritual. Robert H. Deming's *Ceremony and Art: Robert Herrick's Poetry* and "*This Poetick Liturgie*": *Robert Herrick's Ceremonial Mode* by A. Leigh DeNeef both raised Herrick criticism to yet a new level of maturity, building upon previous studies (the poet's interest in the ceremonial has long been noted) but introducing new approaches and fresh perspectives of their own. Both offered alternate readings of familiar poems and alternate organizing principles for *Hesperides*. Both, however, could have benefitted from more fully developed conceptions of "ceremony" and "ritual"; both also exhibited tendencies to emphasize ceremonial at the expense of other key elements of the poetry. Deming's approach comes closest to that of cultural anthropology and is particularly effective in placing Herrick's poetry "in its own milieu, literary and historical, social and artistic" (9). DeNeef emphasizes the ceremonial as a "mode of expression," as the means by which Herrick's artistic vision is poetically realized, and consequently his sensitive readings of individual poems are his study's greatest strength. While it cannot be said that these two books have, since their publication, brought about a critical consensus that ceremony is the key to Herrick's art, they have ensured that future studies of *Hesperides* will (like this one) have to take that art's ceremonial mode more fully into account.

The year 1974 also saw the first of what would become the biennial University of Michigan–Dearborn conferences on seventeenth-century British literature, this one to commemorate the three-hundreth anniversary of Herrick's death. Most of the papers from this conference appeared in revised and expanded form in the only collection of Herrick criticism thus far to see publication, *"Trust to Good Verses": Herrick Tercentenary Essays* (1978), edited by Roger B. Rollin and J. Max Patrick. The wide range of this book's essays indicated the range and the complexity of Herrick's art, while its selected and annotated bibliography (compiled by Ted-Larry Pebworth and others) suggested the scope—and the limitations—of Herrick criticism at the time. This volume came as close to constituting a new consensus about the poet as might be deemed possible in an age of conflicting conceptions of and varied critical approaches to poetry. This consensus holds that

Herrick is a serious and significant artist rather than a minor if skilled craftsman; that his *Hesperides* is an encyclopedic and ultimately coherent work rather than a miscellany of charming but trivial poems; and that many of those poems exhibit patterns of intellectual significance and emotional depth beneath their polished and seemingly simple surfaces. (3)

But the most marked quality of this critical collection is the diversity of its approaches and subjects. Herrick's classicism, lyricism, sensuousness, spirituality, and more are all addressed, as are such varied Hesperidean genres as the meditation, the georgic, the panegyrical epigram, and the political poem. This volume's 15 essays still leave much that is unanswered, even unaddressed, about Herrick, which says something about the complexity of his achievement.

Three questions of continuing interest in Herrick scholarship are addressed in Louise Schleiner's 1976 article, "Herrick's Songs and the Character of *Hesperides*": the poet's popularity in his age, his role as a lyricist, and the impression of "lightness" that his collection can give some readers.[6] That Herrick was England's most popular lyric poet even after he had taken up residence in "dull *Devon-shire*" is seen in the numerous extant musical settings of his poems (77); moreover, his revisions of his song texts into lyrics for reading supply insights into his technical sophistication (80). That same process of "perfecting" his poems for publication may, Schleiner observes, be in part responsible for the "lightweight" character of a number of his pieces: it is probable that many of them are abbreviated versions for reading of longer song texts (82).

Arguably the most brilliant piece of Herrick scholarship and criticism yet published appeared in 1978, as a monograph-length chapter of Gordon Braden's *The Classics and English Renaissance Poetry*. From its title, "Robert Herrick and Classical Lyric Poetry," it would appear to be the kind of study of sources and influences of which Victorian scholarship was so fond. But Braden's meticulous and acute analyses of precisely how Herrick borrows from the Ancients takes the reader into the very mind of the poet as he reads or remembers Greek and Roman poems (or fragments of them) and weaves them into the texture of his own verses. While it is possible to disagree with some of Braden's conclusions about Herrick's imagination and his art, his analysis of the poet's unique *imitatio* of the classics is very persuasive. Moreover, the poet himself would have particularly appreciated the wit and stylishness of this monograph's prose, itself something of a tribute to the wit and stylishness of Herrick's poetry.

Demonstrating the principle that mature scholarship and literary criticism require a broad and deep foundation of prior studies is Ann Baynes Coiro's *Robert Herrick's 'Hesperides' and the Epigram Book Tradition* (1988), the most useful and insightful book-length work on the poet yet to appear. Although many scholars of Herrick have wrestled with the "problem" of his epigrams, Coiro is the first to suggest that Herrick's collection is as a whole "best understood as an epigram book, a genre that allows lyric and epigram to stand side by side in complicating proximity and that was open in the Renaissance to an astonishing variety of intentions and interpretations" (4). Less concerned with explications than with organizing principles, Coiro offers new perspectives on the overall designs that lend unity to *Hesperides* and into some of the internal patterns of theme, subject, and genre that lend it coherence. The extent to which Herrick's collection "is intricately bound to its own historical circumstances" (29) is most effectively demonstrated here, with Coiro (following the lead of Claude J. Summers) applying the coup de grace to long-established notions that Herrick was a poet of "art for art's sake," wholly oblivious to his troubled times. Whether or not this study ever resolves the central crux of *Hesperides'* "innovative mix of pastoral lyric and epigram" (30)—that is, the nature and character of that "mix"—it marks the coming of age of Herrick scholarship and criticism, even as it opens up new territory of the "*Sacred Grove*" for exploration. Moreover, with Coiro's deceptively simple proposal "that *Hesperides* should be read in its entirety" (3)—and in its published order—she poses a major challenge to herself (that she is largely successful in meeting) and to future scholars and critics of Herrick, the challenge of respecting and responding to what she calls the "integrity of *Hesperides*." Her study reminds us that "Robert Herrick is the only Renaissance poet who gathered together the work of his lifetime into one polished, self-presented and self-presenting volume" (4), and this fact alone requires that "the place of *Hesperides* in the Stuart literary tradition should be weighed more carefully than it has been" (4).

The renaissance in literary and critical theory that has taken place in the more than two decades since the publication of the first edition of this book makes it abundantly clear that the definitive study of Robert Herrick's poetry has yet to be written. Such a study would, for example, draw upon psychoanalytic theory and the new historicism to develop a clearer picture of the poet's psychical personality and his creative imagination and their interaction with his world. It would draw upon semiotics to sort out the dazzling array of signs and sign systems *Hesperides* contains. It would draw upon structuralism to explicate the broad and deep patterns of Herrrick's art and upon deconstruction to demonstrate his various subversions of those patterns. Feminist criticism could shed new light not only on Herrick's love poetry and his poems about male-female relationships but also on his celebration of some women, real as well as fictional, and his derogation of certain stereotypes, male as well as female. As mentioned above, the many dimensions of his literary relationships with Jonson as well as with his poetical contemporaries require much more investigation, as do, for example, his prosody, wit, and humor and, above all, the details of his arrangement of his poetic collection.

A new look at the verses Herrick did *not* write also comes under this category. Like all poets he had his limitations; unlike many poets he appears to have been acutely aware of them. *Hesperides* demonstrates that he is one poet who never produces ambitious failures, although he is guilty of some modest ones. Each of his numerous artistic successes is limited more by its conception than by its execution. Herrick seems to have recognized what his artistic strengths were and to have exercised them fairly constantly for several decades. But then, with the publication of his collected works, he evidently stopped. Why? Has there ever been another important poet who, at such a comparatively young age (57), apparently abandoned his art forever? It is a mystery that doth tease us out of thought.

If there is one word for Robert Herrick the poet, it may well be *poise*. His poetry confronts the human condition with a poise that is philosophical and emotional as well as artistic. He had the poise to perceive the way things were without losing sight of the way things might be. He had the poise to be serious without being melancholic, to be joyous without being trivial, to savor both the art of life and the life of art. Although the art through which he expresses and exemplifies this profound poise has not always been in fashion, there can now be little doubt that Robert Herrick was substantially correct when, in the poem that functions as the preface to his *Hesperides,* he claims, "Full is my Book of Glories."

Notes and References

Chapter One

1. *The Poetical Works of Robert Herrick,* ed. L. C. Martin (Oxford: Clarendon Press, 1956), 446; hereafter cited in text as *PW.*

2. Included in *PW* and *The Complete Poetry of Robert Herrick,* ed. J. Max Patrick (New York: New York University Press, 1963); hereafter cited in text as *CP.*

3. *Robert Herrick: A Reference Guide,* ed. Elizabeth H. Hageman (Boston: G. K. Hall, 1983); hereafter cited in text.

4. *"Trust to Good Verses": Herrick Tercentenary Essays,* ed. Roger B. Rollin and J. Max Patrick (Pittsburgh: University of Pittsburgh Press, 1978).

5. Herricks & Beaumanor Society, D. W. Andreas, Honorable Secretary (8 Hastings Road, Woodhouse Eaves, Leicestershire LE12 8QU).

6. *Songs by Roger Quilter* (Andrew Young, tenor; Gordon Watson, pianoforte), Argo RG 36 or Westminster XWN 18152 (includes a song cycle of Herrick lyrics to Julia); *Word Songs* (music by John Dankworth; vocals by Cleo Lane), Phillips Recording #830463 (lyrics by seventeenth-century poets such as Herrick and Donne with modern settings).

7. F. R. Leavis, *Revaluation: Tradition and Development in English Poetry* (New York: George W. Stewart, 1947), 39–41; hereafter cited in text.

8. T. S. Eliot, *On Poetry and Poets* (New York: Farrar, Straus and Cudahy, 1957), 43–44; hereafter cited in text.

9. J. Max Patrick, *"'Poetry perpetuates the Poet'*: Richard James and the Growth of Herrick's Reputation," in *"Trust to Good Verses": Herrick Tercentenary Essays,* ed. Roger B. Rollin and J. Max Patrick (Pittsburgh: University of Pittsburgh Press, 1978), 228, 229, 230–31; hereafter cited in text.

10. A. C. Swinburne, "Preface," *Robert Herrick: The Hesperides and Noble Numbers,* ed. Alfred Pollard, 1, rev. ed. (London: Lawrence and Bullen, 1898), xi; hereafter cited in text.

11. A. Leigh DeNeef, *"This Poetick Liturgie": Robert Herrick's Ceremonial Mode* (Durham: Duke University Press, 1974); hereafter cited in text. Robert H. Deming, *Ceremony and Art: Robert Herrick's Poetry* (The Hague: Mouton, 1974); hereafter cited in text.

12. S. Musgrove, "The Universe of Robert Herrick," *Auckland University College Bulletin* 38, English ser. no. 4 (1950): 6; hereafter cited in text.

13. Thomas R. Whitaker, "Herrick and the Fruits of the Garden," *Journal of English Literary History* 22 (1955): 17; hereafter cited in text.

14. Ann Baynes Coiro, *Robert Herrick's "Hesperides" and the Epigram Book*

Tradition (Baltimore: Johns Hopkins University Press, 1988), 123; hereafter cited in text.

15. Northrop Frye, *Anatomy of Criticism: Four Essays* (Princeton: Princeton University Press, 1957), 194.

16. Claude J. Summers, "Herrick's Political Poetry: The Strategies of His Art," in *"Trust to Good Verses": Herrick Tercentenary Essays,* ed. Roger B. Rollin and J. Max Patrick (Pittsburgh: University of Pittsburgh Press, 1978), 174; hereafter cited in text.

17. Professor Patrick, while acknowledging that the personage portrayed could in fact be Robert Herrick, allows that he "may well be a generalized representation of a poet" (*CP,* 7). But this is unlikely: the appearance of this man is most distinctive, not at all "generalized"; moreover, a poet who took such pains to oversee his book through the press, even compiling a list of errata, is an unlikely candidate to give an engraver a free hand with that book's frontispiece; finally, a poet who inserts himself and even his name into so many of his poems would scarcely be so modest as to decline to have himself portrayed in the front of his own book.

18. Professor Patrick says that the neo-Latin poem is inscribed "on the base of the bust" (*CP,* 8), but the proportions are wrong for this to be the case: the "base" is far too large for the size of the bust, which in fact has its own base. It seems more likely that the bust is resting on Herrick's imagined tomb, creating an appropriate symbol for a poet preoccupied with death and with the transcendence of death through poetry.

19. The translation is by Alexander B. Grosart, *The Complete Poems of Robert Herrick,* 3 vols. (London: Chatto & Windus, 1876); hereafter cited in text as Grosart; reprinted in *CP,* 8.

Chapter Two

1. Frank Kermode, *John Donne,* British Council and the National Book League, Writers and Their Work, no. 86 (London: Longmans, 1961), 32.

2. Allen H. Gilbert, "Robert Herrick on Death," *Modern Language Quarterly* 5 (1944): 67.

3. Louis Untermeyer, ed., *The Love Poems of Robert Herrick and John Donne* (New Brunswick: Rutgers University Press, 1948), 3.

4. John Donne, *Devotions upon Emergent Occasions* (Ann Arbor: University of Michigan Press, 1959), 109.

5. Ben Jonson, *Ben Jonson,* ed. Ian Donaldson, Oxford Authors (Oxford: Oxford University Press, 1985), 221; hereafter cited in text as *BJ.*

6. Epicurus x.125, in *Diogenes Laertius,* 2, trans. R. D. Hicks, Loeb Classical Library (London: Heinemann, 1924), 235; hereafter cited in text as *DL.*

7. A. E. Elmore, "Herrick and the Poetry of Song," in *"Trust to Good Verses":* *Herrick Tercentenary Essays,* ed. Roger B. Rollin and J. Max Patrick (Pittsburgh: University of Pittsburgh Press, 1978), 69.

8. Marcus Aurelius, *The Communings with Himself of Marcus Aurelius*

Antoninus, trans. C. R. Haines, Loeb Classical Library (London: Heinemann, 1924), 651; hereafter cited in text as *MA.*

9. T. G. S. Cain, "'*Times trans-shifting*': Herrick in Meditation," in *"Trust to Good Verses": Herrick Tercentenary Essays,* ed. Roger B. Rollin and J. Max Patrick (Pittsburgh: University of Pittsburgh Press, 1978), 118; hereafter cited in text.

10. Douglas R. Bush, *English Literature in the Earlier Seventeenth Century: 1600–1660,* 2d rev. ed. (Oxford: Oxford University Press, 1962), 4; hereafter cited in text.

11. See Ernest Becker, *The Denial of Death* (New York: Free Press, 1973).

12. See Earl Miner, *The Cavalier Mode from Jonson to Cotton* (Princeton: Princeton University Press, 1971); hereafter cited in text.

Chapter Three

1. See Hageman under 1964.4; 1966.1, 4, 5; 1967.3; 1968.12; 1969.5; 1979.11. See also Leah S. Marcus, *The Politics of Mirth* (Chicago: University of Chicago Press, 1986), 146–49; hereafter cited in text; Peter Stallybrass, "'Wee feaste in our Defense': Patrician Carnival in Early Modern England and Robert Herrick's 'Hesperides,'" *English Literary Renaissance* 16 (Winter 1986): 246–47; and Coiro (1988), 156–58.

2. See DeNeef, 31n; Deming, 150; *PW,* 504–6. In "Herrick's Georgic Encomia," in *"Trust to Good Verses": Herrick Tercentenary Essays,* ed. Roger B. Rollin and J. Max Patrick (Pittsburgh: University of Pittsburgh Press, 1978), 149–57, James S. Tillman suggests that *"A Country Life"* (and a poem to Endymion Porter to be discussed in a later chapter) can be approached as "georgic encomia" as well as pastorals because both employ exhortations that idealize their addressees as "master husbandmen of their estates."

3. In "Robert Herrick's Persona," *Studies in Philology* 67 (1970), John L. Kimmey (hereafter cited in text) argues that *"His returne to London"* (*H*-713) calls into question my hypothesis that Herrick is a pastoral poet because, with the possible exception of *H*-1068, after *"His returne"* "there is no poem praising the country or indicating the persona has gone back to it" (31n). But this ignores the important *H*-724, *"His Grange, or private wealth,"* as well as a poem welcoming Prince Charles to nearby Exeter (*H*-756). Moreover, traditional bucolics like *H*-716, *H*-730, and *H*-984 serve to remind readers that they are still in the *"Sacred Grove"* or that it is nearby.

4. Richard J. Ross, "'A Wild Civility': Robert Herrick's Poetic Solution of the Paradox of Art and Nature," Ph.D. dissertation (University of Michigan, 1958), 93, 132–33; hereafter cited in text.

5. Sam H. Henderson, "Neo-Stoic Influence in Elizabethan Verse Satire," *Studies in English Renaissance Literature,* ed. Waldo F. McNeir, Louisiana State University Studies, Humanities Series no. 12 (Baton Rouge, 1962), 66.

6. See Marcus, 154–55; Stallybrass, 247; see also Coiro (1988), 136.

Chapter 4

1. Gordon Braden, *The Classics and English Renaissance Poetry: Three Case Studies,* Yale Studies in English (New Haven: Yale University Press, 1978), 218–32; hereafter cited in text.

2. Sir Thomas Browne, *Religio Medici,* in *The Prose of Sir Thomas Browne,* ed. Norman J. Endicott (Garden City, N.Y.: Anchor Books, 1967), 7.

3. Hageman (245) lists 24 discussions of this poem published between 1930 and 1978.

4. Louis H. Leiter, "Herrick's 'Upon Julia's Clothes,'" *Modern Language Notes* 73 (May): 331.

5. Ann Baynes Coiro, "Herrick's 'Julia' Poems," *John Donne Journal* 6 (1987), 67; hereafter cited in text.

6. Coiro (1987), 78; Deming, 39–40.

7. Cleanth Brooks, "What Does Poetry Communicate?," in *The Well Wrought Urn: Studies in the Structure of Poetry* (New York: Harcourt, Brace & Co., 1947), 62–73; hereafter cited in text; Deming, 47–57; DeNeef, 54–66; Marcus, 156–65.

8. J. Max Patrick (p. 100) suggests that the "Proclamation" may be "either a particular local proclamation of May Day festivities or possibly a reference to Charles I's 'declaration to his subjects concerning lawful sports,' 1633, which forbade interference . . . with 'having of Maygames . . . and the setting up of Maypoles and other sports therewith used.'" Leah Marcus, 156–65, confirms and expands on Patrick's interpretation. Herrick's usage could also be simply metaphoric, with tradition or even the day itself (because it is conducive to the celebration) "proclaiming" the holiday.

9. See Hageman, 193, 194, 205.

10. Robert Burton, *The Anatomy of Melancholy,* ed. Floyd Dell and Paul Jordan-Smith (New York: Tudor Publishing Co., 1927); see 3.2.1.1 (pp. 643 ff.); hereafter cited in text as *Anatomy.*

Chapter Five

1. Virginia R. Mollenkott, "Herrick and the Cleansing of Perception," in *"Trust to Good Verses": Herrick Tercentenary Essays,* ed. Roger B. Rollin and J. Max Patrick (Pittsburgh: University of Pittsburgh Press, 1978), 208.

2. *John Milton: Complete Poems and Major Prose,* ed. Meritt Y. Hughes (Indianapolis: Odyssey Press, 1957), 728.

3. Achsah Guibbory, *The Map of Time: Seventeenth-Century English Literature and Ideas of Pattern in History* (Urbana: University of Illinois Press, 1986), 150–51; hereafter cited in text.

4. Douglas Bush, *English Literature in the Earlier Seventeenth Century, 1600–1660,* rev. ed., Oxford History of English Literature (New York: Oxford University Press, 1962), 115.

5. William Oram, "Herrick's Use of Sacred Materials," in *"Trust to Good Verses": Herrick Tercentenary Essays*, ed. Roger B. Rollin and J. Max Patrick (Pittsburgh: University of Pittsburgh Press, 1978), 215.

6. *PW*, 527. Although Robert Deming (92) claims that purification prior to participation in a religious service is a prerequisite for Christian worship, it is expected but not mandatory (as it is in Herrick's poem) in Catholic services and is not a necessary feature of Protestant services.

7. *PW*, 520: Ovid's statement (*Metamorphoses* 15.158) may be translated as "Souls are beyond death," that of Tacitus (*Agricola* 46) as "Noble souls are not extinguished with the body."

8. See "*A Charme, or an allay for Love*" (H-587), "*The Night-piece, to Julia*" (H-619), "*Charmes*" (H-888), "*Another*" (H-889), "*Another to bring in the Witch*" (H-890), "*Another Charme for Stables*" (H-891), "*Charmes*" (H-1063), "*Another*" (H-1064), and "*Another*" (H-1065).

9. Miriam K. Starkman, "*Noble Numbers* and the Poetry of Devotion," in *Reason and the Imagination: Studies in the History of Ideas, 1600–1800*, ed. J. A. Mazzeo (New York: Columbia University Press, 1962), 17.

10. Cf. "*Love me little, love me long*" (H-143), line 3; "*Honours are hindrances*" (N-64), and "*The Welcome to Sack*" (H-197), line 11.

11. Claude J. Summers, "Herrick's Political Counterplots," *Studies in English Literature* 25 (1985): 175, 180; hereafter cited in text.

12. Louis L. Martz, *The Poetry of Meditation* (New Haven: Yale University Press, 1954).

13. Although I have come to a somewhat different conclusion about the poem than he does, I am indebted to Professor Deming (104–6) for calling attention to the limitations of my earlier interpretation (in *Robert Herrick*, 1966, 157–60).

Chapter Six

1. See Marcus, chapter 5; Coiro (1988), chapter 9; and Summers (1978, 1985).

2. See, for example, "TO THE KING, Upon his comming with his Army into the West" (H-77); "TO THE KING Upon his taking of *Leicester*" (H-823); "TO THE KING, *Upon his welcome to* Hampton-Court" (H-961); "*To Sir* John Berkley, *Governour of Exeter*" (H-745); "*To Prince* Charles *upon his coming to Exeter*" (H-756); "*A Dirge upon the Death of the Right Valiant Lord,* Bernard Stuart" (H-219); "*To the right gratious Prince,* Lodwick, *Duke of* Richmond *and* Lenox" (H-451).

3. In "Rethinking What Moderation Means to Robert Herrick," *English Literary History* 39 (March 1972), Paul R. Jenkins argues that "The tension [in 'Delight in Disorder'] is not between art and nature [as Jenkins believes my 1966 analysis claims—not on p. 85, as in Jenkins's citation, but on pp. 174–75] but be-

tween that kind of art which seeks . . . to release sensations . . . and 'art precise in every part,'" 54.

4. Achsah Guibbory, "No lust theres like to Poetry": Herrick's Passion for Poetry," in "Trust to Good Verses": Herrick Tercentenary Essays, ed. Roger B. Rollin and J. Max Patrick (Pittsburgh: University of Pittsburgh Press, 1978), 82.

5. Avon Jack Murphy, "Robert Herrick: The Self-Conscious Critic in Hesperides," in "Trust to Good Verses": Herrick Tercentenary Essays, ed. Roger B. Rollin and J. Max Patrick (Pittsburgh: University of Pittsburgh Press, 1978), 57.

6. For an ingenious analysis of Herrick's technique of "spot-quotation," see Braden, chapter 3.

7. Dylan Thomas, "In My Craft or Sullen Art," The Collected Poems of Dylan Thomas (New York: New Directions, 1957), 142.

8. For a discussion of Herrick's images of his book, see Helen Marlborough, "Herrick's Epigrams of Praise," in "Trust to Good Verses": Herrick Tercentenary Essays, ed. Roger B. Rollin and J. Max Patrick (Pittsburgh: University of Pittsburgh Press, 1978), 165–68.

9. For a theory concerning the "narrative order" of Herrick's collection, see John L. Kimmey, "Order and Form in Herrick's Hesperides," Journal of English and Germanic Philology 70 (Spring 1970): 255–68; hereafter cited as "Order," 1970.

Chapter 7

1. Edmund W. Gosse, "Robert Herrick," Cornhill Magazine 32 (1875): 180.

2. Grosart, 1. clxxvi, clxx.

3. F. T. Palgrave, ed. Chrysomela: A Selection from the Lyrical Poems of Robert Herrick. Golden Treasury Series (London: Macmillan & Co., 1877), xx.

4. Leavis, 10–41; Allen H. Gilbert, "Robert Herrick on Death," Modern Language Quarterly 5 (March 1944): 61–67; Eliot, 34–51; Bush, 111–12 and passim; Brooks, 62–73.

5. John L. Kimmey, "Robert Herrick's Persona," Studies in Philology 67 (April 1970): 221–36; "Robert Herrick's Satirical Epigrams." English Studies 51, no. 4 (1970): 312–23; "Order" (1970), 255–68.

6. Louise Schleiner, "Herrick's Songs and the Character of Hesperides," English Literary Renaissance 6 (Winter 1976): 77–91.

Selected Bibliography

BIBLIOGRAPHICAL NOTE

Those interested in doing research on Robert Herrick and his poetry are fortunate in that two relatively recent annotated bibliographies of the highest quality are widely available:

Pebworth, Ted-Larry, with A. Leigh DeNeef, Dorothy Lee, James E. Siemon, and Claude J. Summers. "Selected and Annotated Bibliography." In *"Trust to Good Verses": Herrick Tercentenary Essays*. Edited by Roger B. Rollin and J. Max Patrick. Pittsburgh: University of Pittsburgh Press, 1978, 237–81. Lists and describes significant editions, Herrick bibliographies and selected scholarship and criticism before 1910 (date of F. W Moorman's study of the poet) and since 1910, as well as separately published notes on individual poems. Succinct but useful characterizations and evaluations of most works cited.

Hageman, Elizabeth H. *Robert Herrick: A Reference Guide*. Boston: G. K. Hall & Co., 1983. An "annotated, chronological survey of [Herrick] criticism written in English from 1648 [the publication of *Hesperides*] through mid-1981." Editions of the poetry containing critical apparatus are included, as are a few works of criticism not in English and doctoral dissertations. Ample and and judicious (but nonevaluative) descriptions of the works listed. Chronological listing offers an overview of the vagaries of the criticism of Herrick from its beginnings.

Given the accessibility of these two reliable and relatively recent reference works and given this volume's limitations of space, the bibliography that follows will list only those works likely to be of most relevance to contemporary readers of Herrick, including those published since mid-1981, when Hageman's bibliography concludes. Bibliographical caution: the Pebworth and Hageman bibliographies supersede the unreliable and dated *Robert Herrick (A Concise Bibliography)* of Samuel A. and Dorothy R. Tannenbaum, Elizabethan Bibliographies No. 40 (New York: Elizabethan Bibliographies, 1949).

PRIMARY WORKS

At this writing there is (inexplicably) no edition of Herrick's poetry in print. Most college and university libraries, however, will have one or both of the following:

The Poetical Works of Robert Herrick. Edited by L. C. Martin. Oxford: Clarendon
Press, 1956. Introduction contains an account of Herrick's life and literary
reputation, a study of the text and canon, and speculations on the poems'
chronology. Commentary on individual poems (mainly philological) is incon-
veniently located, along with textual notes, at the back of the book. Not
"reader friendly," but a definitive edition. (Reprinted, minus commentary and
with a few textual notes, as *The Complete Poems of Robert Herrick.* Oxford
Standard Authors. London and New York: Oxford University Press, 1965.)

The Complete Poetry of Robert Herrick. Edited by J. Max Patrick. Anchor
Seventeenth-Century Series. Garden City, N.Y.: Doubleday, 1963. Front
matter includes a brief but insightful critical appreciation, as well as commentary on the publication of *Hesperides'* and its poet's reputation, along with a
biographical outline. Very useful notes conveniently follow the poems, which
are individually numbered for greater accessibility. A definitive edition that
more than meets the needs of most scholars and students. (Reprinted, with a
new foreword and corrections, W. W. Norton & Co., 1968.)

Both of these editions may be used with Malcolm MacLeod's *A Concordance to the
Poems of Robert Herrick* (New York: Oxford University Press, 1936).

SECONDARY WORKS

*Articles and Books to mid-1981**

Berman, Ronald. "Herrick's Secular Poetry." *English Studies* 52, no. 1 (1971):
20–30. Attempts to reconcile the secular and the sacred in *Hesperides.*
Learned, but uses the doctrine of correspondences to sacralize almost everything secular in the poetry. Reprinted in *Ben Jonson and the Cavalier Poets.* Edited by Hugh Maclean. New York: W. W. Norton & Co., 1974, 529–40.

Braden, Gordon. "Robert Herrick and Classical Lyric Poetry." In *The Classics
and English Renaissance Poetry.* Yale Studies in English, 187. New Haven and
London: Yale University Press, 1978, 154–258. Acute and original (if sometimes arguable) insights into Herrick's psyche as well as his creativity, based
on the poet's idiosyncratic techniques of borrowing from the Roman lyricists
and Anacreon. Sophisticated, witty, required reading.

Brooks, Cleanth. "What Does Poetry Communicate?" *The Well-Wrought Urn.*
New York: Harcourt, Brace & Co., 1947, 62–73. A rambling but insightful
analysis of "Corinna's *going a-Maying*" by way of demonstrating how complex the "experience" of a poem can be.

Bush, Douglas. *English Literature in the Earlier Seventeenth Century, 1600–
1660.* Rev. ed. Oxford History of English Literature. New York and Oxford:

*Listed in the Pebworth and/or Hageman bibliographies.

Oxford University Press, 196, 115–19. Perhaps the most useful capsule analysis of Herrick's art and his place in the literary history of the era, though now somewhat dated.

Chambers, A. B. "Herrick and the Trans-shifting of Time." *Studies in Philology* 72 (1975): 85–114. Another effort to reconcile the classical and the Christian in the poetry. Urges reading poems in their immediate contexts in the book and in the context of Herrick's overall design.

Deming, Robert H. *Ceremony and Art: Robert Herrick's Poetry.* The Hague and Paris: Mouton, 1974. Stresses (and occasionally overstresses) the role of classical and Christian ceremony in mediating between basic oppositions of Herrick's poetry.

DeNeef, A. Leigh. *"This Poetick Liturgie": Robert Herrick's Ceremonial Mode.* Durham, N.C.: Duke University Press, 1974. Explains how a reader's response to Herrick is engaged by his "poetic ceremonials," ritual poems of several kinds. Emphasizes the confrontation with death by Herrick's various personas and their various voices.

Eliot, T. S. "What Is Minor Poetry?" In *On Poetry and Poets.* New York: Farrar, Straus, 1957, 34–51. See chapter 1 within.

Jenkins, Paul R. "Re-Thinking What Moderation Means to Robert Herrick." *English Literary History* 39 (1972): 49–65. Attacks the straw man argument that the poetry's spirit is "essentially Roman" as well as the idea, advanced in *Robert Herrick* (1966), that moderation is central to the poet's ethos.

Kimmey, John L. "Robert Herrick's Persona." *Studies in Philology* 67 (1970): 221–36. Argues—contra *Robert Herrick* (1966)—that the Hesperidean persona is not a pastoral poet and offers the New Critical theory that Herrick's speaker is entirely a "fictive character" playing the roles of poet, lover, and exile.

————. "Robert Herrick's Satirical Epigrams." *English Studies* 51 (1971): 312–23. Argues that Herrick, the "keen moralist," emerges from these short poems attacking human imperfections.

————. "Order and Form in Herrick's *Hesperides*." *Journal of English and Germanic Philology* 70 (1971): 255–68. Proposes that Herrick's collection is ordered along the lines of a fictional autobiographical narrative of an aging poet who is not actually Herrick himself. His overall aim is no less than to represent the seventeenth-century secular and religious world. Highly influential.

Leavis, F. R. *"The Line of Wit."* In *Revaluation: Tradition and Development in English Poetry.* London: Chatto & Windus, 1936. Reprinted New York: George W. Stewart, 1947, 10–41. See chapter 1 within.

Low, Anthony. "Robert Herrick: The Religion of Pleasure." In *Love's Architecture: Devotional Modes in Seventeenth-Century English Poetry.* New York: New York University Press, 208–34. Claims that in his secular poems Herrick is very much the Stoic and "one of Epicurus' own sons," displaying a

"Keatsian intensity of feeling" in his pursuit of pleasure. Less convincing in arguing that *Noble Numbers* are also "preoccupied with . . . pleasure."

Martz, Louis L. "Marvell and Herrick: The Masks of Mannerism." In *Approaches to Marvell: The York Tercentenary Lectures*. Edited by C. A. Patrides. Boston: Routledge & Kegan Paul, 1978, 194–215. Suggests that his poetry's imitativeness, "instability," "disjunction," and attention to detail make Herrick something of a "Mannerist" poet.

Miner, Earl. *The Cavalier Mode from Jonson to Cotton*. Princeton: Princeton University Press, 1971. Situates Herrick within the context of this "school" of seventeenth-century poetry. Various chapters treat Cavalier themes. Helpful.

Musgrove, Sidney. *The Universe of Robert Herrick*. Auckland University College Bulletin, no. 38; English Series, no. 4. Auckland, New Zealand: Pelorus Press, 1950. A brief monograph offering an early defense of Herrick against the charge of triviality. Overstates *Hesperides'* Christian orientation.

Rollin, Roger B., and J. Max Patrick, eds. *"Trust to Good Verses": Herrick Tercentenary Essays*. Pittsburgh: University of Pittsburgh Press, 1978. The only collection of essays to date devoted exclusively to Herrick. Introduction offers an overview of the state of Herrick criticism. Essays on the visual and the musical in *Hesperides,* Herrick's poetic temperament, classicism, politics, religion, reputation, etc. Annotated bibliography.

Schleiner, Louise. "Herrick's Songs and the Character of *Hesperides*." *English Literary Renaissance* 6 (1976): 77–91. Offers convincing evidence concerning Herrick's popularity as a composer of song texts, provides insights into his poetic technique, and helps explain why he can give the impression of being a "lightweight." Includes a list of period musical settings of Herrick's lyrics.

Starkman, Miriam K. "*Noble Numbers* and the Poetry of Devotion." In *Reason and the Imagination: Studies in the History of Ideas, 1600–1800*. Edited by J. A. Mazzeo. New York: Columbia University Press, 1962, 1–27. One of the rare attempts to focus on Herrick's sacred collection, suggesting how it "shows us the close boundaries between the devotional and the humanistic."

Whitaker, Thomas R. "Herrick and the Fruits of the Garden." *English Literary History* 22 (1955): 16–33. An important earlier effort to take Herrick seriously by examining "the imaginative world of *Hesperides*." Discusses the Christian-Dionysian tension in the poetry and its exaltation of the world of art.

Articles and Books, mid-1981 to 1990

Chaudhuri, Sukanta. *Renaissance Pastoral and Its English Developments*. Oxford: Clarendon Press, 1989. Notes that Herrick "revitalizes" the pastoral by applying its conventions "to actual English country life," blending "reality and artifact."

Coiro, Anne Baynes. "Herrick's 'Julia' Poems." *John Donne Journal* 6.1 (1987): 67–89. Innovative examination of Herrick's 77 poems to Julia who, in the course of his book, evolves in her role and "becomes a metaphor for language" and its limitations.

_____. *Robert Herrick's 'Hesperides' and the Epigram Book Tradition*. Baltimore: Johns Hopkins University Press, 1988. The most critically advanced study of the poet to date. Essential reading. Does not make entirely clear how *Hesperides* is at once an epigram book "and *more* than a book of epigrams, an innovative mix of pastoral lyric and epigram that complicates both genres." Nevertheless, the only major study of Herrick's vast output of epigrams. Sensitive to *Hesperides'* "local" and general designs. Applies the historical background to the poetry in new ways. Clearly outlines the epigram tradition.

Gerzman, Jay A. *Fantasy, Fashion & Affection: Editions of Robert Herrick's Poetry for the Common Reader, 1810–1968*. Bowling Green, Ohio: Bowling Green State University Popular Press, 1986. Nearly 100 reprints of Herrick's verses—most of them trade editions—between 1810 and 1980 suggest his popularity. Their illustrations exemplify the shifts in popular taste. Of particular interest to bibliophiles.

Guibbory, Achsah. "Robert Herrick: 'Repullulation' and the Cyclical Order." In *The Map of Time: Seventeenth-Century English Literature and Ideas of Pattern in History*. Urbana, Ill.: University of Illinois Press, 1986, 137–67. Explores ways in which the era's literature "reflects a pervasive, deep concern with the pattern or shape of history." Argues that for Herrick time and history were cyclical, implying order in existence. The operation of this principle is seen in art and religion, which for Herrick promise renewal.

Low, Anthony. *The Georgic Revolution*. Princeton: Princeton University Press, 1985. Discusses several of the country-life poems to conclude that "Herrick's georgic is simply a revised version of or a substitute for pastoral" whose theme is "Stoic retreat." Helpful, but the georgic-pastoral distinctions could be more fully developed.

Malekin, Peter. *Liberty and Love: English Literature and Society 1640–88*. London: Hutchinson & Co., 1981. Mentions Herrick's attitudes toward love, sex, and women in passing. Overgeneralizes.

Marcus, Leah S. "Churchman among the Maypoles: Herrick and the *Hesperides*." In *The Politics of Mirth: Jonson, Herrick, Milton, Marvell, and the Defense of Old Holiday Pastimes*. Chicago and London: University of Chicago Press, 1986, 140–68. Herrick's "*Argument*" indicates that traditional popular pastimes associated with the seasons—suppressed by some civil and religious authorities but promoted by the Stuarts—are to be Herrick's subjects. Such "recreations" become a way "to repastoralize England." Several poems discussed to show that Herrick "advocates survivalism [economics and nature linked], sports, and 'the freedom to be merry' as part of a broader fidelity to a vision of political and ecclesiastical conformity."

Patterson, Annabel. "Jonson, Marvell, and Miscellaneity?" In *Poems in Their Place: The Intertextuality and Order of Poetic Collections*. Edited by Neil

Fraistat. Chapel Hill and London: University of North Carolina Press, 95–118. Briefly discusses the debate about the principles of arrangement in *Hesperides* and sees the collection in the context of efforts "to promote solidarity for the crown."

Stallybrass, Peter. "'Wee feaste in our defense': Patrician Carnival in Early Modern England and Robert Herrick's 'Hesperides.'" *English Literary Renaissance* 16 (1986): 234–52. Deals less with Herrick than the title implies. Explains the era's "attempt to reform popular festivities as a means of social control." Thus, "The carnivalesque . . . is used by Herrick . . . to produce a mythic unity of prince, gentry, and people." Cf. Marcus (above).

Stein, Arnold. *The House of Death: Messages from the English Renaissance.* Baltimore and London: Johns Hopkins University Press, 1986. Chapter 9 takes its title from a poem of Herrick's, *"The Plaudite, or end of life,"* and subtly explicates it. Repeats the erroneous cliché about Herrick's "simple, untroubled faith."

Summers, Claude J. "Herrick's Political Counterplots." *Studies in English Literature* 25 (1985): 165–82. Stresses the political sophistication of the poetry. Offers a controversial reading of *"His Returne to London,"* which, it is claimed, exhibits a "counterplot" or subtext "that attempts to distill stoicism from the bitter herbs of the Hesperidean garden in the year of the Puritan triumph, 1647." Less convincingly, a subtext of the devotional poem *"Good Friday"* is held to anticipate the execution of Charles I.

Toliver, Harold. "Herrick's Book of Realms and Moments." *English Literary History* 49 (1982): 429–48. A phenomenological approach to *Hesperides* as composed in a "proleptic mode"—a technique that involves teasing the reader into expecting certainties that often never emerge. The poetry is often elusive, shifting, evanescent. An original and subtle analysis that underestimates Herrick's specificity and concreteness.

Index

The Author

Since 1975 Roger B. Rollin has been William James Lemon Professor of Literature at Clemson University. Between 1959 and 1975 he was a member of the Department of English, Franklin and Marshall College, which department for a time he chaired. He received his B.A. in English and philosophy from Washington and Jefferson College in 1952 and his M.A. (1957) and Ph.D. in English (1960) from Yale University. With J. Max Patrick he organized the 1974 Robert Herrick Memorial Conference at the University of Michigan–Dearborn and edited *"Trust to Good Verses": Herrick Tercentenary Essays* (1978). He has also edited a literature anthology, *Hero/Anti-Hero* (1973), and the collection *The Americanization of the Global Village: Essays in Comparative Popular Culture* (1989).